THE EVERYTHING®
Toltec Wisdom Book

Dear Reader,

It is a great pleasure for me to share the Toltec wisdom with you in this book. Like many others, my first experience with the Toltec teachings came through the books of Carlos Castaneda in the 1970s. When I became an apprentice of don Miguel Ruiz, author of *The Four Agreements*, in 1995, I was introduced to an entirely new perspective of these teachings. Miguel Ruiz wanted to teach us to be at peace with ourselves and all of creation and believed that the old ways based on fear and power would not serve us.

Throughout the ten years I studied with don Miguel, he focused his teaching on common sense, self-love, and self-acceptance as the path to personal freedom. As I carry on the tradition of his eagle warrior lineage, I have done the same, enhancing the Toltec wisdom with my experience as a transpersonal and spiritual counselor.

This book about the Toltecs is not like any other you have read. Don't worry about which one is right; they all are! I am glad you are reading this one and joining me on the Toltec path to personal freedom. Please share your experiences with me at *www.joydancer.com*.

Allan Hardman

The EVERYTHING® Series

Editorial

Publisher	Gary M. Krebs
Director of Product Development	Paula Munier
Managing Editor	Laura M. Daly
Executive Editor, Series Books	Brielle M. Matson
Associate Copy Chief	Sheila Zwiebel
Acquisitions Editor	Brielle Kay
Development Editors	Jessica LaPointe and Katie McDonough
Production Editor	Casey Ebert

Production

Director of Manufacturing	Susan Beale
Production Project Manager	Michelle Roy Kelly
Prepress	Erick DaCosta Matt LeBlanc
Interior Layout	Heather Barrett Brewster Brownville Colleen Cunningham Jennifer Oliveira
Cover Design	Erin Alexander Stephanie Chrusz Frank Rivera

Visit the entire Everything® Series at *www.everything.com*

THE
EVERYTHING®
TOLTEC
WISDOM
BOOK

A complete guide to the ancient wisdoms

Allan Hardman, Toltec Master

Adams Media
Avon, Massachusetts

This book is dedicated to don Miguel Ruiz,
with huge gratitude, for showing me life.

An Everything® Series Book.
Everything® and everything.com® are registered trademarks of F+W Publications, Inc.

Published by Adams Media, an F+W Publications Company
57 Littlefield Street, Avon, MA 02322 U.S.A.
www.adamsmedia.com

ISBN-10: 1-59869-285-2
ISBN-13: 978-1-59869-285-3

Printed in the United States of America.

J   I   H   G   F   E   D   C   B   A

Library of Congress Cataloging-in-Publication Data

Hardman, Allan.
The everything Toltec wisdom book / Allan Hardman.
p. cm. – (An everything series book)
ISBN-13: 978-1-59869-285-3 (pbk.)
ISBN-10: 1-59869-285-2 (pbk.)
1. Conduct of life. 2. Toltec philosophy–Miscellanea. I. Title.

BJ1595.H45 2007
299'.792–dc22

2007010855

This book is available at quantity discounts for bulk purchases.
For information, please call 1-800-289-0963.

Contents

Acknowledgments

It is with boundless gratitude that I acknowledge the love and wisdom shared with me by my teacher, don Miguel Ruiz. Without his patience, persistence, and faith in me I might not ever have awakened from the dream of the planet and reunited with life. I am equally grateful for all of the clients, students, apprentices, and fellow teachers who have pulled this wisdom through me with their presence and desire, so that I, also, could see and appreciate its power.

And to Jessica, who is always there with her smile and love; the eagles; sunshine and clouds; the pyramids and garden roses; my petty tyrants; and to divine presence in my life, I say "Thank you," with all my heart. This book is from and for all of you.

Top Ten Results of Following the
Toltec Path of Transformation

1. You have a clear understanding of your mind and how it works.
2. You feel connected to an ancient and modern tradition of healing and spirituality.
3. Your relationships of all kinds improve—with family and loved ones, at work, with friends, and all of creation.
4. Your inner dialogue is quiet, and your mind is at peace.
5. You are no longer afraid to enjoy life 110 percent or to risk new adventures.
6. You are happy being who you are, and do not need to defend or justify yourself.
7. Your awareness gives you clear choices about your life and how you want to live it.
8. You are impeccable in your interactions with others, and have a strong sense of your integrity and purpose in life.
9. Habits that have controlled you in the past are easily transformed and released.
10. The happiness, energy, and love that shine forth from you are an inspiration to all who meet you.

Introduction

▶ WHEN THE AZTECS founded their city of Tenochtitlán, which is now buried under Mexico City, they found the cities of Tula, Cholula, and Teotihuacán to the north, abandoned and in ruins. They took what art and building materials they could carry away from these sites, and left them alone. The Aztecs had no way to know who built these extensive cities, where they came from, what language the people spoke, or where they had gone.

The Aztecs could, however, appreciate the fine art and building skills of their forgotten neighbors, and gave them the name *Toltec*, which means "artist" in the native Nahuatl language. The Toltec name has survived to identify the survivors of those sites, who drifted out into the Aztec, Mayan, and other civilizations throughout Mexico—and shared their wisdom, astronomical knowledge, building skill, artistic insight, and deep spiritual understanding.

The Toltec spiritual lineages have been passed quietly from master to apprentice for many centuries, until this time of the sixth sun, which has opened all mystery schools to a much wider audience. There are many branches and lineages of the Toltec teachings now available through teachers, books, workshops, and on the Internet (a teaching technology that certainly was not available to the original Toltecs!).

As the different teachings evolve, there is one goal common for them all: a personal freedom that is the result of changing the fear-based agreements and beliefs in the human mind to new ones based on self-love and self-acceptance. Of course, this has been a goal of many religions and spiritual traditions for a very long time. A unique aspect of the Toltec path is the carefully refined tools of transformation that have been passed down through the centuries and are presented here in this book.

At the core of the Toltec wisdom is the understanding that everyone is dreaming a unique and personal dream, based on how they distort and filter their perceptions of the universe. Toltecs teach that there is no absolute right and wrong, or good and bad—except in the minds of humans and the Santa Claus and gods they create in their image.

The Toltec wisdom is based on three unique masteries: the mastery of awareness, the mastery of transformation, and the mastery of intent. The Toltecs have long understood that you must master awareness of the beliefs and agreements that limit the full expression of your being before you can truly transform them into a new and powerful dream. The transformation leads you to the dream of "heaven on Earth," the experience of living your life free of fear, judgment, suffering, guilt, or blame.

The mastery of transformation opens the door to the mastery of intent— the full release of all beliefs and a total surrender to, and communion with, the divine perfection of the universe. This is absolute personal freedom, and the ultimate goal of the Toltec path.

The Everything® Toltec Wisdom Book explains the Toltec path in detail, as a healing journey accessible to everyone. There are no esoteric mysteries here, and very few strange words from other languages to learn—simply a common-sense wisdom and spiritual insight that points the way to awakening and freedom. Anyone interested in becoming happier and more fulfilled in his or her life will find concepts and directions here that will help to achieve that goal.

There are action steps throughout the chapters, and you are encouraged to start a journal to record your experiences along your Toltec path. It is not within the scope of this book, of course, to support you individually if strong emotions or difficult memories arise from these action steps. If you feel drawn to explore the deeper possibilities of this journey into wholeness, you are encouraged to find a Toltec teacher or counselor who can mentor your adventure.

The Toltec path to personal freedom is both ancient and fully modern, and has been followed by innumerable spiritual travelers. It is a journey with no rules, and many valuable tools. You are invited to step onto the path, and find your way to your own personal dream of heaven on Earth.

Chapter 1
Who Were the Toltecs?

The Toltecs were a culture that dominated Mesoamerica for many centuries. Their cities were very sophisticated, and their pyramids and temples grand and complex. The real history, cultural beliefs, and religions of the Toltecs are lost in the past; however, many wonderful myths and partial facts have survived. In this introductory chapter, you will learn a brief bit about the history of the Toltecs, the cities of Tula and Teotihuacán, their god Quetzalcoatl, and what it means to be a Toltec today.

A Brief History of the Toltecs

Many cultures and societies have come and gone throughout the Americas over the past millennium. The Toltec culture of central Mexico has burst into the public awareness in recent years. Many books and teachers have shared the wisdom of these ancient peoples, from various perspectives and often with contradictory information (see Appendix B for a list of authors, teachers, and their books).

There are very few factual details about the Toltec civilization that have survived and are available today. The Toltecs had no written language, and had disappeared from their cities 200 years before the Aztecs settled nearby at what is now Mexico City.

The Aztecs did record what they knew and assumed about the Toltecs' history, including legends and spiritual mythologies they adopted for themselves. Most of the Aztec codices were burned by the Spanish in an effort to erase their culture and convert the Aztecs to the Spaniards' religious beliefs. The Mesoamerican cultures of the period worshiped the god Quetzalcoatl, the feathered serpent, among others, said to be the gentle god of philosophy and learning.

▲ Standing warriors in Tula.

The Spaniards' chroniclers continued the confusion, frequently calling every early civilization in central Mexico before the Aztecs "Toltec." In the Nahuatl legends of that time, the Toltecs were said to be the origin of all civilization.

Dates and Places

The culture now called Toltec was the first of three major groups that came into central Mexico from the north. In the eighth century A.D. they settled in Tula (also called Tollan), "the Place of the Reeds," in the Mexican state of Hidalgo, north of what is now Mexico City. In Tula the Toltecs were familiar with smelting metal and were master stone carvers.

FACT

The Aztecs and many cultures before them spoke the Nahuatl language. It is still the native language of more than a million people throughout central Mexico and beyond. There are many dialects and variations, some unintelligible to each other, and many Spanish words have entered the vocabularies. Nahuatl is recognized as an official national language of Mexico.

Some believe that the Toltecs were strong warriors; others connect them with the pyramids at Teotihuacán, which show no signs of fortification or war. Their culture disappeared in the twelfth century, for unknown reasons, possibly overrun by a second wave of people, the Chichimecas. The Chichimecas' culture slowly disappeared, and central Mexico entered a chaotic dark age until the Aztecs rose to power in Tenochtitlán at what is now Mexico City, in the early 1300s. Their extensive civilization lasted until the Spaniards arrived 200 years later.

What's in a Name?

The Aztecs respected the Toltecs as "men of knowledge," and rewrote some of their own history to show they were related to the Toltecs. The word *Toltec* is said to come from the Nahuatl language of that area, and means

▲ The Toltecs were artists in stone.

"master builder" or "artist." There is no way of knowing what these ancient people called themselves, or what language they spoke.

The founders of the great pyramids at Teotihuacán, northeast of Mexico City, have also been called Toltec by many researchers and teachers. It is important to note that the names and history of these early people have been distorted throughout the centuries to suit the needs of the time. It is significant to recognize that there were cultures of people in central Mexico who possessed deep spiritual understanding and considerable knowledge of astronomy, along with sophisticated systems of government, agriculture, and building.

The ancient people of Mexico and much of Latin America were master artists in stone, gold, silver, and other metals, and used their art to celebrate life and their gods. Although the Toltecs did not leave many clues about their origins, language, religion, or other facts of their daily lives, their art survives as a small window into a time and way of life that will probably remain a mystery forever. Perhaps it is appropriate to call all of the unknown ancients of central Mexico Toltecs—artists of stone and building, and "artists of the spirit."

The Builders of Teotihuacán?

There are many historians and teachers who believe the Toltecs built the inspiring complex of pyramids and urban areas at Teotihuacán, thirty miles northeast of today's Mexico City. It seems to have been built not by a nation or race, but by scientists, artists, and spiritual seekers who came together from the small agricultural villages of the area to build their beautiful city. They formed a society there, perhaps to explore and conserve the art and spiritual knowledge of ones who had come before them.

Teotihuacán is now one of Mexico's most beloved monuments (for a spiritual tour of Teotihuacán, see Chapter 20). The great Pyramids of the Sun and Moon are connected by the mile-long Avenue of the Dead, which is bordered by numerous temple platforms. At its peak in about A.D. 500,

▲ Temple platforms are evidence of the spiritual life of the ancients.

Teotihuacán thrived as a carefully planned city, home to as many as 200,000 people. It was larger and more advanced than any city in the world at that time, and lasted more than 500 years—longer than its contemporary, Rome.

The Great Mystery

The Aztecs found the city and pyramid complex at Teotihuacán in ruins when they settled the area, and the names and mythologies they gave to the pyramids and various structures are those used today. The Aztecs never lived in Teotihuacán, but considered it to be the place where the world was created. They called it "the place of the gods," or "the place where men become God."

ACTION!

Do a Web search for *Teotihuacán* and see the layout and construction of the city. Imagine the pyramids and temple platforms plastered and painted white, with colorful murals and other decorations. Imagine copal incense burning in the many temples, and music from drums and flutes filling the air. Dream yourself there, a new apprentice, in awe.

Evidence of residential groups from Oaxaca and other distant parts of Mexico have been found in the extensive city complex. The pyramids and other structures of Teotihuacán were made mostly of rubble and adobe bricks, faced with stone, and then plastered and painted shimmering white, red, and other colors. Murals with animal and shell motifs decorated the temple platforms and walls. There has been nothing like Teotihuacán in the world before or since.

And Then the Silence

No one knows why the power of Teotihuacán was silenced around A.D. 700. People simply stopped living in the city. Perhaps the residents reached a spiritual state that allowed them to transcend their physical bodies and go home to their beloved sun. There is evidence of a great fire that burned most of the main buildings; however, there is no way to know who burned them, or why. Maybe the residents torched their city when they left, or it was conquered and plundered by a marauding tribe.

Archeologists have not solved these mysteries, and probably never will. Whatever the cause, the great city of Teotihuacán, along with its mystique and magnificence, came to an end. Small village groups continued to live in the area, but the city itself was left alone and silent. The origins and destiny of Teotihuacán remain a secret today. Were these people the first Toltecs, who moved to Tula and began again? Or were they a forgotten group of Toltec masters who came together to manifest a magnificent vision of stone and spirit, and then disappeared into the annals of history?

Although the origins and purpose of Teotihuacán have been lost in history, the site remains alive as a tourist destination, and as a place of great spiritual power. Toltec and other teachers and groups from around the world visit to access the energy there for powerful personal and planetary healing.

Quetzalcoatl: Man or Myth?

Quetzalcoatl, the feathered serpent, was a major deity of ancient Mexico. This was the god of the morning and evening star for the Toltecs, and later, the god of gentle learning, philosophy, and culture to the Aztecs. Quetzalcoatl was especially revered in places where priests and nobility were educated. He was also identified with the planet Venus, and was a symbol of death and resurrection.

Legend says that Quetzalcoatl was tricked and humiliated by his rival, Tezcatlipoca, and either burned himself on a pyre and emerged as the planet Venus, or embarked on a raft made of snakes and disappeared into the Atlantic horizon. Another myth described Quetzalcoatl as a white priest-king, who would someday return from the east.

Quetzalcoatl may also have been a historic figure. He is described in legends as fair-skinned, with a long beard and ruddy complexion—very different from the native people. It is thought that he brought civilization, the calendar, and knowledge of astronomy, agriculture, healing, and social organization to an extensive region, and left on a boat promising to return someday.

▲ Quetzalcoatl was known by Toltecs and Aztecs.

The Aztecs may have believed that the explorer Hernando Cortés and the Spanish came as the realization of the Quetzalcoatl prophecy to return, and were not prepared to defend themselves against the ensuing conquest. The Aztec culture, temples, and secrets of science and spirit were quickly destroyed by the invaders and replaced by a new dream from a different land.

The Mystery School Opens

Although these ancient cultures and societies came and went, the deep spiritual understandings that had been passed down through the generations survived. The powerful truths were given from teacher to student, from master to apprentice, and kept hidden from the masses. For many centuries, the teachings were kept alive as an underground mystery school, spreading throughout Mexico and beyond.

In the Western world, interest in many of the ancient mystery schools from around the world began to emerge during the social revolutions of the

1960s. The time coincides with the time of the sixth sun, a change in the evolution of the human dream, which is described in Chapter 5.

Carlos Castaneda Opens the Door

The first introduction to the Toltec mysteries for most readers was the book by anthropologist and author Carlos Castaneda, *The Teachings of Don Juan—a Yaqui Way of Knowledge*, published in 1968. Ten more books followed, based on Castaneda's experiences with the nagual don Juan Matus in the desert of northern Mexico. (See Chapter 2 for more about what makes a person a "nagual.") Since then, many authors have written about the Toltec tradition, some from direct experience, and others from past lives, apprenticeships, or other connections.

ACTION!

Take a moment to think about reasons for your interest in Toltec, personal power, or freedom. Are they based in fear or love? Are you seeking power to protect yourself or influence others? Know that modern Toltec teachings are mostly directed to helping you learn to accept yourself and creation. Does that interest you?

As the Toltec wisdom leaves the realm of the secret mystery schools and enters into the light of modern culture, it is both enhanced by other traditions and diluted by individual teachers' personal opinions. Some teachers have been seduced away from the power of the teachings by the excitement of using psychotropic plants, while others may be attracted to accumulating personal power and forgetting their original desire for freedom.

Miguel Ruiz Shows the Practical Path

A frequent criticism of the early writings about the Toltec wisdom, especially Castaneda's, was that although the books were fascinating to read, they were not very practical for solving modern issues. Later authors—particularly Miguel Ruiz, whose book, *The Four Agreements: A Practical Guide to Personal Freedom* (1997), captured the minds and hearts of millions of readers all over the world—distilled the teachings into useful tools for personal transformation.

An important change in the Toltec tradition is the shift from fear-based to love-based teachings. The early writers, again especially Castaneda, described the need for personal power to use in defense against attack from all manner of forces, seen and unseen. Castaneda often describes himself shaking in terror, waiting for some force or entity to attack him. Newer writers stress the importance of acceptance and love as the healing power for troubled individuals and the world.

The Toltec wisdom continues to be available to a wide audience, through the love and energy of dedicated teachers and authors (see Appendix B).

From the Ancient to the Modern

Cultural context plays an important part in rituals and ceremonies, with or without psychotropic plants. For the indigenous people living with the historical and personal connection to these plants or shamanic processes, the experiences are interpreted and held in their cultural framework. It is difficult for people from a modern urban cultural perspective to enter the native context and profit from the rich traditions there.

Many seekers who became interested in indigenous people and their spiritual paths set out to find a shaman or master who might take them as an apprentice and "blow their minds." They searched the deserts of Mexico and ate peyote cactus in their quest for truth. They braved the Amazon jungle seeking experiences with magic mushrooms or the powerful ayahuasca vine and its visions. Some found what they were looking for, and most were probably disappointed. As one such seeker reported, "I always came down."

Modern teaching of the Toltec wisdom rarely includes artificially altered states of consciousness. The path to freedom demands a clear mind and focused attention. Although the knowledge from the past has been modified and revised, the essential core of the Toltec wisdom has never been lost: Personal freedom is available to the warrior who dedicates herself to breaking free from the prison of fear-based beliefs and agreements imposed by her domestication and culture—and to becoming the magnificent being she came here to be.

The Toltecs of Today: Artists of the Spirit

Perhaps the greatest artistry of the ancient Toltecs was their spiritual realization. There is much evidence in Tula, Teotihuacán, and other cities of ancient Mexico that the people who lived there experienced and shared deep spiritual truths. The questions they explored about their place in the universe, and life beyond death, were the same ones asked by humans throughout history.

Those questions are still being asked, and answered, on the Toltec path today. The Toltec of today is a "spiritual warrior," struggling against the lies and beliefs that deny his place in the perfection of creation. He uses the tools of stalking, dreaming, recapitulation, and many others from the ancients to break the bonds of his cultural programming and be free.

The Toltec warrior seeks a spiritual life, lived in awareness of his connection with a power or force greater than his individual human story. He recognizes all parts of the universe as perfect manifestations of that single force, and sees the unity of creation as one living being.

The Toltec path offers the potential to change your entire life. To become a Toltec spiritual warrior and free yourself from the conditioning of your childhood is the greatest gift you could give yourself. It is a chance to let go of suffering forever, and be always happy. Your happiness becomes a gift to all of creation.

The Toltec warrior sees his life as a work of art, and himself as the artist. He learns that he is dreaming reality, and he is the master of his dream. He knows that everything he thinks, every action, every choice, and every word he speaks, are the tools of his art. He refines those tools, becoming impeccable with his words and actions, deliberate about the use of his energy, and determined to keep his heart open in love and acceptance.

As an artist of the spirit, the Toltec of today knows there are no rules he must follow, no belief systems he is required to embrace, and no leaders to obey. He seeks complete freedom from fear, and absolute surrender to love and acceptance. The modern Toltec discovers a happiness that is the result of love and acceptance flowing out of him, and he knows there is an endless supply of that love—it is his nature to love. He embraces life, and dances in joy and gratitude for every moment of his existence. This is the Toltec path, and this is the modern spiritual warrior—an artist of the spirit.

Chapter 2

The Wisdom of the Toltecs

The Toltecs have given the world a wonderful gift. Their wisdom of the past has become the common sense of the present, and the perfect solution to many of the challenges of the modern world. In this chapter you will learn that the universe is made mostly of light, and why the Toltecs say you are dreaming all the time. You are invited to walk this path through the three masteries of the Toltecs, and surrender to the unknown as a spiritual warrior.

The Light Is Everywhere

Have you ever gone out into the night and looked up at the stars, and wondered what is in all the space between them? The early Toltecs asked themselves that question, and they realized that the space between the stars was filled with light. You might wonder, "How could that be? It is so dark out there." The ancient Toltec masters saw that if you put any object in the empty space, it would be hit on all sides by light coming from every direction, from every star in the universe!

Every star is a sun, sending out light in every direction. The universe is filled with the light from countless suns.

Have you ever seen one of those illustrations that show how an atom looks, with the electrons spinning around the nucleus? It looks a lot like the planets revolving around the sun, with empty space in between! Modern physics teaches that nothing in this universe is actually very solid—and that is exactly what the old masters saw.

You Are Mostly Light

The ancient Toltec masters did not know about atoms and electrons, but they knew what was later proved by modern science. They knew that what appeared to be solid was only an illusion of the human mind, and that the physical matter in the universe was as open and empty as the night sky. In addition, they saw that the space between all the small particles of matter in the physical universe was filled with light.

When the Toltecs saw that even their bodies were made of tiny little stars, surrounded mostly by space filled with light, they also recognized something very amazing: They saw that there is no boundary between their bodies and any other object. There is no place where one physical object stops and another begins, because nothing is solid and everything is filled with the same light.

The trees, rocks, and birds are filled with light, the air is filled with light, space is filled with light, and it is all the same light. The universe is made of little pieces of matter, suspended in a field of light. Your body is filled with light. You are mostly light!

The Light Is a Messenger

The light that you see with your eyes is a very narrow band of the entire spectrum of the energy that vibrates in this universe. If you could shift just a little to a different vibration, you would come to the infrared band in the

▲ A noble Toltec of Tula

spectrum, but you would not be able to see it with your eyes. There are also x-rays, gamma rays, cell phone signals, and an incredible range of "light" that you cannot see with your eyes. Each receiver is designed to "see" a different part of the spectrum, whether it is a cell phone receiving a call or a human eye seeing the beauty in a flower.

Radio waves are also a form of light. If you were able to hear all of the radio waves that are passing through you as light, it would be absolute chaos. Can you imagine? A rock 'n' roll station would be playing in your head, right along with three talk shows and a sports event! A radio that receives the light as radio frequencies has a system to choose one frequency out of the hundreds that are passing through everything all of the time. You can even receive the signals inside a building, because the radio light waves come right through the walls.

If you are having trouble imagining that the universe is not solid, but is made of light, don't worry. Your mind has believed the "solid" version for a long time, and will no doubt be troubled by this new possibility. It is okay to let your mind relax with this idea for a while.

The light never changes or modifies the message it is carrying. Whether it is a radio signal, or visible light reflected from a distant planet, the light is a perfect messenger.

The Tonal and the Nagual

When the Toltecs saw that the light was everywhere in creation, they understood that it was a living part of the cosmos. The light is the messenger that carries the message of creation to all parts of the universe. They called this messenger the "nagual" and the physical parts of the universe the "tonal." Most people think of themselves as part of the physical universe, and identify themselves with the tonal.

When someone awakens and sees that the universe is made of light, and identifies herself as that light, the person is called a nagual. The great Toltec teachers of the past and present embody this truth, and are referred to as naguals. These masters may or may not choose to accept apprentices and students to guide to liberation from their dream of a solid universe.

The Greatest Gift: You Are Dreaming

When the Toltecs teach "You are dreaming," they are not talking about something the school bully said when you told him you would beat him up if he didn't leave you alone, or what you mother might have said when you told her you wanted to be an astronaut. "You are dreaming" is the greatest gift that the Toltecs have given the world. If you understand this amazing reality, your life will never be the same.

You Are Not Seeing What Is "Out There"

There is more to the mystery of the light than you have learned so far. The light is the living messenger that reflects off the tonal (creation) and brings the message of that aspect of the tonal to your eyes. Remember that illustration in your high school physics book, with the tree and the eyeball, that showed that the light bounces off the tree and comes to the eye?

The light is a perfect messenger. Light passes into the eye and makes an image (upside down, by the way) on the back of your eye. The parts of the eye called rods and cones translate that light image into nerve impulses that travel into the brain and create a little virtual-reality image of the tree in your mind. When you "see" the tree, you are actually looking at that virtual reality in your mind. You are not seeing the tree "out there" at all.

Your Mind Distorts the Light

When the light reflected from an object enters your eye, it travels through channels of perception in your mind. All of your life you have been creating belief systems, collecting opinions, experiencing fears, and making agreements about the world and how it works. You have stored all of that information in the channels of perception in your mind. If your mother said to you, "Your father's a bum and he never comes home. All men are alike," you stored that as a memory somewhere in your channels of perception.

When the light is reflected off an object in creation and enters your eye, it has brought you the perfect message of what is out there. However, when that light enters those channels of perception in your mind, it picks up all the stored memories (old light) in those channels—and the message is distorted! When the light reaches that place in your mind where the virtual reality is created, it has been distorted by the addition of countless pieces of light stored as language, memories, beliefs, assumptions, agreements, emotions, knowledge, and more. Toltecs call this distorted virtual reality the "dream."

Imagine that your mother did say your father was a bum, and all men are alike. As a child, you saw your father, and that stored light distorted your image of him. Even if you became a father yourself, that distorting light is still there. Perhaps you feel guilty about being a father or a man, and don't really know why. If you are a woman, and heard that message as a child, perhaps you can recognize how it has distorted your relationships with men and fathers. You cannot see the world as it is when you are distorting it with the stored light in your mind.

Your Mind Never Stops Dreaming

The process of distorting the light into a virtual reality continues day and night. The Toltecs knew that there is no way to see what is really out in the world, because the light must come into your brain for you to see it. In the process, it is always distorted.

The idea of "light" can be expanded to include the information collected by all of your senses—each one responds to a different frequency in the spectrum. In addition to your eyes, your organs of taste, touch, hearing, and smell collect data from the world around you. They are your "organs of perception."

The image you see as a virtual reality in your mind is not what is out there as "the world." The pure message in the light has been distorted by your mind according to your particular collection of stored data in your channels of perception. Your unique virtual reality is what the Toltecs call your "personal dream."

Remember that all the information your organs of perception collect is a perfect message about what is out there in the world. Unfortunately, your mind is an organ of dreaming—or you could call it an "organ of deception"! Your mind distorts the information into a dream, and then looks at that little personal dream inside your mind and tells you that it is seeing the world. If you believe your mind, you will be very confused about the world. Perhaps you have already noticed that.

At night when you are sleeping, and your organs of perception have stopped collecting information from outside, your mind continues to dream. It simply uses all its stored light to create images. Every image in your night dreams, no matter how strange or bizarre they seem, comes from a lifetime of memories, emotions, and other forms of stored light.

ACTION!

Take some time now to consider these ideas about distorting the light. Write down some ways you might be distorting your friends, family, world events, and even yourself, based on opinions, fears, and other light stored in your channels of perception. Be gentle with yourself if you write "bad" things. It is your dreaming mind writing, not really you.

The Three Masteries of the Toltec Path

These teachings of the Toltecs truly are a path. Like most paths, this one begins somewhere, travels a defined course, and ends in a very special place. It is a path that may wind through unexpected parts of your mind, your history, and your relationships. Yet if you follow it to the end, you will find great treasures there. You will find a richness beyond value. You will know the truth and beauty of who you are and the magnificent oneness of the universe in which you live.

Even though the Toltecs have described this path for thousands of years, it remains unique and personal to each individual who travels it. As you are learning in this book, each person has been programmed to see and understand the world differently, and the world you live in, the paths you walk, are yours and yours alone.

This Toltec path is a path of mastery. In order to help you know where you are beginning and how to get to the riches at the end of this journey, the Toltecs divide their path into three masteries: the mastery of awareness, the mastery of transformation, and the mastery of intent.

Taming Your Mind

One of the goals of the Toltec path is to quiet your mind and resolve troublesome emotional reactions. Imagine you are trying to ride a horse, and it is fidgeting and won't let you stay in the saddle. You try being nice to her, and you try being mad at her, but she still won't let you control her. If the horse has burrs under her saddle blanket, she is never going to settle down so you can ride her. You begin your mastery of awareness when you recognize that your mind and emotions are fidgeting, and you know the problem is the burrs in the saddle blanket of your dreaming mind.

If you just get mad and walk away from the horse, you haven't solved your problem. To help the horse settle down so you can ride her, you must take off the saddle, find the burrs, and remove them. It is the same with your mind and emotions. Once your awareness shows you the real source of any difficulties in your life, you have the information you need to go to the source and remove the burrs. This is the mastery of transformation—your awareness leads you along the path to the true problem and its solution.

Once your mind is cleared of its burrs, you can use it to take you directly and exactly where you want to go. This is the mastery of intent. With your mind cleared of old programming and other distractions, the inspirations and perspirations of your life will take you easily and effortlessly to your goals. You will find yourself creating your life in a new way. You will be an artist, and your life will become a masterpiece of art.

What follows is an introduction to these three masteries, which are expanded and explained more thoroughly in later chapters.

The Mastery of Awareness

Perhaps you have heard the old saying "We don't know who discovered water, but we know it wasn't a fish." When you are dreaming, and you don't yet understand that you are immersed in a reality that is unique only to you, it is difficult to see outside of it. If you take a fish out of the water, and say, "See, there is air, also!" I am guessing that the fish would say "Fine! Great! Now put me back in the water!" With your new Toltec understanding of your dreaming mind, you might say, "Wow, I like the view better out here. I want to really see, without distorting reality!"

Toltec masters teach their apprentices that to "breathe the air" outside of their old dreams, they need to master awareness of how their dreaming minds work. The apprentice needs to become aware of the beliefs, opinions, fears, judgments, and other subconscious attitudes that control his behavior. Remember the example of the burrs under the saddle blanket? The Toltecs know those burrs represent everything stored in your mind that cause you to be stressed, agitated, afraid, angry, hurt, jealous, or depressed.

FACT

The old Toltec masters used some pretty severe techniques to break their apprentices' attachment to their distorted version of reality. They took them close to death by burying them or hanging them upside down in a tree, or gave them hallucinogenic plants. Modern teachers usually rely on love, common sense, and tools of awareness to do the same job.

The Mastery of Transformation

Once you have revealed to yourself the details of your personal dream, you have the opportunity to un-learn everything you know. You came into this world with no opinions and no fears. All the distorting light in your channels of perception was put there by others, and it is possible to clean out those channels. Your new awareness will give you choices about what you want to believe, think, and feel. In this mastery you are offered many tools for transforming your dream.

On the Toltec path there are no rules about who you should be, or how you should think or act. There are only the many time-honored tools that guide you to awareness and the transformation of your dreaming mind. It is up to you to make choices about how you want to live. Once you actually have the choice, wouldn't you like to always be happy, peaceful, and loving in your life?

The Mastery of Intent

Some of the modern Toltec masters call the mastery of intent the "mastery of love." The most important change that people on the Toltec path make is to discard all the beliefs and agreements that cause them to hurt themselves with self-judgment and self-rejection. In their new way of dreaming, they live with self-acceptance and self-love. They learn to be impeccable with their word, and never use it against themselves or others (more about impeccability in later chapters).

The mastery of intent is like holding a big fire hose right at the nozzle, and directing the water (your intent) exactly where you want it to go. Before you reach this level of mastery, you are more like a firefighter holding the hose ten feet back from the nozzle, while it whips around with the water going everywhere.

The Toltecs teach that when you become the master of love and intent, magic will happen in your life, and abundance will come to you effortlessly. You will become the master of your life, and live in the dream of heaven on Earth. This is the ultimate personal freedom, and the goal of the Toltec path.

What Is Personal Freedom?

Can you sense the possibilities the Toltecs offer you in their wisdom? There is a great freedom to be yourself, once you have cleaned out the garbage put into your mind by others, and established your own ideas, rules, and agreements about who you are and how you want to live. With the Toltec wisdom you can live your life free from negativity and fear, and free from the need to prove anything to anyone about your value or worth. This is personal freedom.

In this freedom, you will be able to live your life with impeccability and integrity. Modern people following this ancient Toltec path learn to have access to the truth of their feelings, wants, needs, and desires, and are willing to express those truths to themselves and others. They do not gossip, and they don't commiserate with others about their troubles. Because they are free from fear, they are willing and able to be happy all the time. They go through life with their hearts always open, and everyone who meets them feels uplifted in their presence.

The Serpent, the Jaguar, and the Eagle

People who live close to the land, the changing seasons of planting and harvesting, the movements of the heavens, and life and death are deeply aware of symbols that represent various aspects of their lives. Like many cultures of the past, the Toltecs were very connected to various animals, constellations, plants, crystals, the four directions, and the elements, such as earth, air, fire, and water.

They used these symbols in rituals and ceremonies to help them understand and safeguard their world. Many native peoples, including the Toltecs, used the serpent, the jaguar, and the eagle to represent stages on their journey into spiritual awareness.

The Serpent

When a Toltec apprentice begins to explore her life on this path, she is like the serpent. The serpent sees a pretty small piece of the big picture—its main interests are food and safety from its predators. It moves easily, even gracefully, through its element, but it never sees beyond it.

The serpent represents the new Toltec apprentice, exploring the mastery of awareness. Her view of the big picture of life is still limited to her immediate needs, such as food, the gratification of pleasures, and her fear of being judged or "eaten" by the judging human predators around her. With awareness—like the wise fish learning there is more to life than water—the apprentice desires more. It is time for her to become the jaguar.

The Jaguar

The jaguar is a great hunter. This animal learns the behaviors and activities of its prey by waiting and watching. The jaguar patiently stalks its prey, and moves in deliberately and decisively for the kill. Jaguars are skilled at what they do, and they do not waste any energy doing it. Sometimes they hunt with others of their kind, but mostly they hunt alone.

As you imagine yourself growing in power on the Toltec path, see yourself as the jaguar. You are the stalker, in the mastery of transformation. Your prey are the judgments, fears, and lies that have been programmed into your mind by others. You study your prey carefully, and when you are ready, attack it, grab it by the back of the neck, and shake it until the old lies are gone from it. Changing old lies to new truth is the goal of the jaguar on the path of transformation.

The better you are as a hunter, the worse prey you are. The jaguar has no predator enemies. The mouse has many. The more skilled you become at identifying and eliminating the distorting lies in your mind, the less susceptible you are to their power. Instead of the lies hunting you, you hunt the lies. You become the Toltec jaguar.

The Eagle

The eagle is also a hunter, and is prey for no other. Eagles fly high above the land, and see the patterns, colors, and perfection spread out below them. They have no opinions or judgments about anything they see. The eagle hunts alone, and then soars gracefully with its fellow eagles on high updrafts, in silence.

When you become the eagle, you are the master of your intent, and the master of love and acceptance. You are a seer, open and perceiving without distorting the many magical manifestations of the creation. You do not react to your old judgments and fears, or those of others; you fly free from the old dream. You soar high on your own currents, and live your life impeccably and effortlessly. The abundance of the universe is yours, spread out below, awaiting your choice. You are a master in the Toltec eagle tradition.

The Surrender of the Spiritual Warrior

Have you ever wondered what is possible for you in your life? Have you pondered your potential for juicy romantic relationships, the perfect livelihood, an abundant lifestyle, warm friendships, a healthy body, and more? There is nothing that prohibits all of these gifts from being yours except the limiting beliefs and agreements that you accepted into your mind a long time ago.

▲ Mexico's coat of arms.

Those limitations are nothing more than the stored light in your mind that you learned about in this chapter, and you can stalk and transform them.

QUESTION?

How will I know what my beliefs and agreements are? Isn't it hard to figure out?
The Toltecs have created and refined many simple tools to use for your awareness and transformation. Many of them are described for you in the following chapters, and in action steps throughout this book. Your expanded awareness will show you what you need to know.

The Toltec apprentices of the past became spiritual warriors by surrendering their attachment to what they knew and believed. The masters knew that when an apprentice's surrender was complete, he could create a new dream and become a true artist of the spirit. Are you willing to consider a surrender like theirs? It may feel a bit scary, but it is not dangerous!

Chapter 3

Domestication: Downloading the Dream

The Toltecs say that everyone who is born is domesticated into a dream that already exists in the minds of those around them. In this chapter you will learn how the process of domestication works. You will understand the important part that fear plays in teaching children the rules of the dream, and be alerted to ways in which you are distorting your reality based on what caregivers told you early in your life. You will also discover how you pass your dream on to others, without even realizing it.

3

Who Were You When You Were Born?

You were born into this world as a "bundle of joy." Your mind was free of stories, and you were happy—without even knowing what happiness was. You had no opinions, no fears, no expectations, and no judgments. There was no distorting light stored in your channels of perception. You had no words yet for colors, sounds, objects, or Mom's bad hair day. You had no concept of good and bad or right and wrong.

You simply existed, in a sea of stimulations and events that you experienced directly, just as they were. Your mind had no experience with naming, categorizing, or separating any of this incoming light. You were simply present, in each moment, without self-awareness. You did not even know you had been given a name or gender identity.

The Infant Guru

You were actually like a little Toltec master or guru, present in each and every moment, living in the bliss of love and acceptance. If you could have talked and described your experience, spiritual seekers would have come from miles around to sit at your feet and learn from you.

In those first few months of your life, you lived in the bliss of the oneness that gurus teach and to which spiritual seekers aspire. Because you had not yet learned the fears and judgments of the adult world, your nature was openness and love. Your innocence was like that of Adam and Eve in the Garden of Eden.

Hooking Attention

As your body began to mature, so did your nervous system. You began to focus your eyes on objects, and recognize interesting shapes. Sounds and images of people began to have meaning, and you remembered the meaning from one time to the next. None of this evolution was conscious or intended, of course; it was simply the wisdom of life, maturing your body and awareness.

At first you did not know that your hand was an object separate from your mother's hand. A day came when you realized that by willing your arm to move, you could reach out and grasp an object. Later you tried to move your mother's hand with that same focus of your attention, and it didn't work. You began to learn that your hand and your mother's hand were different, and the one you could control was "yours." Little by little you discovered which parts of the world were you and yours, and which were not.

FACT

By the time an infant is a month old, she has learned to focus her eyes on objects eight to twelve inches away (a parent's face during feeding). By the end of her second month, she has learned to track moving objects with her eyes and recognize voices and other sounds.

Sounds, colors, movement, and touch hooked your attention. The more your body and nervous system matured, the more you were able to direct your attention. At the same time, you were learning to hook the attention of your caregivers. You had simple needs for food, comfort, touch, and relating, and they filled those needs. You also needed their attention, which became the primary food for your maturing body and nervous system.

A channel of attention was opened between you and your caregivers. You learned to hook their attention so your needs could be met, and they began to hook your attention so they could teach you their dream.

The Dream of the First Attention

When you came into this world, everyone around you was dreaming. They had learned to distort the light into their own little virtual reality in their mind, and they believed that their version was the truth. As soon as they could hook your attention, they began to use it as a channel to download their dream into your mind. They took little pieces of their dream and planted them in your mind, and the seeds grew and matured into your own dream.

Because your attention was being used for the first time, the Toltecs call the dream you learned from your parents the "dream of the first attention." Your parents downloaded all the beliefs, judgments, opinions, and fears that became your personal dream as you were growing up. The download was supplemented and enhanced by siblings, friends, and then teachers and religious leaders. You were a sponge, and you soaked up whatever was being offered to you.

Domestication of the New Human

When a new human arrives in the world she is not interested in any of the opinions and judgment of the other humans around her. As her ability to direct her attention matures, her caregivers use that channel of attention to download all of the standards she needs to meet to belong to their family.

The process of domesticating the new human is very much like what one would do to train a new puppy. If the puppy piddles on the rug, it is put out of the house, usually with a swat and a "Bad dog!" When the puppy feels its bladder filling and becomes afraid of punishment, it runs to the door to be let out. When it goes outside, the puppy is rewarded with a cookie, and "Good dog!" The puppy is domesticated to follow the rules through punishment and reward.

Do you see the similarity between domesticating a child and a puppy? The new human child must learn whatever rules, beliefs, and agreements are operating in the system to which she is born. As the child matures, the rules become more and more complex, and the repetition of them makes them more and more real. No matter how well a child learns the rules, there are always more hoops to jump through: new friends, schools, institutions, relatives, religious groups, bosses, lovers, and mates, and all expect different behaviors at different times.

Which Side of the Street?

Have you ever wondered why you were born into your particular family? There are many beliefs and mythologies that have been invented to answer that question. Some people believe that the law of karma is directing these events. Others say a cosmic committee makes the choice, with or without your help, in order for you to learn a life lesson. Other people believe they are being punished or rewarded by an angry or pleased God.

You will learn more about the Toltec view of how the universe works in a later chapter. For now, consider that if everyone has a different dream of why we are born where we are, perhaps there is no answer except "because you were." It is very important to recognize that where you were born, and the family and circumstances you were born into, created the dream you are dreaming right now.

At any one time there are more than a hundred major and minor wars being fought on Earth. These battles are all the result of people with different beliefs fighting about who is right. If you were born on the Lebanese side of the street, you would have learned that the Israelis were your enemies, and vice versa. The same is true for the Irish Catholic and Protestant sides of the street, the Rwandan Hutus and Tutsis (800,000 dead in 100 days), and the American Civil War (as many as 700,000 dead).

Current thinking about puppy training warns against hitting a puppy. Experts say that hitting or hurting a puppy signals the end of a loving and respectful relationship with her. They say that a pup will not trust or willingly obey someone who hits her. Dog trainers encourage lots of positive attention, to balance the training.

Brothers and sisters kill each other to prove their dream is right—and fail to understand that they are only fighting about the dream they were born into on their side of the street. Which side of the street were you born on, and who do you hurt to prove your dream is right?

Here Comes the Judge

The wisdom of the Toltecs teaches that you were born as an enlightened master, free from any suffering, fear, or attachments. Wherever you popped up into the world, whether it was in a family using illegal drugs in a big city, a family of fundamentalist preachers in the rural south, a middle-class American suburb, or a military family in the far north of Russia—no matter where it was, or who was there, you were born free. And no matter where in the world you were born, or into what circumstances, the family unit you were born into was dreaming, and it was their job to teach you their dream.

How They Taught You to Be Good

Your family's dream was the description of every belief, opinion, and agreement they had arrived at about how life is, and how a good person believes and behaves. Your caregivers wanted you to be a good person. More important, they wanted you to be like them. It is important for the family to know who belongs to the family unit and who does not. Perhaps the family belongs to a religious community, a political party, and an extended family of relatives near and far. They might also identify with a profession, a race, a nation, and an economic class.

Until the age of six or seven, children have no logic for discerning truth. They believe what they are told. A four-year-old will absolutely know there is a Santa Claus, while her nine-year-old brother will argue that there is no such person, and that all the Santas at the mall have fake beards.

Your young mind was eager to learn about the world you were born into, and had no ability to filter out lies or misinformation. It absorbed everything, including your parents' love, anger, criticism, beliefs, and all the energy swirling around you. You were truly a fish in the water, and there was no way you could know anything but the dream you were born into, which was downloaded into your mind.

Learning to Fit In

The most important thing they taught you was how you needed to act to be part of the family unit. When a child is told "We don't put our elbows on the table," or "Don't use that tone of voice with your mother," the message is "If you want to belong to this family, and have the identity, food, shelter, comfort, and safety that it provides you, you must do things our way."

The same messages of domestication are used in classrooms, workplaces, friendships, and marriages. "Here is how you need to act in order to belong to this unit, and if you do not act properly, you will be rejected." Kids are expelled from school, bosses fire employees, and mates are divorced because they do not do things the right way for the unit they belong to.

> Parents must be careful not to use this information to judge themselves about their child rearing—past or present. Your domestication included everything you know about being a parent, including what you have learned from "experts" in books and magazines, and on TV. Perhaps you are learning new possibilities here.

This system of domestication creates order from chaos, which cultures need—and denies the uniqueness of the individuals, which hurts both the individuals and the culture. It is quite possible that most cultures go overboard on the side of order, and unnecessarily repress the exceptional gifts of individuals.

Their Way or the Highway

The ultimate tool of domestication is fear, whether training is directed toward a puppy or a child. Remember how you came into this world as a little guru? You were not afraid of anything. There is no way your parents could threaten you with rejection and expulsion from the family for misbehaving, because you had not yet learned that you belonged to it! Once your attention could be hooked, however, and you were taught who you were and where it was safe to belong, you could be made afraid of not belonging.

The fear of punishment and the desire for reward is the key to domestication. "Good dog" and a cookie, or "Bad dog" and expulsion from the house, is everything the puppy needs to understand about the rules. It is the same for a child. "I love you when you get good grades in school" is a message about what is required for acceptance in many families. If in addition to being rewarded for good grades the child is also disciplined for "bad" grades, perhaps by losing privileges or by physical punishment, the message is even stronger.

The Ultimate Fear: Rejection

The ultimate fear powering all domestication is the fear of being rejected. In tribal cultures of the past, to be expelled from the tribe was a sentence of death—an individual could not survive without the support of the community. For a child, rejection from the family feels like annihilation. His only reference point about who he is comes from belonging to his family. He will do anything to be good, to get it right, and to belong.

The authority on what is right and wrong comes from the judgments of those around you when you are young. They are like a judge in a courtroom, looking down at you from a high bench, describing your crimes (you broke the vase, said a bad word, talked back), and deciding on your punishment (no TV for a week, wash your mouth out with soap, a spanking when Dad gets home).

Your Very Own Personal Judge

In time, the "judge" becomes part of the chatter in your mind. He is speaking to you in your dreaming mind, telling you what other people think of you, and what you should be doing to get it right for everyone. The judge is projected outward onto your friends, mate, boss, children, parents, police, strangers, Santa Claus, and ultimately, God—until it can seem that everyone is watching and judging you.

The Toltecs know that the inner judge creates the biggest fears in the human mind, and is the biggest obstacle to living a free and happy life (more on the judge in Chapter 6).

Going Against Yourself for the First Time

The fear of being wrong and being expelled from the family puts a great deal of pressure on a young child. She comes into the world totally open as pure awareness, but as she matures she begins to identify herself and her separateness from others. She has needs, and wants them met. She begins to create a dream of herself and her world, and develops a personality to fit it.

As the new arrival's dream gets stronger, it begins to conflict with the dream that prevails in the family around her. Her parents cannot tolerate her dreaming outside of their box, and so must exert whatever pressure is necessary to make her comply. Each young child finds her own way to deal with this pressure to conform. Some easily abandon their truth in order to be loved; others fight for their right to be themselves.

The Battle for Control

Beliefs about parenting cover a wide range of possibilities. Some children are allowed to run free and wild, while others are made to obey many rules and are punished for minor infractions. Punishments also range from mild rebukes to violent and dangerous beatings. The Toltec wisdom makes no distinction about what is right or wrong with any of the many ways children are parented. It only calls for awareness of the dreaming minds involved, and choices based on that awareness.

QUESTION?

Is it possible for a child to be raised without domestication and a dream?
It might sound ideal, but it is impossible. It would mean not teaching her a language, or engaging her in relationships of any kind. If you parent a child with an awareness of how the dream works, she will be very lucky.

The child and the parents are all dreaming, and battling for their dream to be right. Because everyone is dreaming a personal dream, the Toltecs understand that everyone is right—about his or her dream. When parents are in conflict with their children, it is because they believe their dream is more right than are the desires of the child. This is not to suggest that the desires of the child must always prevail, but only that the dreams of child and parent have equal value.

The Big Battle Is Lost

There comes a time when every new human must abandon the fight for his or her own dream. It often comes by the second year of life. The terrible twos are a rough time for the child—her dream is getting stronger, and it is increasingly in conflict with her parents' demands to be like them. Something must give, and the parents know they cannot lose control.

One of the main principles of modern Toltec wisdom is to be impeccable with your word. To be impeccable means to not use your word against yourself. You will learn more about impeccability later in this book. For now, imagine that a mother and a young boy are in conflict about some behavior or attitude of the child's that the mother wants to change. This time the child is not budging from his position. He wants what he wants, and he will not give it up!

ACTION!

Try to remember a time in your childhood when you lost a battle about something very important to you. If you have no memory of this, imagine what it must have been like to realize you could not win. How does it feel in your body? Does it remind you of anything in your adult life? Write it down.

This final battle may be about something simple, like bedtime, or more important, such as giving up a favorite toy as punishment for breaking a family rule. The child may believe that he is being treated unfairly (again), and this time he is willing to stand his ground. The mother believes that she must win the battle, or she will lose her authority in the family. They both think they are right, and willing to go all the way. Since the parent is bigger, and more determined, she wins, and the boy loses. He gives up his toy.

The boy actually gives up something much bigger than his toy. He gives up his authenticity. In the final battle he surrenders his authority to be right as he is. He uses his word against himself, by telling himself that he is wrong for fighting with his mother, and after that it becomes easier and easier. He must surrender his truth to that of his parents, then his teachers, peers, religious leaders, mate, and anyone else who claims to have authority over him.

It is not the child's fault that he goes against himself, nor is it his mother's fault. They are both doing their best based on what they believe.

Passing On Your Domestication to Others

The beliefs and agreements that constitute your domestication have been passed down through many generations. As the human dream matures and changes, the particulars of the dream and domestication change, but many elements will stay the same—especially the presence of the judge. Nationality, community, religion, and other factors described previously support the bigger dream. For example, people living in parts of the United States known as the "Bible belt" will support each other to maintain a common set of beliefs about church, family, and God. Those beliefs have been passed down to the parents, and will be passed to their children.

In a motorcycle gang, members also support each other to maintain the belief systems that identify who belongs to the gang. Anyone who behaves or dresses outside of the dream will be harassed into conforming or banished from the group. This kind of social domestication is common in all groups, teams, professions, and institutions.

In families, you may have noticed big brother or sister telling a younger sibling "Don't do that; Mommy will get mad." As soon as the little ones can, they start helping to domesticate other little ones. Once they learn the rules, they are ready to pass them on to whoever will believe them. They become the judges, keeping others in line with the rules.

Dress codes at work and school are a form of domestication into conformity. Gang colors are another. These rules define who belongs to a group and who does not. Each group designates one or more people whose job it is to enforce the rules, and mete out punishments for failure to comply.

It is especially interesting to observe the presence of the judge and domestication in personal relationships of all kinds. In romantic relationships people often send messages to each other about how they need to be in order to be part of the love or marriage unit. A wife might tell her husband, "I can't believe you are going to the party dressed like that!" She is domesticating him. He might fight back with, "If you embarrass me again by drinking too much tonight, it is the last party I am going to with you!" He is domesticating her, threatening that her behavior will cause him to withdraw his attention and presence.

Remember, the worst punishment is expulsion or withdrawal—to withhold the attention that is so vital to the development of a child, and also essential to the well-being of adults. This is the penalty the outer or inner judge metes out when he believes you have broken the rules.

Chapter 4
Awakening in the Dream

All humans are asleep, and just dreaming life according to a virtual reality programmed into their minds when they are young. The Toltecs say that each individual who awakens from the dream becomes a spiritual warrior, and master of her own life. This awareness is a gift to the one who awakens, and to all of humanity. In this chapter you will learn more about the "mitote" in the dreaming mind, and the gift of wisdom that comes with the mastery of awareness.

The Matrix: *Fact or Fiction?*

The most important topic you will continue to explore in this book is the idea that you are dreaming all the time, and how to awaken from that dream. There are many stories in ancient mythologies and modern books and movies related to this theme.

Remember stories like "Sleeping Beauty" and "Snow White"? These old folk tales often involve an angry or selfish woman casting a spell on a young woman of whom she is jealous. The spell can only be broken, and the girl awakened, by the kiss of true love.

When these old stories were told and retold throughout the centuries, they retained the core elements of their message—that innocent awareness can and will be put to sleep by jealousy, anger, fear, and power. The only power greater than the one that puts the innocence to sleep is pure love. The charming prince kisses the beautiful sleeping girl, she awakens, and is embraced in that love forever.

Being kissed by a charming prince is nice, but real love and acceptance of yourself and creation is the key to awakening on the Toltec path.

The Matrix: *Fiction*

The story in the movie *The Matrix* is a wonderful allegory for the deep sleep experienced by most humans. In the film, the computers have taken over and are using the humans as a source of power for the machines. They keep the humans asleep by feeding a virtual dream into their minds while they lie in tanks of nutrient solution. Their life force is drained off to power the machines, but the humans are happy living in their dream reality and do not notice or complain.

FACT

The name *Morpheus* comes from the Latin language, and literally means "he who forms, or molds." He is the director and shaper of dreams. The name is perfect for the character in *The Matrix*. Morphine, the powerful narcotic painkiller and sedative, takes its name from the god of dreams, Morpheus.

In the movie, Morpheus (the "Toltec master" in the film) describes the virtual dream to Neo (the "apprentice") this way: "It is the world that has been pulled over your eyes to blind you to the truth."

The Matrix: Fact

The movie is fiction, of course. But do you see the similarities between that story and the one lived by so many people in our Western cultures now? Everyone is dreaming a reality plugged into their minds by others. People are also plugged into machines of all kinds: computers, video games, televisions, radios, media players, and cell phones. These machines invite you to focus your attention into them, and then they download a virtual reality of so-called "news," entertainment, and opinions into your mind.

The machines actually hypnotize you, and then feed the dream into your mind. The hypnosis is also supported by everyone else dreaming the same dream. You are sleepwalking, but so is everyone else, and nobody notices.

The Food of the Matrix

Modern machines even tell people what to eat and drink while they are hooked into the matrix. Advertisements for non-foods such as soft drinks and instant microwave snacks encourage mindless feeding, without attention to the actual nutritional needs of your body. Being plugged into the matrix of news and entertainment also keeps many people from being outdoors and exercising in ways appropriate to maintaining vital human health.

ACTION!

If you use a lot of stimulating foods like coffee and sugary foods, consider cutting back or stopping, and eat real food for a while. See if it improves your energy level, and your ability to be present and aware of the dream around you. The Toltec warrior respects and uses his body well.

Have you ever felt tired and lazy after a big meal? If there were a conspiracy to keep people from being vibrant and alive, seeking and questioning the meaning of their lives, feeding them large quantities of nutritionless food would be a good way to keep them asleep. They would then need to find stimulants to wake them from their stupor in order to function—perhaps drugs like coffee, super-energy caffeine drinks, sugary foods—as well as medical and illegal drugs.

Escape from the Matrix

In the movie version of this dream dilemma, the heroes have awakened from the dream and know the truth about how it works. They are able to go in and out of the virtual-reality dream, and they even know how to awaken others from the dream and bring them back to the "real" world. Of course, the matrix tries to stop them, because its success depends on everyone believing in the same reality—even if it is created from the past, as in the movie, or in the present, as in your daily life.

The Mastery of Awareness

In Chapter 2 you were introduced to the three masteries of the Toltec path. The mastery of awareness was compared to taking a fish out of the water, so that it could discover a different reality. The idea of unplugging from the matrix is the same model. The Toltecs know that for you to have choice in your life, and to be free to create the life you want for yourself, you need to unplug from the beliefs and agreements programmed into your mind. The goal of the spiritual warrior is to awaken into a life "where anything is possible."

Why Your Mind Dreams

The mind dreams because it needs to know. It needs to have stories to tell and it needs to justify everything. The most frightening thing for the mind is to not know the how and why of everything. You are dreaming in this moment. You know who and what you are and what you are doing, because of the power of your mind. You have language and concepts that are stored in your mind, and you are using them to define yourself in this moment.

Would you like to challenge your mind's knowing in this moment? Consider this: You are sitting on a ball of rock with a molten core, a barely stable crust, a little bit of water and green stuff on the outside—out in the middle of space. For all you know, you are sticking sideways off this ball, or hanging off the bottom. You are held on the surface of the ball of rock by some mysterious force while this "Earth" is spinning rapidly on its axis and flying through the solar system at some great speed around a ball of exploding gases we call "the sun."

QUESTION?

Is there any way I can ever know if something is real or if I am dreaming it?
Your mind can only dream. You will never be able to see what is "out there" directly. The Toltec wisdom will help you clean your channels of perception, so that you can perceive more clearly.

The sun and Earth are spinning through the disk of the Milky Way galaxy, made up of about 400 billion other exploding balls of gas and their planets. The Milky Way galaxy has been blasting outward from the center of something unknowable ever since the Big Bang billions and billions of years ago, when the universe was the size of a thimble.

And here you spin, in several different directions, at several different speeds, and it is not even messing up your hair. Your mind does not know what to do with all of the unknowable realities of this existence spinning through space, and the unimaginable magnitude of the universe, so it makes up stories about the meaning of life and God and why you should do something you do not want to do. That is why you dream.

Becoming the Master of Your Awareness

A great teaching tool of the Toltecs is called "non-believing." Now that you know that your mind dreams by distorting reality and generally making up stuff about the universe, are you ready to stop believing it? Are you ready to accept that everything you believe about "reality" is not the truth? That is the first step in the mastery of awareness—to stop believing your mind.

The next step is to learn everything you can about the programming in your mind, and how it distorts reality. The Toltec wisdom offers you many tools for exploring the dream in your mind. At this stage on the path, begin by becoming very skeptical about everything you know, believe, and think. Listen to your opinions and doubt your authority. Catch yourself defending your opinions, and stop trying to convince anyone that you are right about anything and they are wrong.

The Serpent Is Asleep in the Grass

In Chapter 2 you were introduced to the serpent, jaguar, and eagle. The serpent represents the part of you that is asleep in the dream. The serpent moves through life focused on its immediate needs for food, shelter, and safety from predators. As a human, your predators are the people you are afraid of because they judge you, reject you, compete with you, or take your energy in other ways.

Perhaps there is a part of you that has been lulled to sleep by your domestication. Take a moment to look at your life. Are your daily routines always the same? Do you have habits of grooming, eating, or communicating that are so automatic that you don't even notice when you are doing them? What about your thoughts? Listen to your mind. Do you often mull the same topics, or replay hurtful conversations while testing snappy new comebacks? What about recurring fears of losing your possessions, of being criticized at home or work, or losing a mate or lover?

These are the ways of the human as the serpent—going through the motions of life according to the expectations and agreements of the dream, connecting the dots according to other people's pictures of life, following orders, and often feeling disconnected from the passion and juicy fun of life that their spirit remembers from childhood.

The Sleeping Serpent Obeys Orders

Perhaps you can think of examples in history when people did not ask questions, but simply followed leaders, and did what they were told. In the name of both religion and politics, women have been burned as witches, advanced civilizations have been destroyed, and wars have been waged between brothers and sisters of nation or faith.

Throughout history, leaders of all kinds have used fear to convince their followers to go to war against their fellow humans. These leaders, especially in politics and religions, have created false stories of fear and dreamed them into the minds of their followers. They know that people are generally asleep, and domesticated to not question authority. In the mind of the sleeping human, fear is the strongest motivator.

Awakening the Serpent

Because the Toltecs have always been willing to openly explore truth and question reality, they have been able to awaken the sleeping serpents among them. In most families, societies, and religions, this questioning is gently discouraged or vigorously prohibited.

Domestication is not an evil conspiracy or plot to destroy the sensitivities of humans. It is simply a fact of human life, not good or bad, right or wrong—it simply is. As humans awaken to greater possibilities, they realize that they can domesticate their children and each other with mutual awareness and respect.

It is said that every fifty-two years, when Venus completed her cycle in the night sky, the Toltecs examined and destroyed every belief and physical representation of their dream that no longer served them, and then re-created each one. They would not tolerate sleepwalking in their individual lives or as a culture.

There Is a Mitote in Your Mind

What is the sound of a thousand people talking in the marketplace, and nobody listening? No, this is not a mysterious Zen riddle; it is the description of what is going on in the minds of most people when they are dreaming. Toltec teachers use the word *mitote* to describe this babble of the mind. It comes from the Nahuatl language, which, as mentioned earlier, has been spoken in Mexico since the time of the Toltecs.

The Toltec master invites his apprentices to listen to their mitote as an important first step in the mastery of awareness. Most of those voices in your mind are the result of everyone downloading their opinions and beliefs in your early domestication. It is important to keep in mind that whatever you hear there is not bad or wrong, and not to be judged. It is simply the chatter that goes on in most people's minds "behind the scenes" of daily life.

Beliefs and Agreements Rule Your Life

A "belief" is something the mind accepts as true or real, often with an emotional connection that gives it even more of a sense of certainty. When a parent tells a child that she is beautiful or ugly, smart or stupid, the child takes on the belief of the parent with absolute certainty. When a teacher tells a child that he will probably never make it to college, that belief of the teacher becomes the truth for the child. If a parent finds young children exploring each other physically, and tells them they are bad and they must never do that, this becomes a belief in the mitote of the child's mind—and may be there for an entire lifetime.

ACTION!

Write an inventory of ten things you want to do, but don't do, because you agreed they are wrong. Who did you make those agreements with? Do you want to continue to let those people make choices in your life? If not, write new agreements that would serve your life in a more positive way.

An "agreement" is a contract, or a shared opinion between two or more people. During your domestication, you made agreements with parents and others, often against your will or integrity. You had no choice; you had to go along with their way (or the highway). If your Dad said "Hey, we don't pull the cat's tail," you knew you were bad and could be punished if your desire to pull overcame your intention to follow the rules. You made two agreements. The first was that you would be part of the "we" of your family and not pull the cat's tail. The second agreement was subtler. You agreed that if you pulled the cat's tail, or even wanted to, you were a bad person and deserved expulsion from the "we."

When you add up all the things you were told you should do differently, all the wrong things you did (wrong thinking, wrong emotions, wrong actions), and all the things you didn't do that you should have done, you will see how many of these agreements you made. Perhaps you can also understand why the Toltecs teach that these beliefs and agreements are what control your life, and that unless you wake up and reprogram your mind, you will never be free.

Indirect Downloads and Contradictions

There are many beliefs in the mind's mitote that were not learned directly. A child might be frightened by her parents' violent arguing, and make a silent agreement never to fight with her husband when she gets married. From this ongoing experience she would probably create a belief that it is wrong to argue with anyone. As an adult, she will avoid conflict, even denying her feelings and going against herself to keep the peace.

The power of the beliefs and agreements in your mind from the past can have a powerful influence in your adult life. The Toltecs recognize the importance of waking up from the dream and examining those beliefs. When you have awareness of their power, and an understanding that most of them are fear-based lies from others, you have the choice, and perhaps the motivation, to change them.

Have you ever noticed that many of your beliefs contradict each other? The things you were told by parents may conflict with what your teachers said was the right way to behave. Or things your family taught you about love and sex might be in conflict with the ideas of peers and mates.

Here are some examples:

- "Thou shalt not kill" versus "We're looking for a few good men—join the Marines!"
- "Money is the root of all evil" versus "Winning the lottery would be wonderful."
- "God loves all His children" versus "If you are not good, God will punish you for eternity."

This mitote of contradictory beliefs programmed into the human mind cause equally contradictory behaviors. Have you ever said to yourself, "I don't know why I said that! I never intended to say it; it just came out that way"? Or, "I knew that something bad would happen if I did it, and then I went ahead and did it anyway. I don't understand what happened." Inconsistent, conflicting, or unexpected behaviors are the result of these unquestioned beliefs held in the mind.

Knowledge and Wisdom in the Mitote

The Toltecs are careful to distinguish between the information that has been put into your mind by others, and the knowing that comes from the deeper experiencing of "what is." Knowledge is all the stored light in your mind about what is right and wrong, good and bad, or attractive and repulsive. It is information. It is something believed by people in one time, but not another, such as the belief that the world is flat. Knowledge also changes from place to place; for instance, it is not true everywhere that "You should never eat with your hands."

There are times when you will see what is true, without any need to interpret it or filter it through the knowledge or opinions of others. This is wisdom. The goal of the Toltecs is to transform the mitote in the mind so that knowledge does not interfere with wisdom. No matter how many people believe the world is flat, if it is round, that is the truth. If you perceive that the world is round, no matter what other people say, that is wisdom.

Your Mind Is Filled with Knowledge

Domestication fills your mind with knowledge. You were taught the name and value of everything in your world. You learned what is right and wrong, and what is good and bad. You were taught how you should behave at the table, in public, at home, in church, at school, with your elders, on a date, and when you were alone. You were taught the three Rs, the Golden Rule, the Pledge of Allegiance, and to not steal, lie, or cheat. You learned which emotions were okay, and which were not. Chances are that these ideas were also enforced with reward and punishment, making it all the more difficult to reject what you were taught.

Knowledge is handed down through the generations, and is usually accepted without question as the truth. The greater the number of people of the past or present that believe something, the more certain they are about it. The more convinced people are about the truth of something, the more people will believe it. The dream supports itself in the minds of the dreamers.

Knowledge Changes Over Time

Think about what the world was like 500 years ago. The Spaniards were exploring, conquering, and enslaving the people of Cuba and the Americas. The Spaniards knew that it was perfectly acceptable to invade Cuba, take all the land for themselves, and make the native people their slaves. Hernando Cortés was commissioned to wipe out the Aztecs and their city of Tenochtitlán, and build Mexico City. Throughout Europe the system of serfdom, although declining, was still acceptable, and the municipal governments in large Italian cities were establishing brothels to take care of unmarried men and traveling merchants.

The beliefs and agreements in your mind create and describe your dream, and how it manifests as your life. Every action you take, every relationship you form, where and how you live, and your level of financial comfort are all the outward expression of what you believe. It really is true that "believing is seeing."

Theoretically, at least, all of this knowledge has changed in the last 500 years. The world no longer believes it is acceptable for one country to invade another and take over its land and enslave its people. Governments no longer create brothels as a solution to social problems. What was perfectly logical, legal, and socially acceptable at one time changes and is not tolerated at another. This is the nature of the passage of time and the evolution of a society. It is not a bad thing or a good thing; it is just a reality to be recognized and understood.

Wisdom Is the Gift of Awareness

The Toltecs know that knowledge is a major obstacle to knowing the truth. A mind filled with ideas, mostly from other people, obscures the simple reality of what is. To understand the nature of knowledge, then, becomes an important goal on the Toltec path.

Knowledge Changes from One Place to Another

Knowledge changes geographically. What is known and accepted in one place or culture may be unknown or abhorrent to another. In Western cultures, children are scolded and taught never to use their hands to eat. It is bad manners. Young eaters are shown how to use knives and forks, and how to cut and eat food without ever touching it.

In many parts of Latin America, a tortilla is the only utensil needed to pick food from a plate and eat it. In Muslim homes, there are carefully established rules about eating with the hands, including how many fingers to use and from which side of the plate to eat.

Religions and the gods they honor are different all over the world. There are hundreds, if not thousands, of large and small religious groups—and each has different knowledge that is believed, taught, and shared among its members. These religions have changed over time, as well. The gods of ancient Greece and Egypt are no longer worshiped, and now serve only as interesting mythologies for guided tours.

Silent Knowledge, the True Toltec Wisdom

A Toltec master takes delight in watching an apprentice wake up from the old dream and begin to question the virtual reality in his mind. The master encourages the apprentice to surrender his belief in all the knowledge in his mind's mitote, and embrace creation as it is. Each apprentice has the opportunity to transcend a life limited by old belief systems and knowledge, and open his heart in celebration of the beauty and wisdom inherent in all of life.

This wisdom is the recognition of the truth that is life itself. It is common sense, it is the seeing and acceptance of reality as it is, and it is something much bigger. The Toltecs recognize a universal consciousness that animates all of creation. When the chatter of the mitote of the mind has been silenced, Toltecs are able to connect to this consciousness from the essence of their own spiritual presence. Ultimately, the apprentice has access to this "silent knowledge," the true wisdom of creation.

Chapter 5

The Dream of the Planet

All humans are dreaming the individual dreams domesticated into their minds since they were infants. As they dream together, the many common elements of their dreamed realities are called the "dream of the planet." In this chapter you will learn how the collective individual dreams create the bigger dream, and the many ways the dream of all the humans affects the dream of the individuals. You will also gain insight into why no one is willing to be the first to say, "The emperor has no clothes."

The Domestication of All Humans

You have learned about the domestication of individual humans by parents, peers, politicians, bosses, mates, and others. Perhaps you are beginning to see how many of your reactions to people and events are the result of beliefs and agreements programmed into your mind by others.

The Toltecs understand that the collective dreaming by humans also has a powerful effect on individuals, as well as on the evolution of the entire planet. They call this consensus reality the dream of the planet, which describes the common elements of the dream held by most or all humans.

The Dream of Time

A good example of a dream that's commonly held by many humans is the dream of time. The dream of time, clocks, watches, time zones, and changing to daylight-savings time is fairly recent in the history of humanity. People used to say "I'll meet you after the cows come home," or "We always plant those on the spring equinox." Today, time is a very powerful dream. Of course, there's literally no basis to it. The fact that time changes by an hour when you cross a boundary marking a time zone is totally arbitrary.

Everyone agrees to believe the dream of time, and then takes it completely for granted. It is an important tool in the dream of the planet. Many of the functions and details of modern human life depend on more precise timing than cows can offer. Have you ever wondered what time it is on the moon? Does the moon have time? What about the Andromeda galaxy? What time is it there? Where does time come from? How much do you have? Will you run out?

The Dream of Money

Another example of a consensus dream in humans is the dream of money. In most of the Western world, money is made of colored paper, with different pictures and numbers for the various denominations in the various countries. These pieces of paper have no value in themselves, yet the different numbers are very important. The more colored pieces of paper you have, and the bigger the numbers they have, the more power, prestige, and things you can have.

The dream of money is a powerful dream. It is very important to the successful workings of the dream of the planet that everyone agrees about the value of their particular money. The value of the money is vigorously defended by the authorities in charge. If you decide to manufacture your own money, you will be punished, no matter how good of a job you do making it. Your money will be worthless as soon as anyone discovers it is not the official money.

FACT

In Mexico in the early 1990s, the value of the peso had dropped until it took more than 3,000 pesos to equal one U.S. dollar. People were buying milk at their local *tienda* (store) with 10,000-peso notes. When the government took three zeros off of the money, and issued ten-peso notes, people used the old and new bills interchangeably.

The dream of money includes all of the beliefs that everyone holds about whether it is easy or hard to get, what it means to get it without working for it, and what it says about you if you don't have any or if you have too much. Should you save your money for later, or spend it all and enjoy it now? Should you give money to homeless people when they ask? Should you give it to your child, or insist that she earn it? The real answers to these questions are that there are no answers. On the Toltec path, you ultimately realize that there is no such thing as money; there is only a dream we have all agreed to accept.

There Is Safety in Numbers

Since the beginning of time, humans have bonded together in tribes, villages, political units, and families. Their collective dreaming has helped them to maintain traditions, mythologies, and spiritual practices throughout time. The rigid belief in the truth and rightness of their collective dream has, unfortunately, also resulted in the wars and other conflicts that are such a common part of the human experience.

The Toltec wisdom acknowledges the importance of people identifying themselves with dreams larger than their own. The many different religions mentioned earlier are a primary example of how humans have bonded together in group belief systems. In the larger dream of the planet, the need for "a religion" has existed forever, because humans have always needed to explain the unexplainable. Over time, however, the beliefs, mythologies, and power of any particular religious practice have changed or vanished.

These collective dreams are as important and inevitable as the individual dreams from which they are made. The Toltec wisdom teaches that it is the inflexible personal identification with any belief that goes against the awakening and freedom of the individual.

Human Identity Is Based on Belonging

A child is born into a family and learns the rules of the family, in order to belong. He knows who belongs to his family and who does not. As he gets older, he meets the distant relatives from other locations, and expands his sense of who belongs, and what he belongs to.

Some Toltec teachers speak of this phenomenon as though each group dream creates its own unique universe. For instance, everyone in your family belongs to your family universe. If you marry, your mate automatically becomes part of your family universe, and you are accepted into his or hers. If you divorce, the family universes will decide whether each of you is in or out.

ACTION!

Here is a chance to write an inventory of ten or more universes you belong to. Start small and locally, and expand to include larger group identities. Don't forget to include your gender, ethnicity, and nationality. You might try ranking them according to how attached you are to your identification with each one.

If you belong to a religious group, you will know who belongs to your religious family—even if they are strangers from a distant country. They would not, however, be part of your country or family universe. If you belong to a trade organization, union, car-racing club, men's group, hall of fame, priesthood, cult, or street gang, all the other members would be part of that universe with you. It is the same for race, ethnicity, language, and even height, weight, hair color, and drug of choice. You identify with those of similar origin, habit, or organization.

Human Conflict Is Based on Identity

When a person is attached to the identity he gains from belonging to a particular universe, he will need to fight to maintain that identity. An example would be a fellow who is a devoted fan of a sports team. If someone else is strongly identified with another team and she claims it is the better universe to belong to, she is making the man wrong for his affiliation. No one likes to be wrong, so he will argue to be right and protect his identity. She doesn't want to be wrong, since her identity is based on her choice of teams, so she has to fight back and argue for her team's supremacy.

Conflict between sports fans, spouses, teenagers and their parents, countries at war, religions, and all ideologies are the result of humans defending their personal identity. They must protect who they are by being right, and making anyone who disagrees wrong. This is the origin of all conflict.

Believing Is Seeing

You learned in Chapter 2 how the old opinions, emotions, and memories stored in the mind's channels of perception distort the incoming light into a virtual dream. One of the most basic reminders the Toltec teachers give their students is "Don't believe yourself." A healthy skepticism about what you believe gives you a chance to escape the power of your mitote and claim your true wisdom. And if you are not going to believe yourself, you might as well not believe anyone else, including your teacher! The Toltec master simply offers her wisdom and asks you to use it if it makes sense to you.

What an amazing request from a teacher! In many paths of knowledge, the teacher becomes the authority, and assumes that you will believe her and follow the rules of the group. The entire identity of the group and the individuals in it is based on what is believed and known to be true—as defined by the dream of the group. The Toltec teacher knows that attachment to beliefs leads to fear and judgment, and that judgment creates conflict and suffering.

It is important to remember that simply wanting to change a belief or agreement is not always enough to make an instant permanent change. Beliefs are programmed deeply into the mind, and you have collected evidence for many years to support them. If an agreement you changed comes back, it just means you need to go deeper.

Breaking Belief in the Dream

The Toltec teachers of the past often used hallucinogenic plants to break an apprentice free from his belief systems (and some in the present still do). Under the influence of these plants, the apprentice would be confronted with alternate realities so far outside of his normal experience, it gave him no choice but to let go of his narrow vision of the world.

The teacher don Juan Matus, described in the books by Carlos Castaneda, explains to Carlos that the plant medicine he gave him was not important itself; it was only a tool to liberate Castaneda's mind from the grip of his beliefs about reality. Once belief in the beliefs is broken, the true teaching can begin.

The Dream of Beauty and Perfection

Someone once said that if all the women in the world accepted themselves the way they are, the beauty and cosmetic industries would collapse, and the entire world economy would collapse with them. Whether this is true or merely a graphic illustration of this particular dream of the planet, it does illustrate an important reality. Anyone who has waited in line at a modern supermarket can hardly avoid taking in the images of the "perfect" women on the covers of the magazines displayed there. The headlines of the articles inside are equally important to the creation of this dream of beauty and perfection.

Remember that domestication is enforced through reward and punishment. The most feared punishment is rejection or isolation. The images and words on those magazine covers—and all the advertising for cosmetics, clothes, and diets for both men and women—are all intended to remind you that you are not enough. They say you are not pretty enough, tan enough, slim enough, young enough, buff enough, sexy enough, rich enough, or dressed well enough.

Once magazines and advertisers can trigger your "not good enough" domestication from childhood, they can convince you they have the exercise routine, article, deodorant, lotion, or potion that will correct your deficiencies and (finally) make you worthy of love and acceptance. If you believe you are not good enough, you will see truth on the magazine covers. The Toltec warrior does not believe what she sees, but looks inside herself to know who and what she is.

The Emperor Has No Clothes

A wonderful story written by Hans Christian Andersen 170 years ago describes the power of the dream of the planet to influence the opinion of others. It tells the story of an emperor who lived many years ago. He was an average fairy-tale ruler, except for the fact that he was very much identified with his fine clothes.

One day a couple of smart hustlers came to town. They spread the word that they could make a cloth and garments that were so fine that they could not be seen by anyone who was stupid or incompetent. The emperor was quite taken by this idea, because not only would he have some very fine clothes to wear, but he could also learn who was stupid and incompetent in his court and kingdom.

As you probably remember, the hustlers pretended to weave and sew, and the word went out into the kingdom about the emperor's magical clothes. The ruler was a little unsure that he would be able to see the clothes himself, so he sent his trusted aides first. Of course, there was nothing there, but they would not admit they were stupid or incompetent, so they agreed that everything was so very beautiful. When they reported to the emperor, he agreed to dress in his new finery and join a procession through the town to show off his clothes.

Everyone in town was anxious to learn who among their neighbors was stupid and incompetent, so they lined the streets in anticipation. Seeing the emperor in his underwear, regally posing in his carriage, they all forced themselves to exclaim, "How lovely are the emperor's new clothes." Nobody wanted to be thought of as stupid by his neighbors.

The Young Boy Tells the Truth

Finally, a young boy looked up at the emperor, saw the truth, and shouted out, "The emperor has no clothes!"

In the original story, the boy's father grabs him, says "Don't talk nonsense," and takes him away. Then everyone who heard the boy begins to admit the emperor is naked and a murmur rises from the crowd: "The boy is right! The emperor has no clothes! It's true."

ACTION!

Write another inventory. This time, write about times you told your truth when you were young, and what happened to you. Perhaps you did not like a relative, or said a teacher was weird. Was your reality accepted, or were you told not to criticize people? Write it down.

The emperor realized the crowd was right, but he could not admit it, and finished the parade standing proudly in his carriage and in the illusion that he was not stupid or incompetent. Of course, the hustlers who started the whole thing ran off with the emperor's money before he came back.

How the Story Really Ends

Unfortunately, in modern cultures, people are not often so willing to admit that they were hustled. They may wake up to the fact that they have been tricked into their prejudices or their war, but have invested so much of their identity in being right about what they believed that they cannot tell themselves or others the truth. As long as the dream of the planet is not challenged, people will continue to support it. Nobody wants to be the first to say, "The emperor has no clothes."

In the story, although the boy is taken away, everyone who hears him begins to spread the truth, until everyone agrees. If only it was that simple. Have you noticed how most dreamed universes are more intent on preserving their reality than encouraging and listening to challenges?

Earlier you learned how childhood domestication uses punishment and reward to enforce the prevailing dream. In real life, when a child says "The emperor has no clothes" and contradicts the dream of the adults, he is more often punished and silenced than heard. The dream of a group provides identity to the individuals, and to challenge the dream is to challenge that identity. Throughout history, there have been voices that proclaimed the truth about emperors of all kinds, and most have been ignored, punished, or worse.

Challenging the Dream of the Planet

Being born into a dream makes it challenging to awaken. If you have seen the movie *The Matrix*, which was mentioned earlier, you saw how hard and dangerous it was for the ones who were awake to defy the existing reality. The people born free from the matrix dream had to live in hiding, deep in the earth. The masters challenging the dream were always faced with death if they failed.

And yet, the masters always persevered, intent on breaking the hold of the consensus reality on the minds and bodies of the humans. The heroes of *The Matrix* went into the dream, did what they could, fought their battles, and retreated to the safety of their fellows. They were always watching and waiting for someone who could see so clearly that he could break the spell of the dream once and for all. In the movie, even when that hero came, he had to be trained to see his own dream, and, ultimately, the dream of the planet that he had been born into.

The Toltecs say that the various dreams are living beings that use their energy to hold humans under their spell. The dream of the planet uses fear to keep people asleep. It is always dangerous for any human to go against the dream, however big or small. Remember that humans have been living in groups since the beginning of time, and to be found unworthy and rejected from the group is a fear that is buried deep in human minds.

Any group dream must maintain its identity by judging other dreams and making them wrong. Without the perception of "us" and "them," there is no sense of belonging to anything. It is very frightening to the mind to not know who or what it is when it says "I." The Toltec warrior knows that true freedom comes when he has released his attachments to his identities, and can be whomever he chooses to be.

The Sun Is Dreaming the Humans

In the Toltec mythology, the sun is the source of light and life for this planet. The light from the sun carries the message of creation that manifests itself as all life in this solar system. Each and every living thing has its own ray of light from the sun, which manifests as the individualized DNA of that being. No two beings on Earth are alike, because no two rays of the sun are the same.

The dream of the planet comprises all of the dreams of all the individual humans, and all the exclusive realities of every family, race, occupation, religion, nationality, and group identity, large and small, combined. The Toltecs say that this living dream is manifested and guided by the sun, just as is all other life on the planet.

The Evolution of the Dream

Because the dream is alive, the dream of the planet is reflected back as light to the sun. The sun perceives this message, and over time, recognizes the evolution of the human dream. In Chapter 4 you read some examples of how the dream has evolved in the past 500 years. The Toltecs, along among many other traditions, teach that there is a new era coming, in which a new human spiritual awakening will occur. Some teachers believe that this era of the sixth sun began several decades ago, and others believe it will begin in the year 2012. The time is not nearly as important as the fact that human consciousness is evolving.

The traditions of Peru and the Andes also recognize this evolution. They believe there is a day and night cycle of 500 years each. The time of the Incan empire was a powerful "day" cycle, with strong government, abundance and health for the people, and a genuine spiritual relationship with nature. The arrival of the Spaniards 500 years ago was the beginning of a dark "night" cycle, when the Incan empire disintegrated and its wisdom was lost. Now, another 500 years has passed in the Andes, and a new "day" cycle is beginning—a new evolution of the human dream into the light.

The Dream Divides and Polarizes

There is a part of the human dream that creates and eats fear. The Toltecs call it the "parasite," because of the way it eats your energy. You will read much more about it in Chapter 9. The dream of the planet also has a parasite, which feeds on the collective fear of all humans. As the dream evolves away from fear, power, war, and conflict—and toward love, acceptance, and peace—the big parasite is beginning to get very hungry.

ACTION!

Begin to watch for the Toltec "parasite" in the dream of the planet. See how news and political pronouncements create fear. Look at the reactions of your own parasite to the same news. Is it eating the fear from the dream of the planet? How does your body feel? Create a habit of writing down these observations.

Like any animal, when the parasite gets hungry, it begins to hunt more intently, its behavior becomes more erratic, and it eats things it would not normally eat. You might see this parasite behavior in the politics and terrorism of the current political world. As one part of the dream of the planet evolves toward a higher spiritual relationship with life, the parasite in the dream becomes more animated and resistant to the change. It begins to create fear in new places, in new ways, in a feeding frenzy to assure its survival.

As the human dream evolves toward the light, the dark side reacts in its natural way: polarization into fear and resistance. If you look back 500 or 1,000 years, and see how the dream has evolved so far, perhaps you can see that there is nothing the parasite can do to stop it. Imagine what the dream of the humans will be like 500 years from now. The will of the sun will be done.

Chapter 6

The Inner Judge and the Victim Child

In the personal dream of almost every human, the inner judge and victim child are in constant dialogue. The judge and victim are the result of the domestication you have been reading about in previous chapters. Here you get to take a closer look at how the judge uses punishment and reward as the director of domestication, and why the victim child dream is alive in the minds of adults. You will learn the collective dream of the victim, and the path to freedom offered by the Toltecs.

The Judge: Director of Domestication

When you read about domestication in Chapter 3, you learned that fear of punishment and desire for reward are the keys to successful control of a puppy or child's behavior. Children arrive in life free from fear and judgment, and throw their arms and hearts wide open to embrace life without reservation. They have no way of knowing that the judge is waiting to hold court and charge them with numerous violations of the rules in their parents' dream.

The Toltec wisdom teaches that the biggest enemy of personal freedom is the judge. At first, the judge is an outside voice that greets a child when she is very young. As she matures, the voice becomes internalized, like a little recording in the back of her mind. It constantly repeats the criticisms that it has recorded, in an effort to meet all the standards that every different judge has imposed on her during her life.

The Outside Judge Makes You Wrong

Your parents and other caregivers became the first judges of what was right and what was wrong, what was good and what was bad. They were dreaming, and believed their own agreements and opinions—not just about you, but also about each other, themselves, their friends, government, and the events in their lives. They judged, and they began to download those judgments and expectations into your dreaming mind.

FACT

There is no way to know what is right for other people. If knowledge can change over time, and from place to place, and everyone is dreaming their beliefs and opinions, the only "right" is in your own personal dream. You are right when you describe your dream, and so is everyone else when they describe theirs.

Here are some of the things you might have heard your external judge say to you, and learned to believe: "You are so messy! I am so tired of always having to clean up after you! Don't use that tone of voice with me, young man! Why did I ever have to have children? I wouldn't have to drink if it wasn't for you kids. There is nothing to cry about. Stop that pouting. What are you smiling about? Stop all that noise. Go outside if you have to run around yelling like that."

Here is some more judge talk: "Any son of mine has to be tough enough to defend himself against bullies—don't come running to me, sniveling about it! Whoever told you that you could sing? Stop that crying or I will give you something to cry about. Where did you waste your allowance this week? You are so clumsy! What were you thinking when you spilled that? I am not surprised nobody wants to play with you, because you are a very selfish child."

Unique Judges for Every Family

Every family has its own dream, and all parents have unique standards they expect their children to meet. Often, even the parents in a family disagree about the rules, and each enforces different judgments and punishments. They believe (from their domestication) that they need to make their children wrong and punish them for breaking the family rules—and thus make them good citizens of the world. Punishment is the basic standard for child rearing in the dream of the planet. This is not a conscious, deliberate, or mean act by parents—they are fish in the water, knowing only the water, doing what they think is best.

The family also enforces the rules and expectations of all the groups, institutions, religions, occupations, social hierarchies, and political beliefs with which they identify themselves. It is vitally important to parents that everyone around them accept their children. It is even more important to many parents that they themselves are accepted as good parents by the judges around them.

The Inner Judge Takes Over

When a child hears enough of those judgments, she learns to agree she is not good enough, smart enough, or careful enough the way she is. She knows she must get it right, or she will not be tolerated as a member of her family unit. To protect herself from being banished, she learns all the expectations of her family, and all the judgments that enforce them. She internalizes the voices into a recording that can play in her mind twenty-four hours a day, even when she is alone.

As one Toltec apprentice told his teacher, "I always make myself wrong for everything I do! I thought since my mother taught me that way, I should do it that way, too. I have a judge for every occasion!"

Many of the judgments were not spoken directly, nor were they necessarily abusive or overtly hurtful. If no one came when you called them to change your diaper or see a dead worm in the patio, you thought it was your fault. If your parent didn't put the newspaper down when you wanted to show them your school art, or any of the other small ways that even loving parents did not respond to your childhood needs, you were hurt. And the message you told yourself was, "I am not important enough [good enough, interesting enough, and so on] for them to want to pay attention to me and love me. I have to be better." That belief was quietly added to the litany of your inner judge.

The Voice of the Inner Judge

If you listen carefully when the voice in your mind scolds and judges you, you might discover that he speaks to another part of your mind, saying "You should be better!" He is speaking to the victim child, who you will meet later in this chapter. If you hear the voice saying "I should pay better attention," you might ask yourself who is saying that, and to whom?

Here are some of the things the inner judge says to the victim child within: "What is the matter with you? Why can't you get it right? Why don't you pay better attention? You are not beautiful enough, smart enough, tall enough, happy enough, serious enough, focused enough, spiritual enough, relaxed enough, free-spirited enough, mature enough, open enough, thin enough, buff enough, loving enough, lovable enough, stylish enough, sexy enough, healthy enough, old enough, young enough, slick enough, discriminating enough, rich enough, outgoing enough, sophisticated enough, brave enough, humble enough, knowledgeable enough, meditative enough, outgoing enough, man enough, funny enough, enlightened enough, and you can't see well enough."

The judge likes to tell the victim child what she "should" do to be acceptable: "You should be more emotionally available, more friendly, less sensitive, more outgoing, less emotional, more authentic, less nervous, more warm and caring, less afraid, more stylish, less judgmental, more spiritual. You should think more clearly, not be in debt, eat better, pay more attention, and just be more aware! You should be a better person than you are."

As a final blow, the inner judge adds more hurtful messages of childhood: "You are a burden and a nuisance. You are not worthy of love and attention. Nobody could ever really love you for who you are. Your needs are meaningless. You are lucky if anyone loves you, so you had better settle for whatever love you can get."

Characteristics of the Inner Judge

The inner judge is intent on helping you survive, by keeping you in line. He knows that you must be good enough in all the ways he learned when you were growing up. He continues his frantic work into adulthood, driven by the fear of banishment—the rejection from whatever groups, jobs, relationships, or other dreams you want to be part of.

Remember that everything the judge says is a lie. Listen with detachment and curiosity to these voices. They are not you, and they are not your fault. The voices and their beliefs were programmed into your mind by others. The Toltec warrior does not take them personally, because he knows they are not personal.

Because the inner judge is convinced you are not good enough the way you are, he must constantly demand you improve. His rather odd logic is that if he can judge and punish you before others reject you, then you will shape up and do whatever you have to do to be good enough for them to accept you. Your inner judge is actually only concerned with his assumptions about what other people think of you, and will harass you until you meet their imagined standards.

The Apprentice's Story: Free at Last!

A Toltec apprentice described her discovery that her inner judge was making assumptions about other people's judgments this way: "I always knew when I was crossing the street in front of cars that everyone in those cars was watching me. It was so uncomfortable! I knew they were judging how I was dressed, how I walked, my hair, how long I was taking to cross the street, and everything about me.

"When I learned about the assumptions of the inner judge, I decided to find out for myself. I looked carefully into each car to see what those people were paying attention to—and found out nobody was paying any attention to me! They were talking on cell phones, changing radio stations, daydreaming, checking their hair, everything but watching and judging me. Nobody actually cared. In that moment, I became free. I did not have to believe the judge again."

The Judge Is a Liar

Not only do the Toltecs know that the inner judge is the biggest obstacle to your personal freedom; they also know he is a big liar! This is an important wisdom of the Toltecs: The inner and outer judges are liars! The basic message of the judge, which says you should be better or more than you are, cannot possibly be true. Think about it. How could you be different from who you are? If you were different, you would be somebody else! You cannot be someone else; you can only be you.

FACT

The word *should* is often used in the belief that it communicates a reality that is the right thing for a person to do: "You really should have invested in real estate." In fact, the word *should* is always a judge word. It says, "I know better than you what is right for you."

The judge says you "should" be different. You should be all of the good things listed earlier, and you should not be any of the "bad" things. Have you noticed that everyone's judge has a different list of what is the right way to be? While your judge is saying you should be like other people, their judge is saying they should be like you! And the judges are making it all up. It is all lies.

You Can Only Be You

You cannot be different from who you are. You can pretend to be different, you can try to be somebody else, but when the day ends and you lay yourself down, you will still be you, just as you are. And that is okay! In fact, that is perfect. You will learn more about the Toltecs' understanding of the perfection of the universe in later chapters. For now, know that in a perfect universe, all the parts are perfect, and you are a perfect part of the universe, just as you are.

When the judge inside or outside says you should be different from who you are, he is lying, because it is impossible. This is such an important point: It is impossible to be different from who you are. It is also important to note that the judge will never congratulate you for meeting his standards, or for doing something well. His only role is to criticize and (supposedly) motivate you to do more and be better. If you do meet an expectation of the judge, he will simply raise the bar and demand an even higher jump.

The Judge Behind the Scenes

Imagine you are at a job interview, or applying for a mortgage, giving a speech, or meeting your fiancé's parents for the first time. Of course you are remembering to use your firm handshake, your warm smile and eye contact, or whatever else you think will present the best version of you. Can you also hear your inner judge behind the scene, reminding you that you are an imposter, that you are not really qualified for the job, mortgage, or the marriage?

The inner judge is always there, quietly or forcefully, reminding you that you should be different from who you are. If there were a person walking around behind you criticizing how you speak, walk, talk, and all the rest of who and what you are—what would you do? Some people might nod their head in resigned agreement; others would quietly protest and argue in vain.

Some people might react violently. The Toltec master encourages his students to rebel, and "Just say no" to the judge!

Once you know the judge is lying, you can develop the personal power to deny the judge's right to criticize you. This is true for the inner judge and the outer judge. They are lying when they say you should be different from who you are. When you quit trying to meet the expectations and standards of the judges inside and out, you can begin to be you as you are, and get on with your life.

The Child: A Victim of Domestication

Young children believe everything they are told. Because judges are the directors of domestication, children are told some pretty mean things—which you now know are all lies. Children agree to believe lies. They have no choice. If a child is told she is ugly, clumsy, or stupid, she will believe it is the truth. If she is called selfish, that lie is added to the light stored in her channels of perception, and can forever distort how she perceives herself.

Sometimes a judge can be so angry, he thinks you should suffer or die. An inwardly violent judge is often the result of an especially dangerous, neglected, or abusive childhood. If you are hearing that judge in your mind, you are encouraged to work personally with a therapist or Toltec master who can guide you to the truth.

When a child resists these lies, and tries to stand up against the judges, she learns that she has no power. Grownups are bigger, talk louder, and have countless methods of punishment, especially for children who talk back to their parents. This experience of being powerless becomes the theme of childhood, and carries right into adult life. When the inner judge takes over from the outer judges, the hurt feelings continue unabated.

The Victim Dream

The parents' job is to repress a child's reality and enforce theirs. It is simply the necessary truth of domestication, not right or wrong. It just is. When the parents impose their reality, a child cannot express his emotions and truth to get his needs met. The child truly does become a victim of the outside world, without power or control over what happens to him. This happens whether the parents' methods of domestication are gentle or abusive. The message the child learns is the same—only the degree of wounding is different.

The mantra in the victim dream becomes "I am powerless to get my emotional and physical needs met my way. It is not fair, and there is nothing I can do about it." Children learn to be vigilant about the needs and moods of others, and to manipulate adults to meet the children's own needs for attention and safety. They learn to disregard and judge their own needs, and sacrifice them in order to be accepted by the judges around them.

It is unfortunate that when a child leaves home, no one invites him to leave all those agreements, beliefs, and the wounding they cause behind, and go into the world in love with themselves and with life. The dream of helplessness lives on.

The Dream Is Alive

The Toltecs know that dreams are alive and that they reproduce themselves. If you dream yourself as a victim, you will send signals into your world that reproduce and create the world you are dreaming. When a New York City mugger was asked how he chooses his targets, he said, "They already look scared." His victims already perceived the world as dangerous and themselves as powerless—and muggers of all kinds recognize that energy.

This is a good example of "believing is seeing," which you read about in Chapter 5. It is as though you are projecting your individual little virtual reality of life onto a big screen, and everyone around you can see and respond to it. How they respond depends on how they are dreaming. Not everyone becomes a mugger just because someone else appears to be vulnerable. Dreams mate and reproduce with their kind!

The Victim Child Lives in the Adult

What is learned in childhood generally becomes the adult dream of reality. Remember how the stored light distorts the incoming reality? Well, this is one of the big examples of that distortion. When a child is raised feeling powerless, that lie lives in her channels of perception, and creates a virtual reality of a world in which she has no power. She will continue to repress her feelings and truth, because she has learned "it doesn't do any good to express them anyway."

Many people live in this victim dream, usually without being aware of it. They blame their hurt and misfortunes on other people, events, and even life itself. The victim dream can make people angry, suspicious, and resentful. It causes people to take things personally that are not personal. It makes them afraid to take risks or fail, because the judge is there, waiting to make them wrong.

QUESTION?

What does it mean to say the victim child is a living dream?
Everyone has many different personalities buried in their minds, each with different needs and desires. These personalities are distinct and seem to come alive depending on outside situations. They do not have separate bodies, of course, so they are called living dreams in the mind.

It is the inner victim who believes the judge, and knows she is a failure at being who she should be. The living dream of a victim child knows she must hide her imperfections—which her inner judge can see so clearly—from the judges of the outer world. She wears masks and adopts roles to hide the truth of who she is (more on masks in Chapters 7 and 8). The frightened inner victim child uses most of the adult's personal power keeping up the illusion that she is better and more worthy of love than she believes herself to be.

The Victim Dream of the Planet

Since every human on the planet has been domesticated into some system of beliefs and agreements about the world they live in, the dream of the planet also carries a victim dream. Of course, the intensity of this dream varies greatly from culture to culture, and throughout the many different standards of living in the world.

In Chapter 5, you read about how advertising offers solutions to the victim child's fear of not being perfect. You may have noticed that the product or idea being offered rarely actually addresses the deep fears of the victim dream. No one can buy their way out of their dream of a world where they are helpless and powerless. No product, service, or political rhetoric will change the lie in the mind that says "you are not lovable until you get it right."

Conflict and the Victim Dream

Everyone may be dreaming the same victim dream, and yet there are endless variations on how it manifests in individuals and cultures. Some people wallow in the dream: "Nothing ever goes right for me; why try?" Others use it as a way to protect themselves: "Please don't judge me. Can't you see what a big victim I am already?"

Someone who believes he is powerless may become a bully at work or in a bar to prove his judge wrong. Another person may choose to be invisible, as a way to minimize the threat to his vulnerability. And many people compete for power, even while they believe they do not have it or deserve it.

You read earlier in this book about how conflict arises when individuals are attached to the knowledge that defines them, and are afraid to be wrong and lose their identity. The more power the victim dream has in a conflict situation, the higher the stakes will be and the more intense the conflict. The greater the fear of being victimized by losing, the more intense the conflict—whether in a barroom brawl, spouses arguing, or countries at war.

What's interesting to note here is that by fearing becoming victims, people actually put themselves in the perfect position to become victims. The reality is that a petty argument or fight might not be worth having at all, but if it does happen, there are both helpful and destructive ways to view such an event.

Agreements in the Victim Dream

Many agreements about taking care of the victim child inside of other people have been passed down through domestication. One such agreement is that no one should acknowledge the shared feeling of helplessness—people have a need to be seen as strong and self-reliant. People in the dream also agree not to hurt each other's feelings—even to the point of hurting themselves, instead.

ACTION!

An interesting exercise is to listen to the voices speaking in the mitote. Take five minutes and write them all down like a movie script. Who says what to whom? How many characters are speaking at once? What do they say about you trying to write them down? See if you can identify the judge voice.

These agreements also include the guilty fear of being wrong or bad when they do hurt someone's feelings or victimize them in some way. Individuals agree to be careful about how they express themselves and treat each other. No one wants to be accused of being hurtful or insensitive, or be rejected for an offense.

Freedom from the Victim Dream

In many traditions, spiritual seekers have gone to caves or remote monasteries to be free of the distractions of society. Isolation is a very practical way to concentrate on healing the personal dream; however, most contemporary Toltec teachers encourage their apprentices to remain in the dream of the planet to work on their freedom. They know it is the power of the dream, especially the victim dream, that keeps their apprentices in spiritual bondage. Toltec teachers aim to show you that there is another way to think about life and the events that take place.

When you judge yourself, another person, an event, the government, the weather, or God, you are making yourself a victim. You are saying, "This is not fair, it should not be like this, and I am suffering because it is wrong." Begin to notice when you are emotionally disturbed by something, and use that awareness to look inside to see what you are thinking.

If you feel outraged and defiant about being diagnosed with a disease, getting in a car accident, or being robbed, ask yourself why. Are you clinging to ideas of luck, curses, and fate? Did you envision things as being much different than they are? If so, why? What reason did you have to believe that you could know exactly how everything was going to turn out?

If your thoughts are being distorted by the victim dream, perhaps you will want to find a different story to tell yourself. When you understand that you are dreaming, you know you can dream whatever you choose. That is the power of the Toltec wisdom, and the path to personal freedom.

Chapter 7

The Strategies of Protection

Humans develop strategies and wear masks to help them get along in the world. The process of domestication teaches them what they need to do to get it right for other humans so they can be loved, appreciated, and secure. The Toltecs teach that it is important to discover and explore the strategies that have become your adult personality. In this and the following chapter you will be offered a chance to discover your masks, and prepare to release your attachment to them, with love.

The Clever Survival of a Child

The victim child is alone in his struggle with the judges in his life. Although some Toltec apprentices report that they had a parent, grandmother, or other resource they could go to for recognition or unconditional love, most young children are pretty much at the mercy of the dream of the adults around them.

You have already learned how domestication challenges the reality of a child, and how the perceived unfairness of it leads to the child feeling victimized and powerless. When he rebels or expresses his anger, it usually makes things worse. There is nowhere for the child to hide—and he is too little to move in with the family down the street.

The words *mask* and *strategy* are used interchangeably here, and are closely related. A strategy is a behavior or adaptation learned by a child to meet or deny the demands of the judge. A mask is the false persona that the child learns to wear to support his strategy.

Masks and Strategies of the Victim Child

It is remarkable how resourceful children can be to develop strategies to get it right for the judge. Depending on the circumstances of his domestication, a child will develop masks and strategies that help him meet his need for love, attention, acceptance, and safety. Other strategies may be developed to numb the fear and pain of being rejected as unworthy.

Everyone is wearing masks and acting out their strategies, and it is those strategies learned in childhood that are making the choices and creating the dream in adult life. They become the adult personality. Whether it is the fellow who always gathers everyone around for the latest jokes, or the person sitting quietly alone in the back of the room; whether it is the unfortunate soul down on her luck, or the valiant hero who rescues her from her plight; most adult personalities are strategies learned in childhood. Nobody teaches these strategies to a child; they are created by very resourceful children in response to unmet needs for love and approval.

When you wear a mask, you can present any face you want to the world. You can hide your true identity, just like on Halloween. You learned which strategies to use and which masks to wear when your judges told you how you needed to act to be okay. Do you present your masks to the world, hoping everyone will believe they are the true you, while behind the mask, you believe your judge's lies and live in anxiety that your hoax will be discovered?

The struggle to hide behind a mask and not be discovered uses most of a human's personal power each day. The Toltec wisdom teaches the mastery of awareness to discover the masks you wear, and the mastery of transformation to release attachment to them. By ending the struggle, you reclaim your lost personal power.

A Puppet of the Outside World

If you are pretending to be someone you are not, the characters you play include many programmed actions and reactions. When someone says or does something that triggers one of the reactions, you will respond according to that programming. It is like being a puppet, and the outside world controls the strings. If someone is attracted to you romantically, it may cause you to be a happy, dancing puppet. If you are afraid of the attraction and the "fear" strings are pulled, you might be a confused, scared puppet.

The important thing to notice here is that the true you is not in control of your reactions to the outside world. Your emotional life is dictated by what happens around you. If you are dreaming the world through a victim child's perception, many of your reactions will be based on your sense of powerlessness and a fear of rejection. If you see that you repeat the same pattern of unsatisfying romantic relationships, work experiences, or friendships, perhaps it is time to question if you are a puppet, controlled by your old programming. Wouldn't you rather be the puppeteer?

Discovering the Strategies You Learned

Imagine that a child comes home with low grades on his report card. Perhaps Dad has been bragging at work about how smart his kids are, and now this one is not living up to the legend. Dad is angry, perhaps furious: "What are you thinking? How could you do this to me? Are you stupid or just lazy? Go to your room and study! You are grounded until you show me some better grades!"

This child has several options; the most obvious is to please Dad by studying hard until he can get the grades Dad approves. He loves his dad, and he wants his dad to love him. In the dream of the planet, love means approval and safety, and the child knows that he will not be safe until he meets Dad's standards.

The Star Wants to Shine

When Dad demands good grades in return for approval, the child may try very hard, and perhaps succeed, to be a good student. Or maybe Dad wants him to be the best player on the football team, or the best musician in the school band. If the child works hard to meet those standards and is rewarded with acceptance for his success, a "star" is born. The child learns how to earn Dad's love, and works hard to get it. His excellence in school, sports, or music earns praise from many sources.

ACTION!

As you read about the strategies and masks in this chapter, make notes for yourself about which ones you recognize as yours. Always remember not to judge yourself or the strategies you have learned. The mastery of awareness is devoted to witnessing what is true. Keep your judge out of it.

As the boy matures into adulthood, he takes with him the strategy he learned for gaining approval and reward. He works hard, stays late at the office, and becomes the star of his workplace. The star also shows up as the super spouse, super friend, and other types of overachievers. This particular strategy is strongly supported in Western cultures, where production is paramount in the school, home, and workplace.

The Rebel Gives Up

What if the child tries to study and win Dad's approval, but fails? Perhaps he has great artistic talent, but is not very good at remembering math and history. His grades do not improve, and Dad continues to be angry and reject him. There may come a day when the child gives up, and says to himself: "The heck with trying so hard! Nothing works anyway. It isn't fair. The heck with love! I have jumped through all the hoops and it still doesn't work! I quit!" In this moment of giving up, in the pain of failure, the rebel is born.

The rebel mask says, "I don't care about being accepted or about love. I will prove it by doing everything Dad hates, and hanging out with people like me." The boy fails at school, drops out, and spends his time drawing cartoons of angry fathers and hurt sons for his new friends. It is unfortunate that this rebel is not truly a rebel. Instead, he goes from one set of inflexible standards to a new one. If he ever feels good about himself and wants to read a history book, his new friends will judge him and reject him for betraying them. The real rebel is the Toltec warrior, who is guided from within (see Chapter 10).

The Perfectionist and the Procrastinator

The "perfectionist" mask is created much like the star. The emphasis of the outer judge is a little different, because the focus is on doing everything perfectly, according to the judge's standards. The parent or other judges watch the child, criticize, and suggest better ways to do everything she does. The expectations are high for the perfectionist, on the outside and inside.

For the child who is expected to do things perfectly, the best way to keep from failing is to not do anything—at least not do anything that can be judged and for which she can be rejected.

The Perfectionist Has to Do It Right

The perfectionist may be well respected at work and home, keeping everything in flawless order, working long hours to make sure everything is perfect and everyone around her is happy. The downside for the perfectionist is the fear that drives her. She learned as a child, as did the star, that she must perform in order to be of value and be worthy of love. She knows she cannot afford to be lazy or miss any details, because she is being watched.

The Procrastinator Has to Stall

The passive rebellion of the perfectionist is to stonewall the judge. She knows that no matter how well she does something, the judge will say it is not perfect, and therefore she is not good enough. There is no point starting something if it is going to be judged as wrong when it is done. And if something is started, there is no point to finishing it, for the same reason. In the adult, procrastination is the puppet response to the judge's demands for perfection.

Procrastination is a strategy that can sabotage an entire life. Many big ambitions and wild inspirations die because they are put off until the perfectionist is sure she has thought of every contingency, predicted every setback, and controlled every outcome. Of course, life experience teaches her that it is impossible to have perfect control, so the need for procrastination increases.

The inner judge will criticize procrastination as one more failure to be perfect, and often hire the "pusher" to drive his perfectionist to bigger and grander expectations and completions. Of course, the pusher only creates more frustration and procrastination. There is no escaping the judge—until you know he is lying, and quit believing him.

The Many Strategies of the Victim Child

Diverse family situations and the many different possible temperaments of a child unite to create unique expressions of strategies and masks in every person. Some of these strategies are learned by copying parents, and some in resistance to parents. Others simply arise from a combination of experiences. In the mastery of awareness, the Toltec master invites his apprentices to be aware of these strategies and masks, and evaluate their usefulness in adult life.

How can I see my masks if I am wearing them?
The first trick is to acknowledge that you are wearing masks. Then it is good to look in a mirror. Toltec masters and other teachers serve as clear mirrors to reflect back your masks and strategies, without judgment. Then it is up to you to use the tools they teach you to release your attachment to the masks.

What follows are more of the common survival strategies and masks adopted by creative children to cope with less-than-perfect parenting situations. If you recognize any of them as yours, remember to do so in gratitude for the resourcefulness of your child self, not in judgment. It is only by embracing yourself with acceptance and love that you are able to transform your dream on the Toltec path.

The Helper Needs to Help

In families in which parents are distracted by work, alcohol, drugs, depression, or illness, a child may learn that the only way to get attention and get his basic needs met is to help the adults in some way. The variations on the "helper" strategy are the "caretaker," "codependent," "rescuer," "enabler," and "hero."

The helper strategy wears a mask that says, "I am okay, I don't need anything. I see that you need help, and I can help you." To be a helper is to believe that someone needs you to rescue, teach, heal, or support him in some way. The victim loves to see a rescuer coming, because she can surrender and be taken care of. Addicts of all kinds love enablers, who will take care of them by supporting their denial and protecting them from the truth of their addiction. The helper chooses victims for romantic relationships, as employees, and for friends. He knows that he will always be needed.

The selfless appearance of the helper makes it another strategy that is usually rewarded in Western cultures. It appears to conform to religious teachings of self-sacrifice and love, but when help is giving only to get something in return, it is not actually giving at all.

The Victim Needs Help

The victim needs the attention of the helper to give her the approval, care, safety, or empowerment that she craves and believes she does not deserve. By being needy and nonthreatening as a victim, she can attract helpers to solve her problems, loan her money, and listen to her stories about her unsuccessful relationships. The helper lover says, "Go ahead, put your head on my shoulder, it is okay to cry." A helper employer might say, "My door is always open. My employees are always free to come in and share their lives and problems with me."

Helping others is a wonderful way to share your love. When your help is offered freely without any expectation of reward or any attachment to the outcome, you are not using a strategy. When someone helps others in order to get love or gratitude in return, he or she is using a childhood strategy, and not really giving at all.

You will see that many of these strategies find their opposite in adult life, especially romantically, and bond with each other. Each person feels whole through the synergy of the combination, but also secretly judges the quality of his or her opposite. This phenomenon creates much suffering in relationships of all kinds.

A Pleaser Strategy for Every Occasion

When a child is raised in a difficult family situation with intense judgment or arguing among parents and siblings, he may learn to do whatever it takes to make peace. He may become the pleaser, doing everything he can to make sure everyone is happy. Apprentices have told stories of coming home from school at age eight and doing all the housework, in the hopes that it would please Mom and make her happy and loving; or learning to play sports they did not enjoy, in order to please Dad.

The peacemaker might learn to distract arguing parents by interrupting them, or acting out his own anger with siblings—anything to calm his environment and make it feel safer. The doormat might learn to let anyone judge or blame him for anything, in order to avoid creating more tension and anger. This strategy accepts responsibility for things that are not his fault in order to keep the peace.

The Martyr Tries Hard to Please Everyone

The martyr is the ultimate victim pleaser. The martyr's favorite line is "After all I have done for you, this is the thanks I get!" This strategy comes from a child who learns that she has no right to have her needs met until everyone else is satisfied—which means never. She will read in the dark and give up her seat to anyone standing.

Behind the martyr's mask of selflessness is anger and resentment that no one ever takes care of her. She will not let anyone take care of her, of course, because she has learned that she only has value when she takes care of others.

The Thinker, Teacher, Expert, and Talker

When a child's feelings are hurt and emotional wounds unattended, he tends to shift his attention to his mind as a resource for attention and approval. This strategy denies the vulnerability of the victim child, by distracting his attention with thinking and talking about concepts, knowledge, and stories. When the thinker is confronted with feelings, he quickly changes the subject to safer intellectual ground.

As the teacher, he may suddenly begin sharing information about the latest research on longevity, or some detail about the daily news he thinks you should be aware of. The teacher feels safer sending out information than feeling his own or another's emotional reality. The talker loves to tell stories. He loves to dwell on details, and make sure you are getting the complete picture. The talker is often very entertaining, and fun to have around.

The expert can expound on any subject in detail. If he does not know enough about it, he will embellish his knowledge with big words and extraneous information, or simply change the subject to something he knows more about. He will do whatever it takes to keep the focus away from feelings.

The Dreamer, Mystic, Saint, and Guru

Sometimes, the pain in the emotional body is too great for a child to manage. This child is accused of daydreaming in school, and seems disconnected as she floats through life. As an adult, the dreamer will hook her attention inside, in her mind, dreaming about Prince Charming or freedom from the drudgery of her job. Her friends may think she is "spaced out," and she is often late or forgets important commitments.

When a spiritual twist is added to the dreamer strategy, she will float above the cares and troubles of the world as the mystic or saint, claiming freedom from the "negative energy" of life. She may find peace and safety in an ashram in a foreign country. The mystic has learned that it is safer to be quiet and aloof from the ordinary world than to expose herself to its dangers.

When the mystic is also an intellectualizer, he may become the guru, discussing spiritual subjects with great animation and convincing presence. He may judge others as less advanced than he believes himself to be. The guru's goal is the same as that of other members of this category—to avoid the emotional pain of his inner victim child by focusing on "higher" issues and spiritual principles.

ACTION!

If you recognize strategies or masks of your own in these lists, make some notes about the answers to these questions: When you think about releasing a strategy or mask you have been using, what emotions do you notice? Is there someone who stops you? If you experience fear, what are you afraid will happen?

Choosing the Masks You Wear

In this chapter and the next, you are encountering many of the strategies and masks that humans develop to hide the person they are afraid they are. Perhaps you are recognizing some strategies that you have adopted in your life, or seeing them in others. Remember, the awareness that the Toltecs offer you is not a new excuse for your inner judge to make you or others wrong.

No one has choices about their strategies when they are puppets responding to the rules and fears of their domestication. It is only when you use your awareness to transform your dream that you can decide which masks serve you and which don't. As you reclaim your personal power, you will have more options and less fear about letting go of strategies that no longer serve you.

The Nagual of 1,000 Masks

In Chapter 2 you learned about the Toltec nagual, a person who knows the absolute truth of who he or she is. The nagual is free from the games of hiding and denying her truth, and is fully present in life. She knows she is still dreaming, but is completely aware of her choices about how she dreams. The nagual knows she is perfect exactly the way she is.

In the acceptance of her perfection and her identification with the source of all life, the nagual has nothing to hide and nothing to prove. She has no attachment to the strategies, masks, and roles she adopted as a child, and yet accepts them as gifts when appropriate. The Toltecs say, "The nagual is a man or woman of 1,000 masks who is attached to none of them." Freedom from fear and attachment gives the nagual the personal freedom to go through life with her heart wide open, playing the roles that are appropriate to the dream around her, with openness and love.

Practice Makes the Master

Humans refine and rehearse their strategies for most of their lives, and the constant practice pays off. They are able to summon a strategy or grab a mask without any conscious thought whatsoever. If you realize that most people are doing this dance, you see that they are all doing it together. The perfectionist may judge the dreamer, and if the dreamer feels hurt, she might call up her pleaser to get it right for the perfectionist.

There can be no real human intimacy when strategies are dancing with masks, and everyone is pretending to be someone they are not. The Toltecs teach that for individuals to be present and alive in their lives, they must stop believing the lies of the judge and honor the perfection that they are. From that perspective they can show up in life free of fear, and willing to be who they came here to be.

Chapter 8
Strategies to Deny, Protect, and Numb

There are many reasons for the strategies created by the resourceful victim child. In this chapter you will learn about strategies and masks created to hide from the judge, distract the judge's attention, and deny, seduce, or frighten the judge. All these strategies are the result of one universal fear: The fear of being found unworthy of love. The fear demands the rejection or denial of important parts of a human's being. However, the split can be healed and balance restored.

From Addicts to Romantics—All the Same

The Toltecs know that you must reclaim the totality and perfection of who you are to become the complete spiritual warrior. The mastery of awareness offers the opportunity to see your strategies and the masks you wear, and to have conscious choice about how you use them. When used with awareness by a spiritual warrior, they become gifts for yourself and others.

The Addict and Loser

An addict is anyone who is dependent on a mood-altering substance, idea, or behavior—especially if that dependence has a damaging effect on his emotional or physical health. When the pain of childhood survival is too big to contain, many people learn to self-medicate with alcohol, drugs (legal and illegal), food, sex, and general suffering. In the Western culture, the addiction to suffering and the accompanying smallness in life is the biggest addiction.

People can also be addicted to relationships, worry, obsessive thinking, chaos, illness, computer games, recklessness, religion, drama, gambling, television, control, and fear. Any substance or behavior can serve as an addiction, if it numbs the wounded emotional body or distracts the attention from the pain within. Of course, the inner and outer judges are very harsh on people who abuse substances. The very strategy created to numb and protect the hurt child from the judge causes additional judgment, more hurt, and the need for more self-medication. It is a very difficult cycle for an addicted person to break.

The "loser" is an aspect of the rebel who can find no place to hide from his hurt. He is dedicated to proving he is unworthy of love. A loser will reject help, because he knows he does not deserve it. He uses his anger inside to sabotage his life whenever possible, or he acts it out violently with others. He is often addicted to substances, anger, and belief in his powerlessness.

The Prince and Princess, Romantic and Lover

Who could be more deserving of care and attention than a "prince" or "princess"? When Mom or Dad dotes on a child, meeting his or her needs without question, and even calling a girl "my little princess," the strategy is born. Often the attention is given by the parent to meet his or her own needs, not the child's, and beneath the child's glory of attention is resentment about not really being seen.

> As long as your mind is functioning, it is dreaming. Whenever you are dreaming, you are creating a personality, and wearing the mask of that character. The Toltec wisdom is not suggesting that you should or even can live without your identity and personality; it is simply a reminder that you are dreaming it.

Being cute or handsome and well dressed brings its rewards, and so the child grows up using the prince or princess strategy—in spite of the underlying hurt. Such children know they can distract judges from seeing that they are unworthy of real attention by attracting superficial attention. They also expect to be doted on in adulthood, silently resenting those who do not meet their many needs. The prince and princess believe that they are entitled to special attention and care, but even total adoration cannot heal the fear that they actually don't deserve it.

The "romantic" and "lover" distract attention of outside judges by wooing and seducing. They flirt with bank tellers, grocery clerks, their therapists, a police officer writing them a ticket, or anyone who can be drawn into their web. The romantic strategy, like most others, hides the fear of being inadequate, this time by using flirtation, candlelight, sweet talk, and gifts. The lover is often "just passing through," because he believes if he stays still, his partner will see his defects and reject him.

Hiding, Defending, Joking, Blaming— All Afraid

Beneath every strategy and behind every mask is a human afraid of being revealed and rejected as an imposter. Every child who learns that he is not okay the way he is grows up trying to be someone else. The fear is twofold:

First, there is the threat of being unmasked, and rejected because he is not who he pretended to be; second, once unmasked, there is the additional danger of being found out to be defective as a human being—the terrible fear that the judge has been right all along.

The Invisible Child and the Lawyer

The father of an apprentice was a harsh and angry man. When the apprentice was a boy, he learned to slip into the house without being seen, and climb the stairs to his room without stepping on the squeaky steps. He knew if his father saw him, there would be yelling and punishment for some unspecified offense. Alone in his room, he built model airplanes, and dreamed of a time he could be grown up and escape from the home.

FACT

Romantic relationships are generally formed when two strategies recognize each other, and know they will be safe together. Two people who are the same or opposites will join forces. In the beginning it feels so perfect and natural, but as the mutual fears of intimacy reveal themselves, judgment and rejection is sure to follow.

As an adult, the apprentice sits quietly in the back of the room. He married a woman who has a similar strategy, and they don't go out much. They have very few friends, and spend most of their time together watching television or reading. They are careful not to share too much about themselves, and are content to be invisible to each other and the world.

The "lawyer" strategy argues the case of the victim child with the inner and outer judges. "It is not my client's fault, your Honor, he is innocent—his dog ate his homework, the traffic was terrible, he is only human, and it is not fair to punish him." As an adult, the lawyer can be totally tenacious and insistent about his story. This strategy attempts to protect the victim child from all judges by making them wrong for their accusations. Many professional lawyers grew up with judgmental parents.

The Clown and Jokester Versus the Rager, Blamer, and Bully

Remember that all of these strategies and masks are a cover story to hide the pain and hurt feelings of childhood. The emotionally abandoned boy who is finally rewarded with attention for telling jokes or making up funny skits will often continue to use the strategy to avoid revealing any of his vulnerability later in life. Clowns and jokesters can be the life of the party, attracting attention and entertaining for hours. Behind their masks, they are hiding their fear of being seen, judged, and rejected as not good enough.

The human who rages, blames, and bullies others, physically or emotionally, seems to be the opposite of the clown and his fun. If you look more closely at the blamer, you will see the same fear behind his angry mask as behind the clown mask. Both are afraid of being seen and rejected. The bully sets a boundary that says, "Stay away, don't get too close, someone might get hurt."

Hiding as the Judge and Victim

You have discovered many aspects of the judge and the victim child in this book. They are the dominant voices in the mind's mitote, and the ones that give rise to the need for the other strategies here. Without the judge and victim, there would be peace in the minds of all humans. In this section you will find another way in which they express themselves in the outer world—one, by making you superior to everyone; and the other, by making you inferior.

The Judge Makes You Better

The judge is an unlikely "defender" of your victim child, but as a strategy that is exactly what he does. Now he looks outside, and judges those who might judge you. He says to them silently, "I can see through your masks, and I see the defects you are hiding. I know I am better than you, so if you judge me, I don't have to believe it." In its extreme, the defender judge sees everyone in the entire world as less than you.

This defender judge also serves to distract the inner hurt and direct it outside. He judges the government, television programs, his boss's ties, supermarkets, other drivers, and strangers on the street. By putting everyone else down, he tries to raise you up. By rejecting others, he tries to protect you from rejection. Like all strategies of protection, this one has its disadvantages. It separates you from the rest of the world, sheltered but alone, in a cocoon of judgment and rejection.

QUESTION?

Is there anyone who wasn't domesticated and is already free?
Everyone ends up domesticated in some way. Kids want to do what they want to do. When they can't, they think it is not fair and feel victimized, even if what is happening is something that is best for them, or has nothing to do with being hurt or neglected.

Hiding Behind the Victim

Up until now, you have explored the victim as the hurt child within, wounded by the judgments of that eternal inner critical judge. There is also an aspect to the victim that is a strategy. The victim avoids responsibility and judgment from the outside by judging himself and collapsing in pain. He lies down and says, "Don't kick me, I am already beaten down, I am already suffering, so don't judge me! It is not my fault, my mother abused me, I never get anything right, please leave me alone."

There are as many strategies as there are children to learn new ones. They are enhanced, expanded, and improved throughout life. Each and every one is the same, although they may look entirely different. They are the same because they are all created to get it right, avoid the hurt of judgment, or to numb the pain of rejection. Most humans live their lives in fear of being found out as not enough, undesirable, or not worthy of love. The strategies and masks are created to avoid that detection. Even though they all appear to be different, each conceals that single common fear.

Healing the Split

Domestication of a child demands, to whatever degree, that the child abandon parts of herself, in order to become what is expected of her in the family. She disowns the parts that are not welcome, and creates strategies like the ones described thus far to compensate. The star must deny her rebel. The thinker must deny her dreamer, and the dreamer must deny her thinker.

A goal of the Toltec path is wholeness of body, mind, and heart. This means that all of the disowned parts need to be brought back from the shadows into the light. The personality of the average person is divided into many different parts, each with a unique belief system about life. The inner rebel will resist the judge, and the inner star will be afraid of the dreamer. The parts exiled to the shadow will sabotage the efforts of the dominant strategies, and the dominant strategies will work hard to keep the unacceptable parts in the shadow. For many people, this inner struggle results in an outer life of missed opportunities, unexpected reactions, and feelings of powerlessness.

ACTION!

Sit quietly for a moment, and relax into your breath. Feel your physical body. Experience your emotional body. Let your body inform you about any feelings that you have been ignoring in this moment. Use this quiet time to become intimate with yourself. Do not think about it; simply feel.

Fear of Intimacy

Young children are "hardwired" to their feelings. They have no internal resistance to being who they are, and feeling what they feel. They have no judgment about their tears of sadness, or their celebration of joy. Children are what they are, without self-conscious evaluation. If a young child is angry, the emotion is expressed in its raw and natural state. It is not until they encounter the external resistance to their emotional expressions that children begin to question and repress their truth as it rises in them.

As described previously, when a child learns a strategy and assumes a mask to get it right for the dream he is born into, he has to split off the parts that are not acceptable. The more he has to deny who he really is to the outside dream, the more he must deny it to himself, also. It is impossible for a young child to know he is angry, and then talk himself out of expressing it. He must distance himself from his own anger, and become who he needs to be in order to be accepted. He must split off the angry part, and deny it exists.

In this way, the child loses his sense of intimacy with himself. He can no longer know and honor the true feelings that rise in him in response to the world. As he matures, he becomes increasingly skillful at hiding those truths from himself and others, and his strategies and masks become more finely tuned. His fear of being discovered hiding behind his masks also increases. The victim child within remembers his lessons very well, and knows he must avoid the pain of rejection at all costs.

Reclaiming Emotional Intimacy

What has been done can be undone. You came into this world free to know and express the truth of your feelings. You can return to this reality, which the Toltecs call "heaven on Earth." It is the absolute knowing of your perfection as an expression of the "divine" in every action and every moment. In this heaven there is no judgment, and there are no expectations that you be any different than you are. This heaven on Earth is a place of peace and joy, and it lives inside of you. It is not given to you by anyone, and cannot be taken away by anyone or any event.

FACT

Intimacy with one's self is a vital foundation for an intimate relationship with a partner. The Toltec wisdom continues to stress self-acceptance and self-love as the true intimacy. To be open to all of your own emotional expressions, without splitting them off or rejecting them, is the key to intimate wholeness with yourself.

By reclaiming your right to be emotionally intimate with your own feelings, you open your heart to acceptance and intimacy with your world. Your relationships change, because you change. You learn to use your feelings as the guide to your life, and do what you know is right for you—instead of what you think you should do to please others or protect yourself from them.

The Toltec master invites his apprentice to look carefully at his strategies and masks without judgment, and evaluate how they serve him as an adult. The tools of the Toltec path serve the apprentice to change the fear-based beliefs and agreements that anchor those strategies, and transform his life.

The Power of the Assemblage Point

Imagine you are in a city and come to a big wooden fence around a construction site. You find a hole in the fence, and look inside to see a partly finished building beautifully covered with marble. Later that day you see a friend, and tell him about what you saw. He begins to argue with you, saying that he saw the same construction, and there was no marble; there was only an ugly concrete building. You argue back, insisting on the reality of what you saw. Finally, you leave your friend, amazed at how stupid or unobservant he is.

The next day, you are walking on a different route through the city, and come to a different side of the same fence. Curious, you look through a hole and see an ugly concrete building. "Where is the beautiful marble?" you ask yourself. "There must be two different buildings." Perhaps you walk around the fence, looking through holes on various sides, until you realize that it is all the same building in different stages of construction. You realize that your description of the building and that of your friend were both right—and that what you see depends on your point of view.

Establishing the Assemblage Point

The Toltecs know that personal freedom can only come when one is free to see the totality of things from all sides. During domestication, and the pressure to see life with only one set of beliefs and agreements, the wholeness of life is lost. The Toltecs call the place from which we perceive life the "assemblage point." It is the hole through which you perceive and create your personal dream. The assemblage point is fixed in one place for most people. They will look through that single point of view and argue that they are seeing the only reality.

An apprentice went to her teacher because she was sure that her husband was cheating on her, and seeing other women. The apprentice had confronted her husband, who had denied her suspicions and confirmed his loyalty to her, but she remained convinced about her fears. If he came home a few minutes late, or took the telephone in another room to talk, she knew her suspicions were correct. In time, virtually everything he did confirmed in her mind that he was cheating.

In her conversation with her teacher, the apprentice remembered how she felt as a child when her father was out all night, and her mother was crying alone in the kitchen. She recalled the tension in the house when her father came home. She was surprised how vividly she remembered her mother warning her through her tears, "All men are alike! They will all cheat on you, and they will all hurt you!"

Changing the Assemblage Point

The apprentice's mother had (unconsciously) fixed the assemblage point through which the apprentice would always see men and her own husband. There was no other point of view available to her. After her conversation with her teacher, the apprentice realized she had the power to see the situation from many different points of view. She went home and spoke with her husband again, this time listening carefully to his truth. She also asked a close friend, who confirmed the loyalty of the apprentice's husband.

ACTION!

Stop and think about all of your assemblage points. Test them to see if they are rigid and fixed in a single perspective, or if you are flexible about them. Perhaps test this with a political event, a child's behavior, homeless people, illegal immigrants, or a noisy neighbor. How many perspectives can you shift to?

By looking at the situation from all sides, the apprentice was able to see a bigger picture than the one her mother had offered her so many years before. Her assemblage point expanded, and became flexible. This is a goal of the Toltec path: to see the world from a multitude of assemblage points, and marvel at its complexity and perfection.

Survival Strategies Become Gifts

The Toltec master guides his apprentices to recognize how resourceful they were as children. They survived childhoods that were perhaps neglectful, hurtful, humiliating, or even violent. The strategies they adopted and the masks they learned to wear were the clever adaptations of children under stress. No one was standing by when the children left home to remind them they would not need those strategies in their adult world—so they took their strategies with them.

The strategies are held in place by fear—the fear of being discovered as inadequate, not enough, defective, and unworthy of love. The fear gradually diminishes as the spiritual warrior consistently demonstrates the message of unconditional love and acceptance to the victim child. When you have less fear of being seen and more love for your perfection, the strategies will not be held so tightly, and your gifts can emerge.

Many childhood survival strategies have adult gifts hidden in them. For the pleaser to give freely, without expectation of appreciation or reciprocation, is a gift to all. The rebel is a valuable resource when a person needs to deny the social pressures of parents or peers. The clown can be wonderfully entertaining when the fun is offered as a gift of love, and not to avoid being seen.

The world needs mystics and teachers, dreamers and thinkers, perfectionists and procrastinators, lawyers, lovers, and romantics. When the lie of "not enough" is broken, and these gifts are offered from open, loving hearts, they nourish the souls of both givers and receivers.

Chapter 9

The Parasite in Your Mind

The Toltecs say that all humans are sick with a disease of the mind. It is not usually fatal, but it is very contagious. You have learned about it in the preceding chapters as the judge and victim child, the masks and strategies, and all the lies programmed into the mind during domestication. In this chapter, you will learn more about this disease of the mind, which the Toltecs call the "parasite."

Your Very Own Personal Companion

The Toltecs say that humans are sick because there is a parasite in their minds that eats their negative emotions. It not only eats the negative emotions, but it also does everything it can to get the human to dream in fear, so it will have lots to eat.

In most people, the parasite is in charge of the assemblage point. It tells lies in the mind, and the person believes them: "You have to look good for other people. There is a limited amount of love and attention available, and you need them to survive. You have to be good and get it right for other people, to deserve your share of the love." The parasite learned all its lies during childhood, and continues to repeat them in the adult mind. The lies create a single assemblage point, which creates more fear for the parasite to eat.

The parasite is a living dream, dreamed in different ways and degrees by all humans. When you were born into the parasite dream of your family, they began to take little pieces of their parasite and put them into your mind. These were like seeds—little beliefs and lies based in fear—and they grew in your mind. In time, those seeds grew into your unique personal parasite, which has been with you ever since.

Dictionaries define *parasite* as a living being that lives on or in another organism, sucking its energy, and offering no advantage to the host. Often parasites weaken their hosts a little at a time. The parasite in the human mind creates and eats negative thoughts and emotions, drains the human's personal power, and robs his body of its vitality. The Toltecs know that the parasite is the cause of many diseases of both the mind and body.

The Parasite Hurts Its Host

Many people live marginal lives, with just enough energy to get to work, eat, sleep, and go back to work again. They often have little joy in their lives, and no energy for play and creativity. They compensate for their lack of energy with stimulants like caffeine and sweets, or try to change their low mood with drugs and alcohol. They fill their time with minimal-energy activities like watching television.

Without all of their personal power available to them, people whose lives are run by the parasite have no energy for change or growth. Their habits keep them in routines that are safe. This is why the Toltecs know it is very important in the mastery of awareness to understand how the parasite controls the mind, and reclaim personal power from it. They also know that it is difficult in the beginning, because the parasite is very used to being in charge, and does not easily tolerate losing its power.

The nature of the dreaming human is to distort information collected from the outside world into a virtual reality in the mind. The parasite is the sum total of all of the knowledge collected, sorted, and stored there. The Toltecs teach that it is important to examine all of that knowledge, but only if a person is drawn to doing so.

The Job of the Parasite

The parasite's job is to keep you in line, following the rules that the judge knows society wants you to follow, so you will be loved and accepted. The parasite controls your behavior with fear. The minute you try to create new beliefs for yourself, especially based in love, the parasite is terrified. It knows that in the past, going against the outside dream meant rejection, punishment, or worse. The parasite will do everything it can to sabotage your efforts to change your personal dream. It fears for your safety, and ultimately your life. Who could blame it? The parasite learned well, in a very tough school.

If your personal parasite can't control you, there is always the big parasite, the living being that is the dream of the planet. It taught your parasite everything it knows, and colludes with your parasite to keep you asleep. Everyone knows the rules and how to remind you of what will happen if you break them. Remember the story about the emperor's new clothes in Chapter 5? When the boy speaks the truth as he sees it, he is scolded and rushed away from the scene. The parasite is determined to not let that happen to you.

Feeding on Your Fear and Doubt

Can you imagine any other living beings with a parasite like the one the humans have? A small oak tree would be jealous of a larger oak tree, and say, "It isn't fair that you are so big. How come you got the good soil, and I have to be over here in the rocks?" Or, the large oak tree might say: "I had better not grow this year; I shouldn't hurt the little oak tree's feelings by being too successful."

Parasite talk is not going on in the minds of the deer, snails, trees, birds, fish, worms, clouds, wind, galaxies, or rain. It is not even happening in your body. Can you imagine your cells worrying about what other cells think, or your liver thinking it should be more like your kidneys so that it could impress your pancreas? The only part of creation that dreams in fear is the (supposedly) highly evolved humans!

▲ The Toltecs recognized the spiritual wisdom of all life.

The Parasite Creates Fear

This living dream called the parasite feeds on your emotional fear and has the power to create fearful thoughts in your mind. The human mind becomes so possessed by the parasite energy that a Toltec master will often tell her apprentice that he is the parasite. In Chapter 7 you learned that the human can become a puppet of the outside dream. This happens because the person is already a puppet of his or her personal parasite.

ACTION!

Take some time out and imagine yourself as a tree, bird, cloud, or deer. Quietly experience your surroundings from the assemblage point of each of these other living beings. What about a galaxy? What does it think about taxes or the right outfit? Become your liver. Does it worry? Why do you?

There is no limit to the fear that the parasite can create in the emotional body of a human. The rules, expectations, beliefs, obligations, and agreements programmed into the mind by other parasites are an endless source of fear-producing thoughts. After seeing all the variations of fear-based thoughts in his mind, one apprentice reported that ultimately his big and little fears all came down to one story: "I am not good enough, and so sooner or later I will always be rejected, especially by people I care about."

The Parasite Feeds on Fear

The Toltecs say that the food of the parasite is fear. It is as though it uses the human to feed itself, like a farmer raising chickens so he can eat the eggs. It manipulates the dream in the human's mind to create fear, and then it eats that fear. The more fear it can produce, the stronger it becomes. Some parasites are very big and strong, manipulating their humans into angry or violent behavior toward themselves and others. Other parasites are more benign, and only cause mild anxiety and confusion in their humans.

There is a marvelous resource in you. It could be called your truth, or wisdom, or pure knowing. This resource is part of the emotional truth that you were born with, and that was domesticated into exile so that you could be good and welcome in your family. Your truth is the reality of which the parasite is most afraid. It knows that your truth is based in love, and it is afraid it will starve if you feed it truth and love (this is not necessarily true, as you will learn in Chapter 15, but the parasites believe it).

The parasite must do everything it can to make you doubt your truth. It has lots of help from all of the strategies and masks that are busy hiding the real you and creating pretend versions of you to please other people. If you really want that last piece of chocolate cake, the parasite will remind you of your agreement to always leave the last piece for someone who might want it more than you do. It uses words like *selfish* and *greedy* to make sure that you don't break that old agreement. You want the cake, but you doubt your desire, make it wrong, and don't take the cake. The parasite has won another round.

Manipulating Your Perceptions

The parasite is a master at creating fear, even if there is nothing real to be afraid of. Since it has control of the human mind, it can do just about anything it wants with it. The parasite controls the assemblage point. It allows its human only a narrow perspective, one point of view. The result is fear.

If you read a newspaper and it makes you afraid, know that the parasite has channeled the information there through an assemblage point it knows will create fear. It might use your political ideals, your fear of violence, or your identification with the environment. If you are sitting in your car at a red light, and a fearful daydream arises in your mind, that is the parasite creating its food. If you experience tightness in your chest and within moments imagine yourself in an ambulance racing to the hospital, that is the parasite creating its food.

The Parasite Lives in the Past and Future

An apprentice had been married for fifteen years and was never happy. Her husband was sweet to her before the wedding but began criticizing and verbally abusing her shortly after they were married. Her parasite told her to keep trying to make it okay. It convinced her that it must be her fault that he changed, and if she could figure out what had caused him to turn against her, she could fix it. The parasite kept insisting that if she would just keep trying, the future would be better.

ACTION!

Take a moment, put down this book, and see if you can become aware of this parasite dream in your body. Does the parasite have a message for you? Anything you want to say to it? How does your body feel in the presence of the parasite? Make some notes about the conversation.

No matter what she did, no matter how hard she tried, the apprentice's husband continued to be abusive. When she was exhausted from trying, and so hurt it did not matter anymore, she filed for divorce and moved out. Immediately her parasite began blaming her for being weak and selfish. It told her she should have tried harder, and that she would be lucky if anyone ever loved her again. After all, the parasite reminded her, she wasn't getting any younger. Her parasite also told her that she should have left her husband much sooner, and that she was weak and stupid for not leaving him.

When the apprentice began dating a nice man a year after her divorce, the parasite was right there to remind her about the past. It told her over and over that she could not trust her attraction, because look what happened the first time. It made her doubt herself, and she was afraid to commit herself too deeply to her new relationship. In time, the man gave up trying to overcome her fear, and moved on in his life without her. Of course, her parasite used the man's leaving as evidence to create more fear about the future, and more self-judgment about her lack of worth.

The Parasite Uses Other People

A man asks a woman to go out with him on Saturday night, and she replies, "I'm sorry, I can't. I'm busy that night." It may be very true that she is busy, and she might actually hope that he asks her about the next night. If the man's parasite is on the job, what he will imagine he hears her say is "Go out with you? You must be kidding! No thank you!" His parasite can then pull out its list of reasons why nobody would want to go out with him, and why he should never even bother to ask.

The parasite is a ventriloquist, and is able to make its human say things the human would never say on his own. One of the great tricks of the parasite is to ask someone what she thinks of its human. "Do you think I'm fat?" is probably the greatest trick of all. "Do you think this looks good on me?" Remember that the parasite is asking another parasite the questions, and the other parasite will make its human afraid to give the wrong answer and be rejected. The fear nearly guarantees that the "wrong" answer will be given, and more rejection and fear will follow. You can almost see the parasites smiling.

Other Tricks of the Parasite

An apprentice decided that he should meditate for one hour every morning as part of his spiritual work. He was excited, because he knew meditation would help him become a more loving and peaceful person (which meant, of course, that he would be more loved and accepted in his new spiritual community). After doing well for the first week, he overslept one morning and had to rush to work without meditating. All day he was agitated. He knew he would not have time to meditate when he got home, and was angry for failing to keep his agreement with himself. He decided that he would have to meditate for two hours the next morning, in order to make up for his failure.

Religious and spiritual groups are just like any other dream of domestication. There are expectations held by the group about how members should behave and dress, and about the right and wrong words to use— just like a family. The Toltec warrior is always aware, no matter where he is, of these external influences, and resists their effect on him.

When the apprentice was setting his alarm an hour earlier for the next morning, he began to resent the pressure. He was not getting enough sleep, and now he was going to have to get up in the cold and dark, just to sit in meditation. He began to doubt his ability to keep the new schedule, and even started doubting the value of meditating. He fell asleep while trying to decide what to do, and was nearly late for work the next morning. By the time he got home, he was convinced that meditating was a waste of time, and probably wouldn't help him anyway. The next day, he dropped out of his new spiritual group.

The Parasite Talks to Itself

The judge (parasite) made the rule that the apprentice should meditate. The victim child (parasite) created the motivation of love and acceptance. The judge (parasite) made the apprentice wrong for breaking the rules, and then punished his failure with self-anger and the penance of a two-hour meditation. The rebel (parasite) blocked the decision about getting up two hours early, and finally the victim child (parasite) was so hurt and discouraged that nothing ever worked out right that he gave up the whole idea.

Do you see the parasite talking to the parasite? It actually never wanted the apprentice to do anything that might help him become free of its influence and control. So it ran the apprentice in little circles, all dedicated to his "spiritual work." Pushing a human to be perfect on a spiritual path is one of the best tricks of the parasite, because everyone agrees that they and everyone else should be more spiritual. The goal of perfection is unattainable, so the parasite knows his program of sabotage is safe.

The Parasite Lies

The parasite is a big liar. Remember that the judge is the main voice of the parasite, and the judge is always lying. Everything he says about what you "should" have done or been is a lie, because you can only be yourself as you are.

Imagine that you realize that you are going to be late for an important appointment, perhaps a job interview or an exciting date. If you look at the clock and say, "I am going to be late," that is simply the truth. The parasite will look at the same clock and say, "You are going to be late because you are stupid and don't pay attention. You should have known how long it would take to get ready. Now the person is going to be mad at you, and you will probably not get the job (or romance). Nobody will ever like you, and you will probably just get old and die alone."

How can I know whether I am lying to myself or not?
For now, assume that you are always lying. You are describing your dream, and it is not really the "truth"—it is only your perception of reality. And assume that the voice telling you how you should be and what you should do is really a liar!

With that mitote in your mind, you drive to the appointment in a fearful rush, arrive filled with anxiety, rushed apologies, and perhaps excuses about the bad traffic. The person waiting for you might not have noticed the time, or was happy for the quiet time while he or she waited. You would have no way of knowing, because you would be focused inward on the parasite's mitote, and not present in the moment. If the job interview or romantic lunch does not go well, the parasite will blame it on you. Your gift of power on the Toltec path is to learn to blame it on the parasite—the true villain in your mind.

The Power of Your Attention

As the Toltec apprentice begins to clear the mitote in his mind, he also gains power over his attention. In the example of being late that was just described, you saw how the parasite causes the attention to be distracted into assumptions about other people, the future, and the ultimate fear of being rejected by everyone. In the example, there is no attention available for the clear perception of how others are dreaming.

The Toltecs say that your beliefs control your attention until you have reclaimed enough of your personal power to control your own attention. They teach that all the beliefs, opinions, fears, assumptions, and agreements your parasite learned from others make you a puppet of the parasites of the world—including your own parasite. As you learn to separate "you" from the parasite and regain control of your attention, you are on your way to personal freedom.

Beliefs Hook the Attention

An apprentice was excited to be able to attend a talk by a very special spiritual teacher who was visiting his town. Partway into the inspiring talk on the oneness of the unifying presence in creation, somewhere in the large audience a baby began to cry.

At first, the apprentice did not pay much attention to the crying, but soon he was annoyed by it. "How rude," he thought to himself. "Why doesn't that mother take her baby out of here? I am totally distracted, and I'm sure everyone else is, too." His mind began to review all the other times in his life when thoughtless people had distracted him from something important, and he became even more annoyed. As the baby continued to fuss, the apprentice became more agitated. He looked around to see if he could identify the offending mother and child. Perhaps he could say something to her in the lobby after the talk.

The apprentice began rehearsing in his mind the casual way he would mention to the offending mother how inconsiderate he thought she was. He also made a mental note that when he was a father, he would never let his child distract people. He made an agreement with himself to always consider other people, and teach his children to do the same.

The Price Is Paid

Suddenly the room burst into applause, and the apprentice was shaken out of his indignant reverie. He realized that the talk was over, and the baby and her mother had made him miss the whole second half of the program! Now he was even more determined to find the mother and let her know how she had cheated him out of enjoying the teacher's inspiring message about love and acceptance.

What the apprentice failed to understand is that missing the talk was the price he paid for not yet being in control of his own attention. His opinions and beliefs about crying babies, inconsiderate mothers, thoughtless people, rudeness, and everything else his parasite had dredged up in response to the situation was really what cheated him out of hearing the teacher's message.

The Lesson Is Learned

The apprentice returned home from the spiritual teacher's talk agitated and angry. "Why does this always happen to me?" he kept asking himself. "Nothing is ever easy." In the morning, he met with his Toltec teacher to ask for help. "The first thing I always remind you to do in a situation like this," his teacher began, "is to not judge yourself for what happened. You had no choice but to be distracted, because your parasite is still pulling your puppet strings. That is not good or bad, it just is. Let's look at the beliefs that hooked your attention, and see what is true and not true."

Together, teacher and apprentice examined each of the old beliefs and agreements the parasite had used the night before. As they found the lies of "should have" and "should be" in the judgments about the mother and the apprentice himself, the apprentice released them from his mind's mitote and replaced them with the truths of love and acceptance. In time the apprentice learned the power of being in control of his own attention. As you continue on the Toltec path you can give yourself the same gift.

Healing Your Mind

If the parasite is like a disease in the mind, surely there must be a cure. The most important aspect of the disease is fear. The parasite creates fear and eats fear. It depends on fear for its survival. It creates fear in the human mind, and eats the emotions that arise from it in the body. Perhaps by now you are impressed with the skill and persistence of the parasite—both your own and the big one in the dream of the planet. It is a living dream, and lives in the minds of nearly all humans. Surely there must be a cure for this disease.

Could it be so simple that the cure for this disease of fear is its opposite—love? Yes, this is exactly what the Toltecs, and many other spiritual paths, teach. They know that each human comes into this world filled with love and acceptance—and no fear. The new humans must be infected with the parasite disease, in order to be like everyone else. The infection does not destroy or diminish the love that is the nature of every being. It simply overwhelms the nature of the humans, who then forget what they are.

The word *love* is one of the most distorted in the English language. It means so many different things, and brings up so many different emotions and memories in people. If you add all the differences created by other cultures and languages, the meaning is lost. To the Toltecs, love means "acceptance."

The gift given by the Toltec master, ancient and modern, is to awaken the seeker to the truth of who he is as love, as life itself. The master takes the fish out of the water and wakes it from the parasite's dream. She says to her awakening apprentice, "Wake up! You have been suffering in a dream hell created by the parasite! Wake up! See life all around you and within you. You have been asleep in the midst of a wild celebration of life's abundance and magic. It is dancing in joy all around you. Wake up, and join the dance!"

No part of the parasite is capable of waking you up from its own dream. It only knows fear, and the antidote for its disease is love. You need a new resource, a spiritual warrior who sees the truth of what you are and can help you embrace it for yourself. Teachers from all paths of love and truth have acted as that source for their students and apprentices throughout the millennia, and it is wonderful if you can find a modern master to support you.

In this time of the sixth sun, a new way of dreaming is awakening. The teachings of ancient mystery schools such as the Toltec are coming alive and are accessible for everyone. It is possible to awaken a strong resource of love inside yourself. There is a powerful spiritual warrior in your heart. He has been put to sleep by the old dream and overwhelmed by the parasite, but he is there. Perhaps it is time to liberate him from his bonds.

Chapter 10
The Toltec Spiritual Warrior

The parasite has done its best to keep the spiritual warrior asleep in your heart. An important step on the Toltec path is to remember that this warrior is present, and awaken him. Once awakened, he will need to be supported and empowered in his battle against the parasite. This and the following chapters will introduce you to the qualities of the spiritual warrior within, how to empower him, and to the many Toltec tools available to you in the mastery of transformation.

The Qualities of the Spiritual Warrior

In the old times, seekers of new skills and wisdom sought out experts in the field and asked to apprentice with them. Craftsmen of all times, from potters to shoemakers, have had apprentices and novice trainees working with them to learn their trades. Spiritual seekers have also sought out teachers and masters to guide them as apprentices. In this time of a shift in the dream of humans, there are many more spiritual seekers than there are teachers who can work with them personally.

Toltec naguals living in our present time have made themselves available as much as suits their various styles. A list of contact information for many of them appears in Appendix B of this book. The role of these teachers is to model for their students and apprentices the absolute unconditional love of the divine that is the nature of the universe. They also show their apprentices tools and methods they can use to clear the distorting light and see that divinity in themselves.

A New Resource in the Mitote

Because not everyone can have access to a teacher personally, many teachers in this modern technological era have written books, recorded audio teachings, and created Internet communities, to share their love and wisdom with the world. They offer various degrees of experience and personal power, and it is left to the student to evaluate with whom they best resonate.

Ultimately, the best source of love and support is the spiritual warrior within. Even though it is wonderful to find a teacher who can point the way, he can only lead you to the love and wisdom of your own heart. The judge, the victim child, and all the masks and strategies that make up the parasite live in your mind. All the knowledge of right and wrong and good and bad that was domesticated into you as the parasite disease is in your mind.

The secret to healing the parasite disease in the mind is the introduction of the spiritual warrior. The disease in the mind of humans is based in fear. The spiritual warrior, whether outside or inside, is the new resource that brings love to the mind. Love is the antidote for fear. When the warrior within has changed the knowledge in your mind from fear to love, you will be free.

At War with the Parasite

The Toltec spiritual warrior is at war with the parasite—in the mind and in the world. This war is not violent, and should not be confused with the idea of war as armed conflict between nations. This is a war that everyone can ultimately win, both inside and out. It should also be noted that for most people, a benign, gentle approach to the parasite has not worked. The parasite is used to being in control of the mind, and is absolutely opposed to giving up that authority.

Each of the characters in the drama of the mind's mitote has its own dream of the world. Most people are not aware of the different parts of themselves, and believe there is one personality reacting in many different ways. The spiritual warrior understands the dreaming mind, and is witness to all the different dreams.

The warrior in the inner world generally appears as a masculine presence, and the judge almost always does. However, in this section, the spiritual warrior will be referred to as both "he" and "she." If you prefer to think of your inner warrior as feminine, please do. Some people call this new resource in the mitote the "love warrior," because the battle with the parasite is a war between fear and love.

Warriors go into battles fully present, with fear, and with respect for their opponent. They don't know if they will win all their battles; however, they go with absolute confidence and willingness to do their best. The spiritual warrior must fight against the forces and limitations of domestication. The warrior knows it is possible to reclaim the opportunity to live a life of freedom, creativity, and love; and is willing to do whatever it takes to achieve that goal.

The Story of the Sleeping Warrior

Once upon a time, in a land not so far away, there was a new king in a beautiful new kingdom. The king ruled his kingdom with love and integrity, and all of his subjects were happy and at peace. All the other kingdoms around this new kingdom, however, were ruled by kings who were angry, fearful, and jealous. It wasn't long before the true king lost his place on the throne and was replaced by one of the powerful false kings. These kings were not real kings, but simply took over the throne because they had the power to do so.

FACT

The stories about Robin Hood and his merry men are some of the most popular folk tales ever. They were told and sung long before being written down centuries ago. Robin Hood is portrayed as a fearless fighter against tyranny and injustice. He has been a hero of people of all ages, and perhaps represents the rebel in everyone's inner world.

All of the false kings ruled their kingdoms with secrecy, gossip, and intrigue. They made up their own laws, and expected their subjects to follow them, even if they did not make sense, or caused their subjects to hurt themselves. The subjects in the kingdom were not very happy. They had to hide who they were, and what was in their hearts. They tried to follow the laws so they would not be punished, but that only made them unhappier.

The Rebel Lives in Hiding

The subjects vaguely remembered a time long ago when the true king ruled in their kingdom, and sometimes they told each other stories about the love and acceptance of the true king. He had no expectations of his subjects, and encouraged them to be exactly who they were. They felt loved and respected by him, and wished he would return—but they did not know where he was or how to overthrow the false king.

There also lived in the kingdom a rebel. He knew he could not fight the false king, but he also knew he would not follow all the laws that the false king proclaimed. So the rebel lived in hiding, and came out when he knew it was safe to sabotage the false king, to entertain and distract his fellow subjects, or to help them get things they needed. He had to be very careful, because the false king did not like him and wanted to drive him from the kingdom—or worse!

The Warrior Asleep Under a Tree

One day, the rebel heard about a very brave and honest warrior who was in the neighborhood, offering to help restore true kings to their thrones. Seeing how unhappy his fellow subjects were, and knowing that the false king was becoming more and more powerful, the rebel set out to find the brave warrior. He found him sleeping under a tree. "Why aren't you fighting false kings?" the rebel wanted to know. "Nobody has asked me," replied the warrior, "so I have just been waiting here. In fact, I am not sure if I am strong enough anyway, so it's better this way."

"My kingdom needs you," pleaded the rebel. "I can't distract people's attention from their unhappiness any longer. I need your help, and the people need your help!" So, being a brave warrior, he rose and followed the rebel to the kingdom. When they arrived, they discovered that the false king was very strong and very prepared to keep the brave warrior away.

QUESTION?

Are all these parts of the mind actually real?
Well, they are not real in the physical sense, or course, but they are as real as the confusion and unhappiness they cause. By separating them out, giving them names and personalities, you get to learn how they operate in your mind, and how they control the puppet strings of your life.

The warrior and the rebel took their time. They grew stronger together, and learned everything they needed to know about the false king and all of his henchmen. They dedicated their intent to driving the false king from the throne, and restoring the true king to his rightful place in the kingdom. As the word spread in the kingdom, more and more of the unhappy subjects of the false king rallied around the rebel and the brave warrior, adding their support to the cause. They began to remember more stories about the happiness of the past, and excitement spread throughout the kingdom. "Maybe it is possible," they said, "that the true king can come back and claim his throne."

The Master of Self-Acceptance

Perhaps it is time to call the brave warrior of your inner kingdom to come out from where he has been hiding and waiting. The rebel in you has been holding the spark of truth and resisting the ultimate triumph of your domesticators. Together they can challenge the false king (the parasite) to a battle to restore truth, integrity, and peace to your inner kingdom.

The spiritual warrior is separate from the parasite in your mind. Remember that fear controls the perceptions, reactions, and feeding habits of the parasite. Your spiritual warrior is not part of that fear. He is a new resource in the inner world. The warrior brings unconditional love and acceptance to the fear-based knowledge, strategies, masks, doubts, and limitations in the inner kingdom of your mind.

The judge is the master of self-rejection. He makes the victim child within wrong about what she thinks, says, feels, does, cares about, and wants. The judge carries on the work of punishment and reward that began during childhood. The warrior is the master of self-acceptance. When the warrior goes to war against the parasite, they are in a battle for control of the attention of the victim child. Will the child's attention be hooked in fear or in love, in rejection or acceptance?

A Path of Action

To return to the state of self-love and acceptance that is the birthright of every human, the warrior must awaken and take action. He must absolutely know that the judge is lying whenever he makes the victim child wrong. The warrior needs to stop the voice of the judge in the mind, and support the child in love.

When the judge of the inner world demands of the frightened victim child, "What is the matter? You should have known better!" the warrior steps in and tells the child, "Kid, the judge is a liar! Don't listen to him!" He then tells the judge, "Shut up and leave this kid alone. She is perfect just the way she is." He turns to the child and reminds her, "Don't believe the judge. He is always lying."

The warrior knows that to restore self-acceptance to the child, he must take a path of action. He must actively and consistently remind the victim child to accept herself totally the way she is. He must cultivate active self-acceptance for the child, until she awakens from the lie of fear and becomes the master of her own truth and love.

Denying the Dream of "Not Enough"

The warrior is in a battle with the parasite in the mind, and also the big parasite in the dream of the planet. He knows that he must protect the victim child from the judgments that insist she is not enough, no matter where they come from. When she is standing in the supermarket looking at the magazine covers that demand she believe she is not enough the way she is, the warrior is present to deny the lies. It is a war of many battles, large and small.

When the golfer is on the course with his friends, and misses an important putt, the warrior is there to remind him that the barbed joking of his companions has nothing to do with him. He is not wrong, stupid, or not good enough because he missed the shot. When the young woman arrives at the door of the wine tasting with a six-pack of beer in her hands, the warrior is there with her child self to remind her that she is not defective or not smart enough. She misunderstood, and she is doing her best. That is good enough for the warrior, and if the judge tries to make her wrong, the warrior will not tolerate it.

Impeccability: The Key to Inner Peace

Most people would probably say that they are looking for, or wishing for, inner peace. They would like to end the daily clamor of the mitote in their minds, and experience the stillness they imagine is there, too. The strongest intent of the Toltec warrior is to be impeccable with her word. For the Toltecs, to be impeccable with the word means to not use it against yourself.

The warrior is always on guard against negative self-talk, self-judgment, worry, gossip, and other fear-based uses of her word.

The common use of the word *impeccable* means to be so perfect that you are faultless and beyond reproach. Modern Toltecs use *impeccable* to mean to be free of actions or thoughts that go against yourself. To be impeccable with your word, then, means to not use it in any way that would hurt you.

When the Toltec warrior quiets the negative and often abusive self-talk in her mind, she discovers a new world of presence and insight. The incoming light is less distorted, and her dream of the world more closely resembles the reality that is out there. She is no longer a puppet of her emotions and outside stimulation, but lives in centered calm during the changing storms of life.

The Power of the Word

The Toltec warrior knows that every thought, belief, agreement, fear, and doubt, spoken aloud or silently in her mind, is her word. She also knows that her word is the power that creates all of her reality, including her personal dream. The parasite uses all beliefs and knowledge of good and bad against the human to create fear. It is the intention of the warrior to transform the self-talk in her mind into love, support, and acceptance.

To use a phrase from the Bible, the warrior understands that her "word is made flesh" when she projects her inner dream out into the world. The outer world is a reflection of the inner dream. She knows that changing her word will change her world. This is the power of the word, and the power of the Toltec warrior.

Changing the inner dialogue to positive thoughts and beliefs is an important step in quieting the mind. When the judge stops making the victim child wrong, the child can stop defending herself, and the endless mitote in the mind will quiet. The peace the warrior desires will become her reality—both inside and out.

No More Mistakes

The warrior knows that to be impeccable with her word, she cannot use it against herself to judge or make herself wrong for anything she does. She knows that it is the judge and parasite that criticize and second-guess everything that her victim child feels and does. The warrior has a new dream about all the "mistakes" the judge says her child makes. She knows that everyone is always doing their best, and therefore no one ever makes mistakes.

You have already read about the absolute illogic of the judge when he says you should be like someone else. If you could be different, you would be! One of the warrior's favorite illogics of the judge is when he says, "You should know what you learn from your experiences before you have the experience, so you could do the experience differently according to what you learned after you did it." The warrior and the child learn to have a nice laugh together about that one.

You cannot make a mistake if you are doing the best you can do in any moment. When you make any choice or decision, your entire lifetime of experiences, information, beliefs, and fears (even including those from many generations before you) come together in that very moment and create your decision. There is only that moment, and in that moment you look at the situation and weigh the variables and consequences to the best of your ability. Then you act. Ten minutes or ten years later, if something goes wrong with that decision, the judge likes to be right there to make you wrong, because you "should have known better." It is nonsense, and the inner warrior does not believe it.

Support for the Warrior

When your warrior wakes up from where he has been sleeping all these years, it takes him some time to gather his strength and get to know his enemy, the parasite. The rebel may be excited, running around and saying, "Come on, let's get going! Let's go find that parasite and teach him a lesson he won't forget!" The excitement is reasonable and expected, but you need to remember that this is an untested warrior, noble and determined, yet still unsure of his role.

The warrior needs support and training. He must become firm in his conviction that the little child who has been a victim of the judge's criticism and lies is innocent and deserves to be protected and rescued. The warrior needs to be convinced that all of creation is perfect, including the child. The warrior needs to have the authority of his unconditional love for all of creation to overcome the parasite fear-based disease in the child's mind.

The spiritual warrior is the part of you, no matter how small, that is resonating with the idea of your perfection as part of the universe. He is the part of your mind and heart that is agreeing that the illogic of the judge is ridiculous. It may be a small voice right now, but the Toltecs know that even if it only begins as an intellectual understanding, the seed of truth, when planted, grows if it is nourished well.

Nourishing the Warrior

The new spiritual warrior is like a baby eagle in the nest. It has its feathers, and looks ready to fly, but needs encouragement. Any source of unconditional love will strengthen the young warrior. One such source of love might be this book, or others like it that offer insight into the truth of the perfection of the universe. Music with an uplifting spiritual message can also be a valuable ally for the new warrior. Many people find the reflection of their perfection in twelve-step and similar programs. Any source of pure love attracts the warrior—a Toltec master, genuine friends, films, spiritual groups, ceremonies, and nurturing self-care.

ACTION!

Make a list of ways you can think of to strengthen your inner spiritual warrior. Make sure they are all based on love and acceptance. Use ideas from this section, and add your own personal ways to nurture and support that part of you that understands the true meaning of love—a love without conditions or expectations.

Humans of the past that lived in constant relationship with nature—hunting, planting, migrating, and worshiping—instinctively understood their spiritual relationship with the life around them. For modern people, it is important to remember that all life is connected by an intangible presence often called the Divine, spirit, or the many names of gods and deities. The magnificence of mountains, the quiet presence of a tree, or the beauty of a meadow in bloom are all reflections of the human magnificence, presence, and beauty. Nature is the perfect mirror—there is no judgment, no doubt, and no right and wrong in nature. There is only the truth of life, manifesting itself in a multitude of living forms.

Qualities of the New Warrior

The Toltec master calls forth the warrior in his apprentice. He begins by modeling that presence for the apprentice, so she will recognize the experience of unconditional love and a reflection of her perfection from the outside. Then he helps her cultivate that same acceptance inside, through her inner warrior. Here are some of the important qualities of the warrior that the master shares with his apprentice:

- The warrior loves to love, and is separate from the fear of the parasite.
- The warrior holds the victim child in absolute unconditional love.
- The warrior knows the judge is always lying.
- The warrior knows there is no such thing as a mistake, including the victim child.
- The warrior takes action to change the programming of domestication.
- The warrior is connected to the perfect spiritual oneness of all creation.
- The warrior connects with the spiritual oneness through nature, teachers, and other reflections that support his divinity.

The qualities that define the Toltec warrior are present in all humans. The love of the Master is offered as a reflection, a perfect mirror for the apprentice. When she sees herself reflected there, she has the chance to awaken her warrior within.

Your Warrior's Battle with the Parasite

The Toltec spiritual warrior goes to battle with the parasite not knowing where it will lead, or even if he will win. He recognizes that he is battling with both the inner parasite and the big parasite in the dream of the planet for control of the victim child's attention, and he refuses to let them make a puppet of the human any longer.

The warrior holds a strong intention to learn the tricks of the parasite, and the tools of the Toltec path that will support him in his battles. He knows his love must have more authority than do the fear-inducing lies of his rival. When his love and acceptance are powerful enough, he will end the control of the false king, and peace will reign in the kingdom of the inner world.

FACT

The Toltec term *parasite* is related to the parts of the mind called the "ego," the concept Sigmund Freud introduced in the 1920s. The meaning of *ego* has evolved and is used in many different ways, including describing an unrealistic sense of superiority. The word *parasite* includes many of the same ideas, but they are not interchangeable.

You can win this battle with your parasite. As you begin to recognize the illogical voice of the judge in your mind, and the strategies you have developed to protect yourself from his abuse, it is time to rebel! Say "Enough is enough! I don't want to be a puppet of the parasite, not inside and not outside. I want to live my life without being afraid of what people think of me, or trying to get their approval. I want to be free to be me!"

Remember, your word is the creative force in the world. To set an intention for your freedom begins the process. It awakens the warrior in you, and calls him forth to the battle at hand. The possibilities are unknown; the rewards are great. There is no greater crusade in which to engage than the one for your freedom from the tyranny of the judge and parasite. And there is no better time to start than now.

Chapter 11

Transforming Your Dream and Life

In Chapter 2 you learned there were three masteries on the Toltec path. The first is the mastery of awareness, which you have been exploring. The second is the mastery of Transformation. The Toltecs know that you must be aware of the parasite in your mind before you can transform your dream. The awareness gained by an apprentice in the early stages of this path can generate a great deal of transformation. However, when the warrior begins applying the powerful tools of the Toltec path, even deeper transformation takes place.

The Mastery of Transformation

Important lessons from the mastery of awareness include recognizing that the mind is always dreaming, respecting the influence of the parasite, and embracing the possibility of transforming the dream and healing the disease of the mind. The judge is the ruler of the old dream, which the Toltecs aptly call "hell" because of the endless judgment and condemnation involved. The warrior is the architect and true king of the new dream, which is also called "heaven on Earth," because of the foundation of love and acceptance that supports it.

Accepting Does Not Mean Liking

Domestication and the dream of the parasite create a fear of being rejected. The Toltec warrior knows that the antidote for this fear is love and acceptance. It takes time on this path to change the lies in the mind, which create the fear, into truths that support acceptance. As the warrior grows more certain of the reality that this universe is perfect in every aspect, he expands to greater acceptance of every part of it, including himself. He sees that there is no beginning or end to any event, no primary cause or effect, no victims and no perpetrators. (The idea of a perfect universe is explored more deeply in later chapters.)

The idea of accepting things you do not like may be perplexing to you. Remember that "acceptance" is being used here to recognize the reality of what is. Events and people are what they are. To argue that they "should" be different cannot change the truth of what is. You can accept the truth without liking it.

Along with his appreciation and acceptance of the perfection of the universe, the warrior learns that he does not necessarily have to like what goes on here. He knows if someone wants to abuse him it is the perfect expression of how they are dreaming, but in his self-love he will not tolerate it. This understanding frees the warrior to live his life in openhearted communion with every person and event in creation, while at the same time making choices on his personal path based on what supports his growth and happiness.

Acceptance as a Spiritual Path

The word *spiritual* has appeared in these chapters without being specifically defined, because it is a general concept that can be used in many different ways. The Toltec path of personal transformation is called a spiritual journey because the goal is to recognize and identify with the spiritual (nagual) nature of the universe, in balance with the material (tonal) reality.

Since there is one whole, there can be no authority outside of that unified whole to take it apart and judge the individual parts. Without a judge making parts of the universe right and wrong, we can only say the parts and whole are perfect. The human mind, through the parasite, is the only part of the universe that thinks it has the power to make itself and other parts wrong—and it is dreaming a lie!

The Toltec warrior may only accept this truth as an intellectual concept at first; however, when he works to clear his channels of perception and transform his dream, he can truly perceive the perfection of the universe. In the acceptance of the universe as it is, the warrior enters into a relationship with the spiritual or divine reality of creation. Thus, his acceptance becomes his spiritual path.

ACTION!

Take a few moments to think about people or events that you judge as bad or wrong. Write down some thoughts about how you feel emotionally when you are judging. Then imagine yourself in open acceptance of the same people or events, and notice any changes in your emotional state.

The purest state of love is total acceptance. Love as acceptance is the healing balm for fear. Thus, the warrior is the antidote for the disease of the parasite in the human mind.

The Dream of the Second Attention

As a child, your attention was hooked for the first time, and you were taught a dream. The Toltecs call the dream that you were taught during your domestication (and subsequent societal reinforcements) the "dream of the first attention." As you learned in Chapter 3, it was a dream based in judgment and fear. With your new awareness you are ready to hook your attention for the second time, and transform your personal dream. You are ready to create the "dream of the second attention."

The work of the second attention is to examine and clean the distorting memories and lies from your channels of perception, so that you can see reality as it is, rather than as you have been programmed to interpret it. This is a very powerful state of consciousness, and attainable for anyone with the desire and willingness to surrender the old dream for the new.

Surrendering the Human Form

Not everyone is prepared to surrender the relationships, habits, and comforts of their old dream, even if they sabotage their ambitions and drain their life force. Not everyone is called to battle as a warrior. The Toltec masters of the past chose their apprentices carefully, and were very respectful of their own energies and the investment they were willing to make to take the apprentice all the way to freedom. In these new times of the sixth sun, as the teachings of the Toltec and other mystery schools are becoming available to a wide spectrum of humanity, there are more opportunities for individuals to travel their own path, in their own way.

For those who are prepared, there is an opportunity for total surrender of attachment to everything they "know," and the identity they create with their knowledge. The "human form" is the physical and psychological expression of the sum total of every opinion, agreement, habit, and domesticated belief of good and bad in the human dream. This form is the identity that the parasite calls "I." It is the human form that is defended in conflict and hurt with insults. It is a rigid structure that is part of the parasite's survival strategy in a world it fears.

The mastery of transformation holds the keys to softening the rigidity of your human form, releasing those parts that go against your highest good, and cultivating a new dream—this time based on your choice, using your attention for the second time.

Taking Out the Garbage

A guru once told his students, "I can show you where your garbage is—it is that brown paper bag over there with the grease spots on it—but you are the one that must take it out." The Toltec warrior, whether inside or out, can help identify the garbage in your mind. He can show you what it looks like; he can help you identify how it affects your emotional body; but you must do the work of changing it. In Chapter 2 you learned about the channels of perception in the mind, and how the stored light there distorts your perceptions. That is the garbage.

QUESTION?

If I let go of everything I know and believe, won't I be lost in my life, and not know right from wrong?
Since right and wrong are arbitrary beliefs themselves, downloaded into your mind by others, there really is no such thing. You are invited to follow your heart, and never go against yourself.

In the dream of the first attention, the judge has been writing a book of laws. He has been writing down everything you should be, and should not do, to be okay. Your judge has been writing and enforcing the laws in his book your entire life, without your awareness or permission. Now that you are aware of what the judge has been doing, would you like to change the rules?

Your New Awareness Gives You Choice

In the dream of the second attention, you get to rewrite the judge's book of laws. It is a time to clean the old distorting garbage out of your channels of perception. It is a time to un-learn everything you think you know. On a planet that is hurtling through space, coming from somewhere unknown and going somewhere unknowable, there really is nothing true and no knowledge worth suffering for.

As you break your human form of rigid beliefs and opinions, you will be able to re-domesticate yourself into a new dream—this time by choice. This is the mastery of transformation of the Toltecs. Here the warrior takes action to create a dream of heaven on Earth, based on love and acceptance. The rigid structures of the old dream are replaced by a fluid movement through life with all of its changes and challenges.

The Choice: Love or Fear

The choice is simple: love or fear. It is not necessarily easy, but it is simple. In any moment, do you choose love or fear? They are two tracks of life, and from what you have read so far, it is probably clear where each leads. Fear is the energy the parasite uses to keep you small, safe, and out of trouble. Love, the simple act of accepting what is, opens your heart and frees you to enjoy life, be creative, and play.

The Toltecs realize that even though the choice is simple, and even obvious to most people, it is not necessarily easy. The parasite has been in control for a long time, and is not willing to relinquish its authority in your life.

The parasite knows that the strategies it has developed to keep the shameful truth of who you are hidden from others are the only thing that keeps you from being banished from human company and dying impoverished and alone. The parasite wastes most of your daily human energy allotment on its lies, big dramas, and keeping you hidden. Perhaps it is time to find out how big you can really be!

The Choice: Happiness or Suffering

How happy can you be? How happy do you have permission to be? The parasites of the world like to bond through suffering and commiserating. They say things at their pity party like "Oh, dear, the worst thing happened to me yesterday. . . ." Another parasite replies, "Oh, that's nothing. You should hear what somebody did to me! They told me I was. . . ." It is as though the parasites are trying to one-up each other in a contest about how unhappy they can make their humans—by seeing the world as hurtful, unsupportive, or filled with danger and betrayal.

The Toltec warrior realizes that the parasites inside and outside are afraid of too much happiness. It makes the humans too big, which is dangerous in the dream of the parasite. The parasite says maybe you can be happy sometimes, but you have to suffer to balance it, or you will not recognize the happiness or be grateful for it. The warrior knows this is another lie. You can be happy all of the time. On the love track of life, there is only happiness. On the fear track, there is suffering. The warrior is dedicated to risking being happy all the time, and being as big as he can be.

ACTION!

Take a moment to think about ways that you stop yourself from being *too* happy. What are the agreements you've made about happiness? What do you feel when you think about being really happy? Does your parasite commiserate with other parasites about how bad it is? How does that serve you? Make some notes for yourself.

Accepting Responsibility for Your Life

The dream of the planet is deeply entrenched in its judgment, blame, and revenge. People, governments, and even religions blame each other for their unhappiness, inconvenience, emotional reactions, and wars. These people and institutions feel discouraged and powerless when their blame and judgment does not change the world, so they resort to revenge and punishment of those they believe hurt them.

The warrior knows he is dreaming his own unique version of reality. He understands that his universe is his creation, and so takes full responsibility for it himself. He knows that his personal power arises from his aware choice of his reactions to the world as it unfolds around him. When he chooses acceptance, he experiences inner peace no matter how crazy or violent the world appears. A warrior experiencing inner peace will dream a world "out there" at peace in its perfection, regardless of the appearances.

The Big Shift

An apprentice grew up in a household where judgment and blame were the main forms of communication. Her parents blamed others constantly for all of their problems, beginning with each other, and then on to friends, strangers, bosses, and the government. The apprentice learned to dream like her parents, and was invited to commiserate with them about the lousy world they all had to live in.

When you remember that everyone is dreaming their own personal dream, you know you are free of responsibility for other people's dreams of you. Their emotions and judgments of you are coming from how they have distorted you in their dreaming mind, and have nothing to do with you. You are free to be you.

When she matured and went into the world on her own, the apprentice took the victim dream of judgment and blame with her. She blamed her lovers for not being present with her, and her bosses for not recognizing her worth and power. In her world there was no support, and no one she could really trust to be there for her.

The first questions her teacher asked when he heard the apprentice's stories were, "Are you present for yourself? Do you recognize your own worth and power?" The apprentice was stunned. She had never considered her responsibility to herself. She had only learned to see why they were wrong, and what they were not doing for her.

As the apprentice's awareness grew, she could see that she had abandoned her responsibility for herself and her happiness, and had projected that abandonment out onto everyone in her life. She made everyone "out there" responsible for her well-being, and then judged them when they did not meet her needs. When she realized she had the power to change her world by changing her perceptions, she was liberated from her victim dream. She is now free.

It's Nobody's Fault

When the apprentice stopped blaming others for the choices and decisions she was creating in her life, she saw that her problems had never been anybody's fault. She was able to forgive all those she imagined had let her down, and forgive herself for not knowing how she had been programmed by her family. It was not her fault that she was domesticated into a way of dreaming, nor was it her family's fault—they had been domesticated, too.

As she awakened, the apprentice began to see the universe as one divine whole. In a universe of perfect wholeness, there can be no victims, no perpetrators, and nobody to blame. Nothing can be anybody's fault, because everyone is doing their best, based on how they are dreaming. Certainly, if even the most angry parent, hardened criminal, or corrupt politician had a better choice for their actions, would they not take it?

Staying Awake in the Dream

Much like the young women in the fairy tales "Sleeping Beauty" and "Snow White," most children are put into a deep sleep during childhood—and can only be awakened by the kiss of true love. In the Toltec story, that kiss of love comes from the presence and intention of the spiritual warrior. Often, the first warrior to awaken a sleeping princess (or prince) is an external teacher. The challenge for the apprentice is to stay awake, surrounded by a dream of the planet designed to keep her asleep.

In the film *The Matrix*, the guide Morpheus tells the hero, Neo, "I am trying to free your mind, Neo. I can only show you the door, you're the one that has to walk through it." The best any teacher can do is be a signpost pointing the way. The danger for the student is the temptation to stop and worship the signpost, instead of continuing on the path.

Wake Up! Wake Up!

Just as an alarm clock helps you wake up in the morning, it helps to have an alarm that says "Wake up, wake up!" when you are learning to be awake in the dream. There are many possibilities, but anything that will jolt you out of the old dream is fine. There is a perfect wake-up tool you can find on the Internet called the MotivAider. It fits in a pocket or on a belt, and vibrates to remind you to wake up!

ACTION!

Try some wake-up tools. What can you use to jog yourself out of the old way of dreaming and awaken to the truth of life? This precious experience of life is unfolding in every moment all around you. Life does not exist in the past or future. To be fully engaged in life you must awaken to each precious moment.

Other wake-up tools include colored stickers in strategic places in your life—on the car dashboard, front door (coming and going), mirrors, computer monitor, work station, clothes closet door—anywhere you need the nudge to remember the truth of who you are. Apprentices have also hung their shoes on the doorknob at night, made a picture on the wall crooked, or changed the location of their coffeemaker. Whatever it is, the wake-up asks, "Are you on the love track or the fear track in this moment?"

It Is Okay to Fall Asleep Again

The parasite is like a hypnotist that can put you back to sleep with a silent word—a bit of fear about the future, a sudden thought about failure or rejection—and make you lose the love track. It is okay to forget. It is okay to fall asleep, over and over and over. It is part of the process of changing your dream, just like waking up. Awake and asleep are both perfect expressions of your dreaming mind. If you prefer one over the other, set your intention to remind yourself about your preference.

You will know when you are awake in the dream of life. A new light will shine from all parts of creation, and there will be a lightness in your heart and step. You will know that everyone is dreaming, including you, and you will be at peace with their dream and yours. You will not take anything personally, because you know nothing is personal!

You will also know when you fall back asleep again—after you wake up! Life will feel heavy and sluggish when you are asleep. You will worry about getting things right for other people. There may be a tightness in your shoulders or belly. When you are asleep you will not notice this, because it is very familiar. When you awaken you will recognize what happened to you. It is okay to fall asleep, and it is okay to be awake.

A New Relationship with Your Feelings

This time of transformation is your chance to create a new relationship with your feelings—to know them as your guide to this human life. When you were young you were domesticated into denying much of the truth of what you were feeling. Perhaps your parents told you to stop crying, to go outside if you were going to make so much (joyful) noise, to play quietly, not be afraid of the monsters under the bed, share when you did not want to share, and to be seen and not heard. Most of the reasons you were ignored, shamed, or punished was because of the natural bubbling up of the truth of what you were feeling. And what you were feeling was the truth of who you were.

FACT

Feelings arise spontaneously from the belly and heart. The information contained in feelings is totally personal to each individual. They are not a problem to solve or a disorder to fix. Having awareness of the feelings and taking actions based on them is the power of a warrior's life well lived.

There is no way for a young child to experience her feelings and not express them. When she feels sad or hurt, she cries. When she feels happy, she laughs, and when she feels angry, she yells. That is the nature of feelings. In order to stop expressing her feelings, she has to learn to stop being aware of them. Learning to cut herself off from the experience of feeling her own truth is one of the great masteries of childhood. Children learn to reject their own feelings, and then, in the absence of that very important information, use their minds to mock up acceptable emotional expressions. In a perfect world, a child would be encouraged to express and discharge her emotional energy. Her parents would not react or take her emotions personally, because they had learned to embrace and celebrate their own emotional aliveness. In a perfect world, that is.

In this imperfect world, it is the warrior's job to bring a relationship of love and acceptance back to the victim child's feelings. The warrior knows that her feelings are not a problem to be solved, but are important information arising from the truth of her being. She knows she can use that truth to guide her choices and decisions, and ultimately her life. The warrior is dedicated to listening to the victim child within, denying the lies of the judge, and restoring the emotional aliveness that is the child's birthright.

Chapter 12

The Warrior Exposes the Judge's Lies

When the new Toltec warrior has gained sufficient awareness of the limitations programmed into her mind by others, she prepares herself to go to war with the parasite. She knows that her integrity, clarity, and freedom of choice are at stake, and is determined to reclaim them for herself. In this chapter you will learn how the warrior goes deep into the mitote to explore the judge's book of lies, and prepares to use the many Toltec tools of personal transformation.

Deeper into Your Mind's Mitote

The Toltec warrior who has perceived the dream in his mind and wants to change it knows that the process is a simple one: change his fear-based thoughts and beliefs to those based on love. He also knows that the process is not necessarily easy. He recognizes that he has been domesticated and programmed for many years, both by other people and by himself. He is prepared to use the time-tested and powerful Toltec tools of transformation to reprogram his own mind.

The Toltec path is said to have "no rules and many powerful tools." As you learn about the various tools in this and the following chapters, note that some may be perfect for you to try, and others may not resonate with you at all. That is okay. There are many possibilities, and they are here for you to explore.

A Reminder about the Warrior's Love

It is very important to remember that it is the spiritual warrior who uses these tools of transformation. If the judge is allowed to be involved, he will use them in his ongoing story of "not doing it right" and "should do more." The judge loves to have new goals and intentions he can make into rules, and then make the victim child wrong for not following them. If the new warrior is not strong enough to keep the judge out of the process, or at least catch his interference in a reasonable amount of time, he may need to continue strengthening his personal power before going on.

It takes constant vigilance to keep the judge from interfering with the warrior's progress. The judge will do everything he can to sabotage the quest for freedom from the old dream. He is the gatekeeper of the prison of domestication, and he takes his job very seriously.

When the warrior is sufficiently aware of the tricks of the judge and parasite, he can bring his intent and love to his transformation and use the tools to free the victim child from his old dream of fear—the "hell" of the mind's mitote. The love and acceptance that the warrior brings to the victim child are the ultimate keys to healing the parasite disease in his mind.

The Power of the Lies in the Mind

It is sometimes surprising to the new warrior how deep, hidden, and pervasive the lies in his mind are. The parasite has spun a complex web of fears, worries, beliefs, denials, and self-rejections that often seem to have no beginning and no end. When the warrior tries to pull out one lie, it is attached to hundreds more that hold it in place. The beliefs and fears support each other with their power, and their long history of being the "reality" in the personal dream.

Not only are the lies of the old domestication deeply rooted in the mind, but they are also the very fabric of the dream of the planet. Almost every human is dreaming the old dream based on the parasite's lies of fear and rejection. The Toltec spiritual warrior must confront both the lies in his own mind and the reflection of the same beliefs and agreements in the culture around him.

The dream of the planet is afraid of personal freedom, and the dream of the individual parasite is afraid of freedom. The fear of freedom is programmed into each human's mind, along with all the other lies. Only love can overcome this fear, and only self-acceptance can heal the wounds of self-rejection. The warrior seeks to reclaim his personal power to overcome the lies and live in the truth.

A New Resource for the Victim Child

As the warrior breaks old agreements and transforms belief systems, she reclaims more personal power. Her awareness and power can then be directed to deeper work in the mitote, reclaiming even more freedom. You learned in earlier chapters that the judge is lying when he says you are not okay the way you are. Now it is time for the warrior, knowing the truth, to expose the lies of the judge and parasite, especially for the victim child. This is the time of the jaguar, stalking the parasite in the jungle of the inner world.

▲ The jaguar-serpent of the underworld.

Like any child, the victim child in the inner world needs to bond with an adult figure. Left alone with the inner judge, a bond is created that is often difficult to break. The victim child is always working hard to achieve the perfection that the judge demands, and the judge is always watching and pointing out the child's "mistakes." It is a strong alliance, which is also projected out and reinforced in the outer world in relationships of all kinds.

The Victim Child Bonds with the Warrior

When the warrior becomes strong enough to deny the lies of the judge, the victim child takes notice. The child may not believe the warrior when she first tells the child she is perfect just the way she is, but the child listens. The process is much like adopting a child who has been abandoned and abused in an orphanage. It takes patience and time for the child to understand that her circumstances have changed, and she is free to relax and be herself.

The love of the warrior is patient. She accepts the reality of the child within, and offers her love. The warrior has no expectations about the outcome of her loving; she simply offers it freely. She knows that the child came into this world as love, with the freedom to play and dance in life with joy.

She recognizes that this love and joy still live in the heart of the child, and trusts that the child will remember her birthright when it is reflected to her by the warrior.

ACTION!

Take a moment to be quiet, and feel yourself as the loving warrior. Check in with the victim child, and let her speak to you about her hurt or fear. Open your heart, feel compassion for the child, and let her know that you are learning a new way to protect, listen to, and accept her.

New Hope for the Victim Child

As the warrior continues to recognize the perfection of the child, and accept her every thought and feeling, the child learns to trust this new resource in the inner world—and their bond grows stronger. With the warrior at her side, the child pays less and less attention to the ranting and worry of the judge and parasite, and basks in the pure love of the warrior's acceptance.

In order for the child to learn and conform to the dream of the planet, she had to go against herself and her nature. It was hard work, and she protested and fought until she could fight no more. She put herself to sleep, along with the other humans, so she could survive in her family and culture. Now, in the loving embrace of the warrior, the victim child can reclaim her power and spiritual nature as a unique expression of the divine, and come alive once again. She is delighted to discover that it is much easier to return to being her true self than it was to deny herself and pretend to be something she was not.

The Judge's Book of Lies

When the new Toltec warrior understands that the universe is one living whole, perfect in its wholeness and in all of its parts, he also understands that any ideas about imperfection are not the truth. All of the "shoulds" that have been programmed into the mind's mitote from the outside are not the truth. Any notion that anyone, anything, or any event could be different from what it is in any given moment is not the truth. In fact, the entire dream in the mind's mitote is not the truth—it is based on lies, compounded by more lies, and held together by lies about the lies.

It is often confusing to talk about "lies" and "truth" when using the words in the context of the old dream. The Toltecs know that you are always describing your dream, and it is true for you, but not for anyone else. They teach that there is no absolute truth; there is only what is dreamed.

The biggest lie about all the lies in the human mind is that they are the truth! They are not the truth, because they deny the essential perfection of the universal whole and its parts. Your judge sits high up on his bench in your inner world, looking at a book filled with lies, and judges you against them. He has collected the lies for many years, from many sources, and believes they all are "right." The inner judge compares the actions, needs, fears, desires, and feelings of the child within to the standards in his book of lies. The judge finds the child guilty, and punishes him over and over.

All the Characters Believe the Lies

Every one of the strategies and their masks that you learned about in previous chapters is dreamed by a child part of the inner world. Each of those strategies is based on a lie that says the individual human should be different from what he is. The strategies are born of fear, and remain rigid and unchanged until the judge has been removed from his bench by the warrior.

The complexity of the inner world makes unraveling the lies and creating a new dream an interesting challenge for the new warrior. At times, the possibility of success may seem remote or nonexistent, but the Toltec teacher will always encourage his students to persevere. He reminds them that it is always the most difficult in the beginning, when the old habits and fears of rejection are still a powerful force in the mind. The teacher remembers his own battles with the parasite, and offers his experience, wisdom, and love to support whoever is ready to rumble.

The Warrior Versus the Judge

The Toltec warrior focuses on two aspects of the battle to free the victim child from the tyranny of the judge: He must protect the child from the judgments, and he must teach the child that the judge is always lying. In the past, when the judge looked down from his bench and his book of lies and told the child that his desires, actions, or feelings were wrong, the child would cringe and try to get it right for the judge (or would rebel, procrastinate, and so on).

As the warrior's presence in the inner world grows stronger, he hears the judgments and says, "No, judge, that is a lie, and you are a liar! There is nothing bad or wrong with what the child does, wants, or feels, and I will not let you talk to him like that!" Don't you wish you'd had someone like that around when you were a child, to protect you from criticism and rejection? It is not too late.

▲ The god of fire burns away the lies.

At the same time he is stopping the judgments, the warrior also turns to the child within and reminds him of his divine perfection. While the judge is carrying on about what is wrong with the victim child, the warrior is telling the child he is perfect exactly the way he is, and exactly the way he is not. He offers his love and acceptance to the child as the healing antidote to the fear and rejection of the judge.

An Apprentice Tells Her Story

"I have never wanted to acknowledge it, but I have finally accepted that my childhood was abusive. I know my parents did not intentionally hurt me or decide to mess up my life. Their parents hurt them, and they had no choice about the way they treated me. Their pain became my pain. They told me so many things about myself and life in general that were not true. And I believed them, because they were the only authorities in my life.

"The hurt my parents brought from their childhoods and the way they related to me, along with my already sensitive nature, caused me to suffer a great deal of hurt inside. I am ready to call it 'abusive,' when someone causes a beautiful, innocent child to hurt that much. To say that my childhood was abusive doesn't make anyone wrong, but it has given me a chance to look at it and say 'Wow, no wonder I have this pain. No wonder my relationships don't work, and I take things personally.' Throughout my whole life everything was personal, everything hurt. The people I needed to be there for me were not there for me, and that hurt.

QUESTION?

I have done lots of therapy, but still seem to be stuck. What can I do?
Make sure that the counseling you are using is based in self-acceptance and love. If not, it will only give your inner judge more expectations for you to meet. Ask the victim child within how she feels at therapy.

"'Abusive' is a very charged word, but I need to accept what happened to me. I was told so many things about me that were not true. They told me no one would ever love me. They said I wasn't worth paying attention to, unless I did everything they wanted. They said the world was a dangerous place, and I should always be afraid of it. I finally understand why I feel so frightened and alone. I know it is not my fault now, and it is not some psychological defect I have to live with.

"It is no wonder I feel the way I do. It came from the outside, I was taught to feel this way about myself, but it is not the truth of who I am. I was taught to believe it by people who were angry, hurt, disinterested, and afraid. I do not need to make them wrong anymore. Now it is my job to change my personal dream. I am changing the lies to truths, the rejection to acceptance, and the fear to love. It is my chance to give myself the childhood that I never had. They say it is never too late to have a happy childhood, and by god, I am making it happen!"

Reading the Book of Lies

The mastery of transformation follows the mastery of awareness because you must be aware of what you want to transform before you can transform it. If you wish to transform your dream and your life, it is very important to know everything you can about the judge's book of lies. It is a great act of power for the new warrior to enter the mind's mitote, look at the program, see the lies, and make choices about what to change.

The warrior must enter the book of lies like an explorer, with no agendas or judgments. She must be interested in what is there, but with detachment, or she will be sucked right into the mitote, and lose the battle. The explorer makes a map of what she finds—including the beautiful, the ugly, the safe, and the dangerous. With a thorough map, she will be able to navigate the inner terrain, enjoying what is beautiful and transforming what does not please her.

Lewis and Clark of the Mitote

The warrior explores the mitote like the great explorers Lewis and Clark, during their adventures on the great rivers of the West. Their perspective was fascination, discovery, awe, some trepidation, and plenty of wonder. The new Toltec warrior is the mapmaker of the mitote. She discovers the agreements, beliefs, fears, judgments, hopes, opinions, love, dreams, laws, and lies that make up the program in her mind.

ACTION!

Create a sacred journal for yourself and write down what you learn as you explore the judge's book of lies. Make absolutely sure you are writing as the warrior, and not the judge. If you find yourself judging the judgments in your mind, put the journal down and come back to it later.

The warrior does not try to predict or control the river, nor does she judge it. Can you imagine Lewis or Clark saying, "This stupid river is too slow. Why is it taking so long? This ridiculous river shouldn't turn south here, we are trying to go west! Oh no! More rapids, this will never work. I am going to quit."

You Are the Director of Exploration

In the spirit of acceptance and love, there is no timetable for investigating the lies in your mitote. You can choose to go fast or slow, camp out in a quiet spot on the river and work on your map, or shoot the worst rapids all at once. If you hear a voice telling you that you "should" work faster or fix everything and get on with your life, know that it is the judge again, and add him to your map.

Eventually, Lewis and Clark came to the Pacific Ocean. Perhaps, as they gazed out across the endless sea, they recognized that the rivers they had surveyed were simply parts of a larger whole—each a perfect expression of the influences around it, and yet all part of the same source. Once they had discovered the source, they turned around and went back. This time they knew the way and what to expect. Their journey was much easier, just as yours will be when you have mapped your mind's mitote, and all of its lies.

Traps Along the Way

If you choose to explore and study the book of lies, it is a good idea to write down what you find. It is also a good idea to work with an experienced Toltec teacher or therapist, who can support you and guide you through the rough spots. There may be many unexpected rapids on the journey, and deep emotional pools that have been forgotten or denied.

Be careful not to let the mind rationalize or fix emotional "problems" that you find on your inner journey. As the warrior, you need only become aware of the book of lies that the judge has been enforcing all these years. The awareness itself will produce a great deal of transformation. Also beware of the mind's attempts to intellectualize or gloss over painful events and try to make them okay: "Yes, Dad beat me, but I have forgiven him and moved past all of that." It could be true, and it could be a lie. Remember that memories and hurt are held in the dream of the victim child, and the warrior's intent is to listen and love, not minimize or deny.

FACT

The Toltecs who lived two thousand years ago had no form of writing. Modern teachers often adapt ancient teachings to the tools and needs of their times. Even though the teachings may remain unchanged, contemporary methods empower students to receive the best possible results from their experience with these ancient wisdoms.

Also remember that the parasite will be quite disturbed by your reading and transcribing the secret book of lies. It will do everything it can to sabotage your intentions, in order to stay in power. You might hear a voice saying, "I don't really have the kind of quality time I want to put into reading the book of lies now, so I will do it later. I really should not start it until I have created an altar (cleaned my room, built a private Toltec temple in the backyard). I am tired now; I will write in the morning. I will write tonight when it is quiet." If you hear this sort of chatter, remember who is talking, and who you are, and then make a choice about your next action.

The Warrior Has the Power of Choice

The awareness of the warrior is the key to choice, and choice is the key to personal freedom. When you are a puppet, reacting to the world around you through the dream programmed into your mind by others, you are the parasite. You do not have the option of clear seeing, clear thinking, or clear acting. The first step to reclaiming your integrity and clarity, and liberating your choice, is to become the warrior and learn all the lies in the judge's book.

Imagine your life after you have explored your mitote and learned all the lies the parasite uses to keep you small and afraid, and after you have used the tools of the Toltec path to free yourself from the tyranny of those lies. Imagine what it would feel like to go out into the world with no fear of other people's opinions and judgments of you. Imagine how relaxed and free to create, love, and play you would be if you did not take anyone's emotional reactions to you personally. Imagine being free in each moment to choose what is best for you, and taking action based on those choices.

As a new Toltec warrior, you are standing at the threshold of great possibilities. It takes courage to face the parasite, both within and without. The parasite will not give up its power easily. The spiritual warrior chooses to battle for his freedom from the tyranny of the parasite because he knows he has no choice. Once he senses what is possible, he will bring to the battle all of his resources and the power and tools of the masters, both ancient and modern. Those tools are available to you, right here, right now.

Chapter 13
Toltec Tools of Personal Transformation

The Toltec path is a path of action. The Toltec warrior utilizes the tools of transformation to challenge the old dream and create a new life based in love and self-acceptance. In the new dream, lost personal power is reclaimed, suffering is ended, and the warrior becomes present in the vitality and joy of each moment as it unfolds. In this and the following chapter you will be introduced to some of the tools the Toltecs have used and perfected throughout the millennia.

Changing Your Life by Changing Your Mind

Nearly everything you believe and know, all of your opinions and judgments, and all the ways that you compartmentalize creation have been programmed into your mind by others. The great gift of the Toltecs (described in Chapter 2) is the awareness that every human is dreaming, and every dream is unique. There are no two identical humans, and no two identical human dreams.

Each human lives in a totally unique universe, one that is created in the mind by the way each person dreams his or her reality. This point is vital to the Toltec wisdom. There is no reality outside of each unique human's dream. There is no universal right or wrong, no authority that speaks for any or all humans about how they should act, think, or believe. There is only the dreaming mind.

Many people who read that there is no *absolute* right or wrong are disturbed because the idea conflicts with their morality, religious teachings, and other beliefs they have accepted. The Toltec wisdom has no new rules to follow; it only invites you to open your mind to all possibilities.

The good news offered in the Toltec wisdom is the opportunity to change your life and the world you live in to make it anything you want it to be, by changing how you dream it. Escaping from the "matrix" of the old dream (discussed in Chapter 4) opens the possibility of applying the time-honored tools from both ancient and modern teachers to change your life by changing your mind.

The transformational tools of the Toltecs challenge every aspect of the dream of the first attention, and prepare the new warrior to dream in the second attention of love and acceptance.

Letting Go of Your Personal Importance

The Toltecs teach that believing that your dream is the only correct perspective of the universe can only lead to suffering. This understanding has been presented in several different ways in this book; now it is time to learn more about how to change that old way of thinking. Whenever you are fighting to be right, it means you are forgetting that you and all other people are dreaming. The mistaken view that your beliefs and opinions are true for anyone outside of your own dreaming mind is called "personal importance."

In order to be completely free, the Toltecs teach that you must let go of your personal importance. This is not easy when you are emotionally charged and absolutely convinced that you are an expert about how the universe "should" operate! Many of the tools of transformation described in this chapter are designed to help you through this difficult transition out of an old way of dreaming.

Ptolemy and the Center of the Universe

Two thousand years ago, a Greek astronomer named Ptolemy studied the heavens and taught that the Earth and the humans on it were the center of the universe. He created mathematical formulas and observations that supported his theories, which were widely accepted and taught for nearly 1,500 years.

ACTION!

Make a list of ways you are used to thinking of yourself as the center of your universe. Make notes about any personal theories or strategies you might have created to convince yourself and others about how and why they should orbit around you. Example: Are you a talker or a listener? Do you argue?

Over time, the believers in Ptolemy's theories had more and more difficulty explaining the celestial phenomena they were observing that did not fit the model of the Earth as the center of the universe. They struggled to create theories and mathematics that would continue to support their ideas.

The Catholic Church agreed with Ptolemy, and threatened anyone who challenged the accepted doctrine.

After scientists struggled for centuries to make this model work, Copernicus came along in the 1500s and disagreed. Copernicus believed that the sun was the center of the universe, and the Earth was orbiting the sun. He proposed that his model would explain in a much simpler way the daily rotation of the stars and planets. The Catholic Church and scientists of the time liked believing that they were in the center of the universe, and for a long time refused to accept this new theory.

The Warrior Releases Personal Importance

When a child is little, he is like Ptolemy's Earth. Everything orbits around him, and he truly is the center of his universe. In the beginning, his parents agree, and give him all of their attention. The child learns to believe that everything is happening to him for his benefit, or against him to frustrate or hurt him. The "center of the universe" attitude is the beginning of personal importance in the human. As the child gets older, he experiences confusion and conflict when he tries to keep his theory alive, and those around him have contradictory new ideas about the location of the center of their universe.

As a spiritual warrior, you can give yourself the gift of understanding that you are one celestial body orbiting in an infinite and unfathomable universe of other celestial bodies. You are not the center of the universe. You are no more or less important than any other aspect of creation.

QUESTION?

If I am just an insignificant speck drifting in the universe, what's the purpose of life?
There is no point to life, except that you are alive, conscious, and here. From that understanding, choose your purpose and be passionate about it. There is nothing you have to do, and nothing to risk by doing it all.

The good news is that when you let go of your perspective of personal importance, you will not have to work so hard to defend and justify your point of view. You will not have to make up strange formulas, as Ptolemy did, to explain why you are victimized or not responsible for your actions.

The Power of Self-Acceptance

It is not natural for humans to reject themselves. It is a learned "skill," and young children must be forced to learn it in order to fit into the culture of their birth. There is no other species on earth that rejects itself. Trees do not see themselves as superior or inferior to other trees, or to bushes or grass. Squirrels do not compare themselves to other squirrels, or to monkeys, which have better tails for leaping through the treetops. Comparing, compartmentalizing, and judging are all a special gift endowed only to humans.

Humans have perfected the gift of comparing and rejecting, especially in regard to themselves. In Western cultures, almost all commerce is dependent on people's dissatisfaction with who they are and what they have. As noted in an earlier chapter, a majority of advertising is specifically designed to create or stimulate the "not enough" judgment of self that motivates consumption of the solution to the lack. In a culture that has perfected the art of self-rejection, this is very smart advertising.

The Art of Active Self-Acceptance

Toltecs are artists of the spirit, and the highest form of their art is absolute and complete self-acceptance. Liberation from the old dream has been achieved when there is no longer any personal importance standing in the way of total acceptance of the self. Self-rejection was learned, and so self-acceptance must be actively relearned. The warrior applies herself diligently to cherish the truth of her perfection—in spite of the judge and parasite comparing, rating, and rejecting her.

The Toltec warrior knows that the parasite will do everything in its power to sabotage her personal growth. Her constant motivation is liberation from the limiting lies of the judge and parasite in her mind. The warrior is an artist, and she creates her life with her thoughts, words, and actions. As she continues to stalk her mind as the Toltec jaguar, her prey is all of her negative self-rejecting thoughts and judgments. Whenever she finds self-rejecting judgments, she attacks them with all the love and acceptance she can muster. With her love, she transforms self-rejection to self-acceptance, and fear and negativity into love.

Living in Active Self-Acceptance

To totally accept yourself the way you are is an amazing act of power. It means that you, the warrior, have convinced the victim child that she is okay just the way she is—and just the way she is not. The child has relearned that she is worthy of love and acceptance without meeting anybody's expectations, without bargaining, and without getting anything right. She is comfortable and happy just as she is.

Living in complete acceptance of yourself means that you never believe criticism or judgment from others, because you know they are not talking about you; they are simply describing their dream of you. Your mind is quiet, and if the judge happens to arise, nobody in your inner world believes him anymore.

The real magic of self-acceptance is your peace with the rest of creation. When you accept yourself the way you are, that acceptance radiates out of you to include everyone and everything. You accept yourself the way you are, and you accept all of creation exactly as it is. When you accept yourself the way you are, you cannot be a victim of people or events, because you know and accept their perfection. You are free to be in the world with your heart wide open, celebrating life in every precious moment.

The Origins of the Petty Tyrant

An apprentice was raised in a very serious family. There was not much laughter or fun, and he learned to deny his more frivolous parts—both to himself and others. He was domesticated to know that serious, intellectual, and grounded people were good, and frivolous and foolish people were not good. He developed a very competent and logical personality, which served him well in his family, and later in his work as a computer technician.

The apprentice never questioned his intense irritation with people who were not as logical and practical as he was. Even children bothered him, and he vaguely knew that he never wanted children of his own. It all seemed perfectly logical, because it was clear to him that frivolous, foolish, and spontaneous people were obviously not worth his attention.

Nearly every human is required to disown part of the self in order to fit into his or her family and society. It is necessary for societies to have rules that govern or restrict the expression of behaviors that could harm the cultural structure. It is important to choose which of these rules are valuable to you as an individual.

The Disowned Selves of Domestication

During the process of domestication, when a child is rejected or punished for certain feelings and behaviors, the part of his personality that represents those experiences is sent into exile. It is a deal reached between the child and his parents, and later is enforced by the child's own inner judge—often for the rest of his life. In the example cited here, the apprentice agreed to reject his own frivolous and spontaneous parts in order to be acceptable in his family system. In time, he became rigidly stuck in only one half of his total being.

As a result of the bargain the apprentice made with his parents, he judged those light-hearted parts of himself and others. When he was in the presence of children or adults who were being childlike, he was uncomfortable, judgmental, or sometimes quite angry. Until he understood the Toltec wisdom, he did not realize that it was his victim child within who was resentful about having to keep the deal to deny important parts of himself.

The Creation of Petty Tyrants

The Toltec warrior learns that he reacts to certain types of people with anger, judgment, or even envy because they represent those parts that he agreed to judge in himself. People who push his buttons or trigger him are what the Toltecs call "petty tyrants." If, as a child, your being "needy" was judged, you might have become independent and self-sufficient—

and you learned to judge needy people. If you were shamed and rejected whenever you expressed your emotions, you will be triggered by emotional people. If you were very talkative as a child, and your enthusiasm was ridiculed, you might have become very quiet or invisible—and irritated by boisterous people.

ACTION!

Take a close look at the strong parts of your personality, your favorite strategies and masks. See if there is a corresponding opposite that was judged and denied that needs to be brought back into wholeness. Make a list, honor the strengths, and see what qualities you are ready to reclaim.

The petty tyrant shows up in life as the opposite of the strategy you adopted in your family. If you were always forced to be clean, neat, and tidy, you had to exile the casual, messy part of yourself. You will react to people who are messy or disorganized because of the fear that keeps you clean and neat. If you are serious, you will react to the jokester, and if you are the jokester, you will react to someone who is always serious. These are the petty tyrants in your life, reflecting your disowned selves.

The Petty Tyrant as the Perfect Teacher

There are many powerful tools of transformation in the Toltec tradition. However, for the new warrior who truly understands the subtleties and potential for using the petty tyrant, it could be the only tool necessary to achieve total freedom. The petty tyrant serves you by illuminating your judgments of the "wrongness" of behaviors and emotions in yourself and all humans, as well as events, ideas, opinions, wars, and the weather.

When the warrior learns to accept the perfection of every aspect of the universe, including and especially herself, all judgment, suffering, and conflict end. The result is peace of mind, wholeness, and a free communion with the spiritual aspect of life itself. This is the life of the spiritual warrior. This is personal freedom.

Using the Petty Tyrant

The petty tyrant is like a mirror that reflects back to you the parts of yourself you agreed to send into exile. The warrior goes into the world in search of her petty tyrants, and they are not hard to find! She knows that anyone she judges for the way he or she acts, dresses, talks, eats, frowns, thinks, or votes is her unique personal petty tyrant. Anyone who irritates her, annoys her, triggers her, or pushes her buttons is a gift offered to her for her growth and transformation.

Every quality of another human that the parasite sees as "wrong" is the reflection of a child part of herself that she has split off and exiled. When the parasite reacts, the warrior looks deeply into her judgment, to refine it from the initial "her laugh bugs me" to a more precise "I think she is insincere, and I can't stand insincere people." From that truth, the warrior can recognize that a part of her that can sometimes be insincere has been rejected and judged within.

The Gifts from the Petty Tyrant

The warrior recognizes that her petty tyrants are getting to do things or behave in ways that she does not allow herself. Every disowned part of herself will show up in the petty tyrants of her world. When she is triggered by someone who is messy, she sees the reflection of her own exiled messy part. When she reacts to a companion's burst of anger, she sees a reflection of the anger she has denied to herself.

If you choose to use identifying your petty tyrants as a tool of transformation, wonderful possibilities will be opened to you. The petty tyrants of your world will alert you to all the important parts of you that were exiled during your domestication, and offer you the opportunity to embrace them and reclaim them as your own. If you learned to always be serious, you can learn to enjoy a little frivolity sometimes. If your strategy is to stay invisible (and loud people push your buttons), you can welcome the energetic, visible part of you back into your life.

The Reunion with the Exiled Selves

Imagine yourself going to the orphanage and bringing home all the kids that were taken away from your inner family. Enjoy the reunion! Bringing home your messy, serious, visible, quiet, and other parts does not mean you have to become them all the time. It does mean that you can enjoy them when it is appropriate, and reclaim the personal power you have been using to keep them in exile.

An important goal of the Toltec path is reclaiming the wholeness of your being. Domestication and other influences forced you to disown parts of yourself—perhaps your anger, tears, fear, or joy. By using the tools of the Toltecs, you can reclaim those lost parts, increase your personal power, and return to wholeness.

The ultimate benefit of using your petty tyrants to recover your banished parts is that you will no longer be irritated and triggered by the tyrants in your life. Once you can embrace and accept the formerly judged parts of yourself, you will be able to love and accept the same behaviors in others. You may still choose to not be around certain people, but it will be a choice made from self-love, rather than from rejection of yourself and others.

The Power of Not-Doings

Because of the strategies, masks, and exiled parts that humans have to deal with, they have adopted ways of being in their lives that are rigid and not very spontaneous. Perhaps you have noticed this in yourself, friends, or family; behaviors and emotional reactions are predicable, habits are unconscious, and wardrobe choices are limited. These are the signs of someone domesticated into a sleepwalking dream.

There are two essential reasons for the new Toltec warrior to use what are called "not-doings" as a tool of transformation: The first is to awaken from the domesticated sleep by changing routines and habits, and forcing himself to awaken and be present. The second reason is to challenge his rigid habits and test new ways of being in the world.

Awakening and Staying Awake

It is the intention of the Toltec warrior to wake up and stay awake in the dream. He uses the not-doings to support that goal. The inventive warrior will find many ways to wake himself up and be alive in the present moment. Anything he can do to break habits, change routines, react in new ways, or simply remember to be present in his body in the moment will be a not-doing.

The warrior uses not-doings to go beyond simply waking up in the moment. His goal is to challenge all of the habits, strategies, and domesticated routines that unconsciously run his life. He knows that he has been practicing the old routines for many years, and it will take effort and intention to change them. He wants to be fully alive!

Challenging the Doings of the Old Dream

Not-doings can be used to challenge the rigid strategies and masks from the old dream, by consciously "doing the opposite." If you are always late, start being early. If you always have to arrive early, then choose to be late sometimes. If you are always serious, learn some jokes. If you are normally boisterous, try being quiet and mellow. If you are generally messy, try being neat. Neat? Be messy.

Choose some not-doings that make you uncomfortable, and try them out. If they are too scary, check with the child within and don't push too hard. Here are some examples of doing the opposite that expand on the wake-up tools described in Chapter 11:

- Drive to school, work, or the store by a different route every day.
- Trade wardrobes with a friend; change hairstyles.
- If you love to talk, try silence for an hour or day.
- Eat or write with the unaccustomed hand.
- If you usually stay home, go out. If you usually go out, stay home.
- Change bathing and grooming routines every day.
- Skip morning coffee or other daily habits.

- Wear makeup or a tie if you normally don't. Don't wear them if you always do.
- Sleep on a different side of the bed.

These suggestions, and many more like them, are not-doings the warrior can use to break the sleepwalking routines of his or her life and wake up to be in the present moment. In the awareness of the moment, the warrior is empowered to make choices about his or her life with self-acceptance and love.

ACTION!

The not-doings are an effective way to take action to change your dream, and to open yourself to new possibilities. With patience and love, you can try out ways of doing the opposite, and see what emotions arise. If you become anxious, you are probably in the right place, challenging an old strategy. Be gentle, and keep going!

The child within who learned and has maintained the old strategies and routines will be afraid of changes. If you were punished for being messy as a child, and learned you were safe and accepted when you were neat, allowing yourself some disorder as an adult will alarm the child within. Doing the opposite shows the child that nothing bad will happen. After many years of being afraid you will be judged for being late or messy, perhaps you will learn that no one even notices now! Or you may find that people love your jokes, or your new mellow self.

The child's excitement will be boundless when he learns that the past with his judging parents is over, and there are new opportunities to express the truth of who he is. He will want to try even more ways of expanding his personality and choices. With the warrior standing by to protect and encourage the victim child, love replaces the fear that has held the personality in bondage, and new possibilities for expansion and expression of wholeness become unlimited.

Chapter 14

Tools of the Ancients for Today

The transformational tools of the Toltec path are directed toward one goal: freeing the apprentice's mind from the lies and suffering created during his domestication. The result is the freedom to live a life filled with self-acceptance, creativity, and joy. In this chapter you will learn more about the tools that have been passed down from the ancients to support new warriors on their path to personal freedom. Although most of them originated in the past, all are relevant and beneficial in today's world.

The Angel of Death and Life

In Western cultures, the idea and reality of death are often dismissed from people's conscious awareness. To individual humans, death is something that might come in some distant future, in some vague way. They don't like to think about it. Many people die alone, away from home in hospitals or care facilities, separated from their friends and families. Funerals are somber, detached events, with little or no contact with the reality of death, seeing lifeless bodies, or even real grief.

Religions and spiritual paths have always provided mythologies and rituals associated with death and dying, because, although ignored, the issue is very important to the human mind. When humans identify themselves with the tonal—the material world of their mind, parasite, body, possessions, and personal identity—death means the end of everything they are. The idea of loss of identity creates fear, and the fear is met with denial. Denial of death is an important part of the dream of the planet.

The Angel of Death Walks with You

The Toltecs say that the angel of death always walks with you, behind your left shoulder. She is the most powerful guide to a joyful and creative life on the Toltec path. She is there to remind the warrior that everything in life is temporary. In the Toltec tradition, the angel of death is the source of all your possessions. She owns everything that you have—your car, your home, job, relationships, money, youth, even your body and life itself.

The Toltec warrior surrenders with the knowledge that he is not losing anything, but actually gaining much. To surrender the attachments and illusions that create suffering is a gift the Toltec gives himself with love. The parasite resists, but the warrior expects its resistance, and includes the parasite in his love and acceptance.

The angel of death has lent you everything you possess, and when she is ready, she will ask for it back. The warrior knows that the angel is always there, and that he cannot control when she will take something from him. As one Toltec teacher said, the warrior can be grateful for the angel of death, because if it were not for her, every car the warrior had ever owned would be parked in front of his house, and every relationship he had ever been in would be waiting for him inside!

Surrender to the Angel of Death

Your parasite wants to carry the past with you, so it can remind you about your mistakes and personal deficiencies, and then judge you for everything. The warrior knows the past is dead, and the angel of death has already taken it. The warrior wants to live in each moment, fully present and alive.

The warrior lives in gratitude for everything the angel has lent him, rather than in fear of losing it. The biggest surrender on the Toltec path is letting go of the illusion that you own or can control any of your possessions—including your life. The angel of death is always with you, inviting you to live in the present, to love freely, to live the life you want to live. She reminds you that this life is temporary, and you will die—it could be this moment or any time. You can be ready by surrendering to her what is already hers, and live in absolute gratitude for her abundant generosity.

That is the life of the Toltec warrior. That is personal freedom. The angel of death is also the angel of life, because when you surrender to her, you are free to live your life to the fullest expression of who you are. She is your guide to life, in all of its abundance and wonder.

The Power of the Toltec Inventory

Many of the powerful tools of personal transformation on the Toltec path are used to become aware of the programming in the mind's mitote, and change it from fear to love-based. A thorough inventory and recapitulation is the most effective action the warrior can take to insure her freedom. The inventory is the first step, and serves as the basis for the recapitulation described in the next section.

Memories are held in your mind because of their emotional content. If there is no emotional content to an interaction or event, the mind has no reason to hold on to it. Experiences in the past in which you perceived yourself as a victim have the strongest hook in your mind. They are the ones the parasite uses to drag your energy down and keep you distracted from the present. To become aware of those memories with the inventory and release them through recapitulation is a powerful achievement of the Toltec warrior.

FACT

Many different healing disciplines, most notably the numerous twelve-step addiction programs, have used personal inventories to access forgotten or denied memories and feelings. Each one is directed to a slightly different goal, but all forms of inventories offer increased awareness and personal transformation.

Beginning the Inventory

The Toltec inventory is a list of virtually every memory in your mind—of every event, person, possession, and place. All the memories your mind is holding become part of the inventory. As you write, memories will arise from the most amazing places in your mind; use all of them, too. The more thorough you are when creating the list, the deeper and more healing your recapitulation can be.

The first step is to make a list of all of the major categories of people, places, and things in your life. Here are some examples of people and places:

- Lovers (including first sexual encounter)
- Mates
- Parents
- Brothers and sisters (including not having any)
- Relatives (could be separate category for each)
- Friends
- Roommates
- Places you have lived
- Schools you attended
- Jobs

- Churches, spiritual groups, cults, fraternities/sororities, gangs you have belonged to
- Jails or prisons you have been in; probation officers

As you begin to write these lists, let your memories emerge, and add them as you go. You will also want to include possessions, traumas to your physical body, and mistakes your judge says you have made. Some examples would be:

- Cars, motorcycles, tractors, boats, bicycles, and other vehicles you have owned
- Money lost, inheritances squandered, investment mistakes
- Lawsuits
- Accidents
- Abortions
- Surgeries (especially lost body parts)
- Robberies, muggings, violent crimes
- Physical or emotional injuries you have caused others

When you have completed a list using the major topics suggested here, you will begin to expand on each one. Note that any time you were a perpetrator against someone else, your judge will make you wrong, thus making you a victim of the judgment. The memory will be held by the emotions caused by your internal victimization.

Expanding the Inventory

Once you have established the major categories suggested in the list, you will begin to expand each of the categories in a new list. For example, if you are working with "friends," you will create a list of all of your friends—beginning with the most current, and going back to the first ones you can remember in your life. Do the same with "jobs," "mates," and each category on your first list. You will probably remember people you have not thought about for many years.

There is more: Begin another new list, using the first person on your "friends" or other list, and break down the relationship with that person into important time periods of the friendship. Always start with the present, and work back to the beginning. Do this with each person or event on each list. Examples of time periods with a friend might be: "Yesterday, when we had lunch"; "The month she didn't call me"; "First great six months."

ACTION!

Many new warriors read the instructions for the Toltec inventory and pretend they cannot understand it, or their parasite convinces them that they do not have the time or energy for such an undertaking. If you are passionate about your freedom, now is the time to make a commitment to yourself. Take action!

There is one more list. Look at the list of time periods, and starting with the most recent, such as "Yesterday, when we had lunch," let your mind scan back while you feel for any emotional reactions in your body. Make a note of any moments when a communication (or lack of same) caused hurt, irritation, sadness, anger, or other emotion. Write down a word or two to remind yourself of the incident and feeling. Do the same for each previous time period, on each list. These feelings are what you will recapitulate when you are ready.

Ready for the Transformation of Recapitulation

The more energy and intent you put into your inventory, the more powerful it will be. As you might imagine, the experience of creating the inventory itself is both illuminating and transforming. You will see patterns, choices, victimization, successes, and tricks of the parasite. Remember that you are doing this as the warrior, who has no judgments about the unfolding of your life.

The incidents you remember from the past are actually dead and gone. The only thing that is real is what you believe about them. You don't really know what the other person actually did, or why he or she did it—and if you asked, you'd find that his or her story would be very different from yours!

It is important to honor your memories and the feelings you carry about people and incidents, because they are what have shaped your belief system and emotional reactions. When you have sufficient information in your inventory—which could be one moment in one relationship, or every detail on every list—you are ready to recapitulate.

Beginning the Recapitulation

Start your process by creating a secure sacred space and time for yourself. Perhaps you will find a place in nature, a quiet room or closet with a personal altar (more about this later in the chapter), or you might build a small wooden box to sit in. Whatever you choose, do it with care and respect for the power of the process you are entering.

Begin with one item from your inventory—a person, incident, event, or other emotional memory. Relax into the memory, and use your breath to pull it toward you. Inhale, pulling the memory from the past into the present, and begin to feel it in your body. Your body's experience of the emotions involved is more important than your thoughts about the incident.

Continue to draw it in with your breath, until you are experiencing the incident fully. Be careful not to get lost in the feelings or victimized by the emotions. Feel and know the truth that you believe about the incident. Remember that it is the victim child who dreams these memories and emotions. It is the judge who keeps them alive by renewing the charges, finding the child guilty, and punishing him—over and over. It is the warrior who releases them.

The Toltec Eagle Flies

When you are fully in touch with the incident or memory, become the Toltec eagle, the master of intent and love. Fly high above the incident, and look down on that moment in your life, and the people involved. See the long stretch of time before and after the incident. Perhaps you can see several generations of families, and see their pain, fear, strategies, and their parasites domesticating the participants—including you.

As the eagle, see the absolute perfection of it all, and how this moment in time could not have been any different than it was.

Perhaps you are recapitulating a time when your mother punished you very harshly for something you did not do. Or your mate fell in love with someone else and left you. Or your landlord threw you out of a house you had just painted. Your boss gave your promotion to someone else. A friend was late to your lunch date again. Your probation officer refused to believe your story about why you did not call him. Your mother disowned you because you got arrested for drunk driving. Or you feel intense guilt because of an abortion.

▲ The artistry of the ancients captures the power of their warrior vision.

The Eagle Sees the Truth

In recapitulation, the eagle warrior sees the bigger truths: Your mother did not punish you because there was something defective about you; she was simply being the mother she was. Your mate left because your mate left. The landlord threw you out because he wanted to rent the house to his girlfriend. Your boss gave the promotion to someone else because she was actually more qualified. Your friend is late most of the time. Your probation officer is overworked, and didn't listen to your story clearly. Your mother was afraid of how her friends would judge her about your arrest. You did your best when you chose to have an abortion.

The heart of recapitulation is the moment when the eagle warrior shows the victim child that her mother, mate, landlord, boss, friend, probation officer, and the child were simply doing their best. In all those hurtful, angry, or sad incidents, the child was actually one player in a vast drama. She and others came together being who they were, and in the shortest little twinkle of time they passed each other and went their ways.

There never was a victim or a perpetrator—there was simply the interconnected action and reaction of an unfathomable universe, a living dream in the minds of all humans. With this truth alive in the heart of the child, she releases old stories and repeated self-rejections, and reclaims her integrity, vitality, and self-acceptance. New energy comes alive in her, and she is free to love life in joy and celebration. She becomes the eagle, and soars high in the new dream of heaven on Earth.

The Ultimate Forgiveness

During recapitulation, when the victim child shifts to the new assemblage point described here, the warrior feels a corresponding shift in his body. The heavy energy associated with the memory lifts, and he is set free. He uses his exhaled breath now, to gently release the person or incident. He continues his gentle breathing out until the experience is totally cleared, and he is at peace. The diligent warrior repeats this process with each item on every one of his lists, until recapitulation is complete, and his peace is eternal.

In the old dream, there is a "forgiveness" that is actually based on personal importance. It says: "You have hurt me, I judge and condemn you, but I am a better person than you, so I will forgive you." There are many variations on this theme, but they all reflect the old dream of wrongdoing, judgment, and victimization. It is not actually forgiveness at all.

When a Toltec warrior clears an incident with recapitulation, there is no longer any hurt, no perpetrator, and no victim. The entire incident is released. There is no need to forgive, because from the eagle's perspective, there is no offense to be punished or forgiven. There is no blame. In the Toltec wisdom, this is the true forgiveness: knowing that there is nothing to forgive.

If lies cause suffering, then truth will create happiness. This universe is animated by life itself. There are no lies in life; lies exist only in the human mind. When the warrior awakens to see that each human is life manifesting itself as infinite truths, he releases the lies of judgment and fear and opens to love.

This forgiveness results from a change of the assemblage point away from victim and perpetrator to the eagle's view of the perfection of the universe. The cleansing power of this truth releases poison from old emotional wounds. When the warrior applies the poultice of self-love to those cleansed wounds, they heal with only the trace of a scar. When someone touches that place, there is no longer a need to protect it, so the warrior can step forward with his arms wide open to embrace the world.

Living Altars for Recapitulation

The essence of recapitulation is in finding the lies in the mind's mitote, and changing them to the truth. The warrior stalks the old dream with its beliefs and agreements based on fear, and releases them to reveal the natural truth of love and perfection hidden under them. The description of recapitulation given thus far is a detailed formal method for mining deep into the mind in search of every memory held by fear and judgment. It has freed many warriors from the prisons of their domestication.

There are many other effective tools of transformation available to the warrior that complement formal recapitulation. Some students work best in the outer world, rather than the inner world of their minds, using objects instead of ideas. Two of those outer world tools are the "medicine bag" and "living altars."

The Medicine Bag

You can carry this three-dimensional recapitulation altar with you wherever you go. To create a medicine bag, begin with a small bag that you can wear or carry with you. Something made by hand with good energy is ideal. You will need a small cloth, such as a bandana or silk handkerchief. This is your mesa, or the table for your altar. Spread the cloth and place an object in the center that represents the source of all perfection in the universe—a small round mirror or a Mexican coin with the eagle and serpent symbols are possibilities.

FACT

Medicine bags have been an important source of power and healing since the beginning of time. Shamans have created and collected power objects and other symbols to use in ceremonies to cure individuals, beseech gods for rain or fertility, and protect their people from enemies. A medicine bag can be a powerful source of personal magic.

On the mesa, arrange small objects that represent issues or memories you want to recapitulate, or beliefs you are changing. If you are letting go of the hurt of a past relationship, for example, place an object to represent the person on the mesa, and perhaps place a small rose quartz heart or other symbol of love and acceptance next to it.

Let you heart show you what needs to be done. You will move the pieces according to the energy that wants to move in you. Perhaps you will add a symbol for the parasite moving closer to the heart, trying to create lies and suffering. You move it away. Maybe you put the heart between the person and the parasite.

Continue to add objects as your heart suggests, and release them from the mesa when their work is finished. All of the suggestions in the inventory lists in this chapter can be used in the medicine bag. No issue is too big or too trivial for this portable altar. When your work is finished, fold the mesa cloth around the objects, and slide the bundle into your medicine bag. Carry it with you, and, like a mother hen incubating eggs, know that with your awareness and intent, the seeds of your transformation are being nurtured and will hatch into new love and freedom.

Living Altars at Home and Work

In the same way that you create a three-dimensional representation of your recapitulation process in a medicine bag, you can make a more permanent altar in your home or workplace. Keep your living altar alive with your issues and processes each day. Here you will be able to use larger objects, such as framed photos, flowers, and candles.

ACTION!

Create an altar dedicated to your healing process in your home or workplace. Keep it alive by lighting candles to begin the day, and replacing objects as they lose their relevance. You may also choose to include written intentions on your altar, perhaps burning them in a ceremony when they are complete.

When including candles on altars or in ceremonies, many people use them to represent the ever-burning flame of life that is at the center of every living being. Light the candles on your altar, and in the glow of their light, remember that the light of the divine essence burns in every cell of your body, in every thought and feeling, and in every perfect expression of "you."

Personal History Is Erased

When the warrior has broken the spell of her domestication by releasing her personal importance, reclaiming the exiled parts of herself that she finds in her petty tyrants, challenging her habits with her not-doings, making the angel of death her companion in life, and recapitulating a thorough inventory . . . she will discover that she has little or no attachment to her past or other stories about herself.

The warrior who has walked this path, and used these powerful tools of transformation, will no longer have a personal identity to defend, justify, judge, or rationalize. She will be at peace within herself and with the world. Without the old emotions attached to her memories and stories, the human form they created becomes very fluid. She moves through the world with no resistance to it or from it, because she is free to flow with it. It is a beautiful way of life, and can be achieved by anyone who desires it with enough passion and tenacity.

The Toltecs say that when the warrior has reached this level of mastery she has "erased her personal history." She remembers her childhood, relationships, and other events of her life; however, without their emotional content, the memories float in the background, without substance or attachments. She is free to live in the richness of each moment of life.

Chapter 15

Redeeming Your Parasite

In previous chapters you learned about the parasite as the enemy to personal freedom. As the warrior travels the path of transformation, he realizes that the parasite is a more complex issue than he first understood. Now, strengthened by his journey, the warrior has the opportunity to re-examine his relationship with the parasite. He has gathered enough personal power to embrace his parasite in love, and to make his knowledge and his body his allies.

You Do Not Really Know Anything

Perhaps it has become clear from reading this far that the beliefs, opinions, judgments, and agreements that you have preached and defended most of your life are really just a lot of smoke. They have no substance, no "reality" outside of your own personal passion for them. That is not to say that you shouldn't be passionate. When the warrior breaks her human form and lets go of her need to defend or justify her beliefs or actions, she is free to be very passionate about life and all it brings her.

An Apprentice Realizes She Knows Nothing

"Before I began on the Toltec path, I was convinced that I knew a great many things . . . some of them very grand and special. I knew many facts about many things, and many wonderful theories about other things. Botany, biology, and science fascinated me in college, along with my classes in art and drama. I always considered myself to be properly educated in a well-rounded sort of way.

"It was a great relief and release for me when I reached the point in my transformation when I realized I did not know anything. The first thing I noticed was the changes in the relationship with my parents. They have always been very opinionated, and judge anyone who does not agree with them. As a child and young adult, I was very afraid of their displeasure. Later I just quit relating to them, so I didn't have to deal with their criticism and nagging about my life.

To know you know nothing is a great knowing. It is the basis of the Toltec wisdom. The virtual reality you are dreaming in your mind is a description of everything you think you know. It is not real—except in your mind. Truly understanding this concept leads to the freedom that is the goal of the Toltecs.

"Letting go of my personal importance about my beliefs allowed me to listen to theirs without judging them. In fact, I realized I was judging them for judging me! Wow. Now I can call and visit them and let them be who they are. I know they are going to dream me however they dream me, and there is nothing I can really do about. The best thing is, it doesn't really matter. Their dream of me has nothing to do with who I am. I just love and accept them, and accept their love, whatever form it comes in."

The Warrior Never Assumes to Know

Once the warrior understands that there is nothing she really knows, she stops imagining that she can read people's minds. In the old dream, all the humans are trying to keep their truth secret, while they are trying to figure out what the others are thinking. Since one of the rules in the old dream is "Don't ask questions, you might embarrass someone," everyone learns the trick of assuming the answers.

Nobody stops to realize that their assumptions are very often wrong. When the only way to know the answer is to make it up, the odds are pretty good that you will be wrong. The basic rule in the dream of the planet says that if you embarrass someone, you are a bad person. Your inner judge is in charge of enforcing this rule. The fear of being made wrong and punished by your own judge is actually more important than your concern about the other person's feelings.

The Toltec warrior does not believe her judge, and is very willing to ask questions when she does not know. She will ask people how they are feeling emotionally, if they are pregnant, what size they wear, how long they have been out of work, how they lost their leg in the war, or if they like being a mother. She asks out of love and a desire to know the story, and trusts that if someone is offended, they can take care of their feelings themselves—she does not have to protect them. If they do not want to talk about it, she does not take it personally.

The Parasite as Knowledge

When the new warrior begins on her Toltec path of transformation, it is important to perceive her parasite as the enemy of her freedom. She strengthens her personal power as she battles with the parasite for control of her attention. She learns to be vigilant about whether her attention is hooked in fear (parasite) or love (the warrior). The more she brings her attention back to agreements and beliefs based in love, the stronger she becomes, and the parasite's energy weakens.

As the warrior clears her channels of perception of old domesticated garbage, she sees her own mind in a new way. Her love and acceptance for herself expands, and she embraces more of the truth of who she is. In that embrace, she begins to see that it has been her mind full of knowledge that she has been using against herself all of her life.

Domestication Is the Root of All Knowledge

The process of domestication you learned about in previous chapters is the Toltec description of how knowledge is downloaded into your mind. There are two broad categories of knowledge, the first being facts and information, the kind of things you learned in school. The other type of knowledge is all the concepts humans are taught concerning right and wrong, good and bad—and what it means to be a good girl, a bad boy, a good father, a caring husband, a loyal wife, a bad daughter, a good student, a valuable employee, and all the rest of the judgments and expectations programmed into their minds throughout their lives.

The Toltecs know that this second type of knowledge is arbitrary, and changes with time and place. It is based mostly on fear and self-rejection, and is used by the humans' inner judges to condemn and punish them. Humans who are asleep in the old dream do not realize how unhappy it makes them to believe all the judgments based on the knowledge domesticated into their minds by other humans.

As the warrior matures on the Toltec path, her teacher will show her that the knowledge about right and wrong, good and bad that the parasite uses to judge and punish her victim child is, in fact, the parasite. Knowledge used against yourself is your parasite.

No Justice from the Judge

The inner judge does not dispense true justice. Even in the world's most severe systems of trial and punishment, perpetrators are charged with their misdeeds, evidence is brought, a judgment is handed down, and punishment is carried out. Once the process is finished, it is not started over for the same offense. In the inner world of humans, the judge brings up the charges and hands down punishments over and over for the same offense.

ACTION!

For the next few days, listen to your inner judge, and make notes about his favorite charges against you. Note how many times you are charged and punished for the same supposed offenses. Perhaps there is something you would like to say to the judge about this habit of his.

The judge is reopening the case every time he says, "You should have known better than to marry him! How could you be so stupid?" Or, "You'll never make money. It didn't work the last ten times; why are you trying again?" Or, "Every time you open your mouth, something lame comes out. Just be quiet." Or, "If you were a better husband, your wife wouldn't be depressed."

It is no wonder the victim child's mantra is "It's not fair!"

Love: A New Food for the Parasite

The first thing the new warrior learns about the parasite during his training in the mastery of awareness is that it creates and feeds on fear. In Chapter 9 you learned all the tricks of the parasite, and its feeding habits. In the previous section, you were introduced to an expanded concept of the parasite: It is your knowledge used against you, to judge and condemn.

It is true that the parasite feeds on fear, but it is not the entire truth. The parasite feeds on emotions, and it started out in life feeding on love. In the openness of the infant, there was only love; the only knowledge was love. The process of domestication introduced fear as a way of teaching and controlling the behavior of all the human infants. The knowledge they were given was based in fear. This was the beginning of the shift to feeding on fear, and the birth of the parasite as it has been described here.

Changing Knowledge, Changing the Parasite

The warrior changes the diet of the parasite by changing his knowledge. By clearing the distorting light from his channels of perception, and recapitulating memories that the judge drags up from the past to punish him, he eliminates much of the fear-based knowledge in his mind. By purposefully adding positive and love-based knowledge to replace the old knowledge, the warrior frees his mind to love, and thus offers his parasite a new emotional food.

The new warrior needs support and outside resources to help him remember the truth and deny the old lies. He turns to good friends, spiritual practices, loving teachers, nature, pets, recovery programs, and other sources to empower himself. He seeks companions who are impeccable with their word, and intent on learning to love.

At first the parasite fights love, like a child being fed lima beans. In time, however, the parasite remembers that its original food was love, and begins to accept it. The warrior feeds it self-acceptance and knowledge based on the beautiful truth of life manifesting itself perfectly as this universe. The warrior finds resources in the outer world that support his awareness of the perfection of this universe, and shares them with the parasite.

Taming the Wild Parasite

It takes time to change the diet of the parasite from fear to love. The idea is simple; however, the mind has been stuck in old ruts for a long time, and needs to be gently coaxed into an entirely new way of dreaming. The process is much like befriending a wild animal. If you know what the animal likes to eat, you can put some food out for it, but not too close to you. You must put it a distance away, and then sit quietly when the animal comes out to eat.

Each day you can move the food a little closer to you, sitting still so that the wild animal does not feel threatened. Over time it will learn to trust the food and you. Little by little, and ever so gently, you and the animal can feel safe with each other. You might begin to speak out loud to it, and move gently. With enough patience, a wild animal may begin to eat from your hand, and let you touch it.

The Parasite Becomes Your Ally

The victim child within is very much like a wild animal. She has been hurt by the inner and outer judges so often that she probably does not feel safe coming out to play just because the new warrior wants her to. The warrior must tame the child, the judge, and the entire complex of strategies, masks, and other adaptations you have learned to call the parasite in earlier chapters. The warrior must change the parasite's diet, and feed it love and acceptance.

FACT

The Toltec wisdom has been passed down and taught by many teachers for thousands of years, and the core beliefs have remained the same: To be free from the conditioning of your domestication, you must identify it in your mind and reject it. Then you can learn to accept yourself the way you are.

Every time the warrior reminds the victim child that the judge is lying when he is critical or shaming, the warrior is feeding the parasite love. Every agreement the warrior breaks about having to do it right to earn love, replacing the old agreement with self-acceptance, is a bit of love food for the parasite. The warrior continues to offer the new diet to the parasite, and little by little the parasite is befriended.

Using Knowledge with Self-Love

An apprentice's story: "All my life I believed that the way to improve myself was to judge myself for the things I did wrong. That is how my mother 'helped' me to behave, to pay attention, and to be good, so I did it to myself, without even thinking about it. I was very attentive to my actions, and even if I kept the extra change from a store clerk who miscounted, I scolded myself for weeks about my lack of moral integrity. Like I said, I never really thought about it, I just did it because that is what you do to improve yourself. I also did not notice that I was a pretty unhappy person.

"When I began to explore the Toltec way of life, I knew I wanted to be an artist of the spirit, an artist of my life. I began to stalk and inventory all the ways the voices in my mind talked to each other. Wow, was I ever surprised to hear what they were doing. The judge sounded an awful lot like my mother! Yikes. I thought I had left home many years before, but I guess I took her with me. One day my teacher pointed out to me that it is rare that anyone is actually motivated to improve themselves by being judged, shamed, or criticized.

"I knew he was right. I was hurting myself with everything I knew about how I should be and what I should do. I was filled with knowledge and I was using that knowledge against myself. So, I changed it. It wasn't easy, but I kept stalking and listening, and little by little I stopped the mean talk in my mind. I taught those voices to say supportive and loving things to each other and me. I taught them new agreements about life, love, and my worthiness as a human. Now I bask in the light of self-love and my entire life has changed. I am a very happy person."

Redeeming the Parasite with Love

When you think of the parasite as all your knowledge, perhaps you can understand why it is important to inventory and recapitulate everything in your mind if you want to be free. There is great magic available to you when you change those thoughts that judge and scold you into voices of love and compassionate support. When all the beliefs, agreements, and knowledge in your mind are working for you instead of against you, your mind becomes a powerful tool for creating a beautiful life.

The Toltecs say that when you redeem your parasite with love, it becomes your ally. When you change the knowledge in your mind from fear-based rules and judgments to love-based wisdom, your mind becomes an ally, and you become the artist of your life. This is the Toltec wisdom, and the Toltec way of life.

Healing the Relationship with Your Body

In Chapter 11 you read about the importance of creating a new relationship with your feelings. The shift from rejection to acceptance of feeling the truth of who you are is a fundamental part of the path of transformation. Most of the knowledge in the mind of a domesticated human consists of beliefs and agreements that support the rejection of his feelings. Feelings arise in the body. To deny the feelings that arise, humans learn to deny their bodies.

Because of the demands of domestication to deny feelings, humans have also learned to deny or reject other messages arising from their bodies about hunger, sexuality, pain, indigestion, exhaustion, stress, lust, and aging—as well as the noises and odors associated with a functioning body. There is shame and embarrassment associated with the normal needs and processes of bodies, and all of it arises from the knowledge that has been domesticated into the human mind. Infants and young toddlers have not yet learned about being ashamed of their nakedness or the needs of their bodies.

ACTION!

On this path, you have been invited to be a warrior battling your parasite. Now that the warrior is strong enough, it is time to accept the parasite as part of you, and no longer reject or fight it. The power of love is in acceptance. To heal the parasite and create an ally, it is time accept the parasite, just the way it is.

An Old Memory Liberates an Apprentice

"I was doing some recapitulation around issues I have with my body—I have always been too short, and I am aging, losing my hair, and gaining too much weight—when I suddenly remembered a story I read in a magazine when I was a kid. I think it was about Margaret Mead, but I'm not sure. She talked about getting up at dawn and walking down to the river where she heard the natives bathing and laughing. Most of the women from the village were in the river, and they were all naked.

"When she approached them, they shrieked, covered themselves in embarrassment, and ran to their shelters. She was confused, because they were always naked, and she had lived among them for a long time. It took her a while to find out they were embarrassed because she had seen them without the bones in their noses. I have remembered that story for most of my life, but it wasn't until I was recapitulating the beliefs I have about my body that the importance of it hit me: I was just like those women in the river!

QUESTION?

If I don't judge my body, does that mean I have to like it the way it is?
Your body is a great gift, and to judge it is to judge the life that gave it to you. Accepting does not mean liking. Change what you can, and accept what you can't—with love.

"Other people taught me how I should look, and what would be accepted and not accepted. All those rules and agreements that I learned, everything I knew about my body and other people's bodies was a social belief system, just like bones in noses, and had nothing to do with any reality. I was embarrassed and ashamed because of lies I had been told.

"Suddenly, I was free! I knew what I had to do, and I did it. I made an inventory of every lie I had been told about my body, about sex, my hair, attractiveness, eating, and aging—and I let them all go. I told myself the truth, that I am perfect the way I am, and worthy of the abundance and love of creation no matter how young or old or skinny or fat I am."

In Love with the Tonal

The Toltec warrior who is identifying himself as the nagual, the messenger of creation, rather than the tonal, creation itself, is free to love and respect his body. When he says "I" he is identifying with the life force that animates his body, not his human body and mind. As the nagual, the warrior is in love and acceptance with all of creation, including his own body.

One Toltec master has pointed out that most humans treat their pets better than they do their own bodies. They are concerned about their pet's diet, health, and comfort, and they accept their pets just as they are. In contrast, they feed their own bodies junk foods, alcohol, medicines, and other toxic substances, and do not pay attention to their body's reactions.

The Wisdom of the Human Body

The human body is a walking, talking miracle. Most of what is happening in your body as you read this has nothing to do with your conscious mind. Your heart is sending blood and nutrients to the trillions of cells in your body, air is moving in and out of your lungs, your liver is regulating blood sugar, your wounds are being healed, you are reading and comprehending the symbols on this page, and countless other processes are being directed by your body itself.

If your conscious mind were in charge of the processes of your body, it would stop working in just a few moments. You would not able to keep up with all the details. There is a life force present in your body that knows what it needs to do, and it does it well. It has matured your body from the first moments of conception, maturing through puberty, right up until this moment. You, as the awareness reading this, are here, able to do what you do, because of the body you created and maintain.

ACTION!

Write and repeat an affirmation like this: "My body is a gift from life. I express my gratitude to life by caring for this body the best way I know how. It is the instrument through which I enjoy the abundance of food, sunshine, air, love, and everything that I do. Thank you, life."

The Toltec warrior develops a loving communication with his body, and listens to its wisdom. He respects his body, and is mindful of his body's needs for good-quality food, exercise, and rest—and does his best to keep it free from toxic substances and thoughts. He listens to his body, and refrains from overriding its messages with medications or denial. The warrior loves, accepts, and respects his body, in recognition of the important partnership between himself as the nagual and as the tonal.

Chapter 16

Reclaiming Personal Power

The Toltec warrior seeks to conserve and increase his personal power, so that he can live the most effective, successful, and happy life possible. In the old dream, the power of the human is claimed and controlled by the parasite. The warrior knows he must win the battle for control of his attention to reclaim his power for himself. His power is the power of life itself, and the authority of his self-love and acceptance. He uses the Toltec tools, along with his determined intention, to reach his goal.

The Power of Your Power

To understand the transformative potential of the Toltec wisdom, it is often important to return to the beginning of the domestication process and remember what humans are like when they come into this world. Humans are born free. They have no opinions, judgments, fears, shame, denial, addictions, broken hearts, and no sense of self to defend or justify. Especially at the very beginning, human infants are pure awareness, with no stored light in their minds to distort the incoming light of reality.

In the early chapters of this book you learned how humans store light in their channels of perception, and how that light distorts their awareness of reality. The Toltecs call the resulting virtual reality in the human mind the personal dream. The more distorted a human's personal dream of reality is, the less effective and happy he will be in his life. Domestication is the path away from the truth of the spiritual nature of every human.

Remembering the Goal

The goal of the Toltec path is to clear the distorting light and return to the spiritual awareness that is a human's birthright. The path to that birthright lies back through the domestication and its stored emotions and hurts, and the warrior travels there like an explorer hacking his way through the jungle looking for a lost city of gold. The treasure the warrior seeks is his original state of pure awareness, which has been covered and lost under a tangle of lies and childhood hurts.

The warrior knows he cannot return to the state of pure innocence of his infancy, and he does not intend to. He knows the treasure he longs to recover will be a product of his clarity and wisdom as an adult. The warrior is prepared to use his tools and his energy to find his way back through the jungle of his domestication and out the other side—into the light of pure awareness and spirit. He will not reject, deny, or misuse the knowledge he has gained throughout his life, though he knows it is not the truth.

A Life Lived with Awareness

The parasite is not interested in, or capable of, imagining a life lived without the parasite. Remember the definition of the parasite as "knowledge used against yourself" from a previous chapter? What would it be like for you to live with knowledge as your ally, always supporting, accepting, and loving yourself and everything you do? Can you imagine what your personal relationships, work, spirituality, leisure activities, and creativity would be like if you lived free from fear of judgment, and doubts about your perfection?

There are many paths to a life of awareness and freedom, and they all share an essential truth: In order to change your life, you must change your mind. To change your mind, you must be awake and pay attention to the beliefs in your mind, and have the personal power to change them.

There is incredible personal power available to humans who have freed themselves from the tangle of their domestication—power to create, play, love, laugh, and enjoy life in every moment, no matter what happens to them. A life of personal freedom and joy is available to any human who frees himself from the control of his parasite and returns to the truth of his nature.

The Resistance of the Parasite

When a child experiences her emotions of joy, anger, sadness, hurt, excitement, fear, or the multitude of other ways she might express herself, and those feelings are rejected, ignored, punished, or worse, she is hurt. When it happens repeatedly, along with the shame and embarrassment she feels, she learns to believe it is her fault. In fact, she is often told it is her fault: "I wouldn't be so angry if you weren't so careless."

Parents in the old dream believe that their emotional reactions to their children are the children's fault. And they insist their children believe the same lie. Innocent young humans are punished for their spontaneous emotional responses to their lives. Many children learn that if they are seen, they will be hurt—so they learn to hide, either physically or emotionally. Young children cannot psychologically tolerate rejection for being who they are, so they learn to be someone else.

The Parasite Wants to Take Over

The parasite learns the strategies it needs to feel safe. It does its best to protect the child from the dangers of rejection and other punishment (see Chapters 7 to 9). All of the knowledge about good and bad, right and wrong, and how to get it right for the punishers forms a powerful resource of protection in the human mind. The parasite knows that when a new warrior declares her desire to be free, it must swing into action and sabotage the warrior's madness.

FACT

Children are hurt by many parental actions besides yelling and hitting. A mother might be having fun with a small child, then get a phone call that distresses her, and not return to their play. The child is disappointed, and if the mother is then sharp with her, she will take it personally.

The parasite knows without doubt that if the warrior manifests her desire to be big, alive, creative, and playful, and expresses her feelings with wild abandon, she will be in danger of rejection and hurt. The parasite will use all of its strategies and cunning to resist the very thing it has worked a lifetime to avoid. It must protect against the hurt that it knows will come if the warrior reclaims her personal power.

The Warrior Uses Love and Acceptance

The warrior knows that more judgment and rejection will not stop the parasite from "protecting" her. She has learned the healing power of love and acceptance, and she has claimed enough of her power that she can now hold the parasite in an embrace of love just as it is. She understands its history, and she has compassion for its fear. The warrior can also acknowledge the power of the parasite, while quietly claiming her own. She knows her power comes from love, which will ultimately heal the parasite's fear.

The parasite's resistance will slowly melt away when it sees that the warrior is ready to take over as the protector. The parasite was born out of a need to protect the young human from hurt of all kinds. Now the warrior says, "I have enough self-love, my ally is strong, my body has matured, and now I am ready and able to protect myself."

Releasing Attachments That Bind

Have you ever watched a rocket launching? At first it sits on the launch pad, with fire pouring out of the bottom. Very slowly, it begins to lift into the air. As the rocket begins to gain speed, all the bracing and fuel lines begin to fall away, and it accelerates and roars off out of sight. Like the rocket, the new Toltec warrior must also be willing to release his bracing and support lines in order to blast completely free of the old dream.

The Toltec tools of the not-doings, the angel of death, and many others are offered to the new warrior to help break his attachments to the baggage of the old dream. There are many ways humans become attached—to ideas, people, places, possessions, emotions, expectations, outcomes, being right, and more. People are even attached to being wrong, failing, and to their fear itself. Anything that helps a person feel safe, and that they are afraid of letting go of, will keep them stuck on the launch pad of life.

Leaving Old Baggage Behind

There is a carefully calculated weight limit on the rocket described earlier. There is no room for old baggage and worn-out things. It is the same for the warrior who wants to blast free from the limitations of the old dream. He must lighten his load by letting go of his baggage from the past. He uses recapitulation, forgiveness, and other tools to release agreements, heal wounds, deny judgments, and let go of resentments.

The process of releasing baggage and attachments does not happen all at once. The warrior is patient and persistent. He keeps his goal of personal freedom always in his awareness, and silently asks himself, "Am I responding with love or reacting from fear?" The answer in each moment gives the warrior feedback about his actions, and empowers him to make choices that support his continuing liberation.

An Apprentice's Struggle

"When I discovered the Toltec path I was very excited. I wanted so much to be free from the worry and fear that had plagued my life. I wanted to be free to speak my truth, follow my passions, and live my dreams. Then I found out how afraid I was of letting go of the people in my life who were comfortable and kept me grounded—especially my wife.

"My wife and I had not really been in love for years, but we silently agreed neither of us wanted to risk going into the world single, and 'starting over.' We settled into a comfortable routine, friendly . . . and maybe a little resentful. I think we blamed each other for the lack of passion between us. I know I blamed myself. I thought I was doing something wrong, and knew if I could fix it, everything would be okay again—but I couldn't figure out how.

There is no way to predict what will happen from telling the truth. The warrior is willing to tell the truth about what he wants, feels, and needs, and let the outcome sort itself out. The warrior releases all attachment to controlling outcomes and focuses on the reality of the present.

"When I got to know the angel of death, she invited me to let go of anything I was holding onto out of fear. She didn't say I had to leave my wife, but simply explore my fear of telling the truth about our marriage. I was really afraid I might have to let go of my comfortable life with her. I finally realized that I couldn't be free if I was holding on to that safety, so I opened up and told her the truth about my attachment and fear.

"An amazing thing happened: My wife opened up, too, and we started really talking for the first time in years. We had nothing to lose anymore. Our sharing became very deep and intimate, and we fell into love together, in a whole new way. We are still together, but I am not afraid of telling the truth, and I am not afraid of letting go of my marriage if it is not right for either one of us. My marriage is a choice I make every day, from my own self-love."

The Power of Life

The life force that creates and animates all of creation is an amazing phenomenon. When it manifests as a human infant, it has the power to sustain that infant and get all of her needs met. From the beginning, life knows how to communicate about hunger, discomfort, and other basic issues. It can call forth a corresponding action in adult humans to care for the infant, and meet her needs. The life force resonates with the adult, because it is the same life that animates the child.

The power of life is everywhere in creation. From eagles to earthworms, and from trees to toads, in every form life takes, it knows how to grow, eat, mature, reproduce, and get all of the needs met for that particular form. What a tremendous power! It is true for strands of DNA and for galaxies— everywhere in creation, the unfolding of life has the power and intelligence to know what it needs to do to be what it is.

The power of life created you and animates you in every moment. Without it, your body simply stops acting as a complete organism, and returns to the smaller bits of life that were gathered together as you. Most of what you are is life animating you, not the specks of physical matter it animates. You are the power that is life. In Chapter 2, you learned the Toltec wisdom about the light. The Toltecs knew that the universe, including you, is mostly space, filled with light. The light is life; it is the nagual that animates the tonal.

If you are life, and life has the power of creation, do you see the power you have? It is the unlimited power to create. It is unlimited power to be present in life, to enjoy creating and to enjoy your creation. This is the power that life gives each human on this earth, and it is available and accessible to everyone.

Because of the hurts and fears of domestication, most humans are unaware of the power they have as life. Their vision is limited, their world is distorted, and they have forgotten who they are. They live in an illusion of lack, in a body and world actually created by the very essence of abundance itself! They live in continual need, when in fact they are the life that fulfills all needs. And most heartbreaking of all, as victims, they feel powerless, when in fact they are the power of life itself.

Breaking the Old Agreements

To reclaim her personal power, which was lost during domestication, the warrior must break all the agreements she made that cause her to reject herself and judge creation. She also must expose and deny the lies she learned to tell herself about lack, need, scarcity, and even death. Every agreement and belief that is held by fear in her personal dream limits her power of creation and her freedom to be herself.

QUESTION?

How do I start to reclaim my personal power when I am worn out from working all day, spending time with my kids, and cooking and cleaning?
One of the roles of a teacher is to support you with his encouragement, accountability, and unconditional love. You don't have to do the work alone—ask for help.

The Toltec tools for transforming the limiting agreements have been described in earlier chapters. The important thing to recognize here is that it takes power to reclaim power. Someone who always lives in the victim dream has no power available to stalk and transform agreements. All of her personal power is being used by her parasite to defend her victim dream and deny her pain. It is often beneficial for a new warrior to "borrow" the personal power of a teacher or master to support her as she begins her healing journey.

Every agreement the warrior breaks, and every belief she changes from fear to self-affirming love, recovers power from the parasite for her to use in her quest for freedom. As she accumulates more power and gains more awareness, her stalking becomes stronger, and she is able to break even more old agreements. The warrior's most difficult journey was the one away from her truth as life. The return to the truth of that source is welcomed and facilitated by life.

Nothing Is Personal

All humans are dreaming a dream that is unique to themselves. The light they are distorting and projecting into their minds is creating the only universe of its kind. The awareness of this phenomenon is the biggest gift of the Toltec wisdom. If you understand that everyone is dreaming, you will know that their "dream you" has nothing to do with you. You are not who they are dreaming you are. There is a different you being dreamed in every unique universe, including your own!

The most powerful agreement in the mitote of the old dream says, "What other people say or believe about you is the truth." Nearly all new humans are taught to accept this agreement, and then they live their lives worrying about, and trying to control, what others think of them. They teach the agreement to the new humans, and reinforce it in each other. It is the most powerful agreement and the biggest lie in the mitote.

If you rely on what other people think of you to determine your value, your life will be lived on an emotional roller coaster. You will go up when you are liked, down when you are judged. Don't believe them, either way. It does not matter what people think about you, because they are dreaming you, not seeing you.

This agreement that makes everything personal is one of the foundations of the dream of the planet. The warrior knows she must break its hold on her mind before she can be free. She consistently brings her awareness to her perfection as a manifestation of life, exactly as she is. She remembers that all the humans are dreaming, and when they speak of her, they are describing their dream image of her, not her. She knows they are not talking about the reality of what she is.

The warrior knows she is dreaming, also, and does not believe herself or the universe she dreams. She does not take anything personally, because she absolutely knows the universe is not personal. She is free to be in the world, but not attached to it. The warrior can keep her heart open, knowing she has no identity to defend and no beliefs to justify.

You Are the Source of Love

The dream of the planet depends on all the humans believing that they must have the approval of other humans in order to be okay. The fear that permeates the old dream is the fear of rejection and expulsion from the family, workplace, tribe, religious culture, friendships, and love relationships. The old dream teaches that God and Santa Claus are both watching you, making a list, checking it twice, and will punish you if you're not nice.

The Toltec warrior knows she came into this world as love, and she claims her right to love and be loved just the way she is. She breaks the old agreement that she must prove herself worthy of love, and claims her truth as the source of love and life. The warrior, empowered by her love, offers unconditional love to the victim child, judge, rebel, and all the wounded mask-wearing parts of her inner world. In the light of her love, every part of her finds new joy and peace.

Conserving and Increasing Power

Power in the dream of the planet can come from many sources. A fat wallet, a coveted body image, fame or infamy, a high position in sports, government, the arts, or business—all offer a human power in the old dream. This power comes from the outside, and may or may not affect the person on whom it is bestowed. It is power that is often misused, because it does not arise from love, personal integrity, or impeccability.

The personal power sought by the Toltec warrior arises from within, reclaimed from the parasite, and recognized as the birthright of the human. The warrior's intention is to continue to conserve and increase his power, and use it with love and acceptance to better himself and all humanity. The true power of the warrior comes with knowing the truth of who he is as love and acceptance. This power is the authority to be himself, as he is, without any fear. His self-love is his power.

The Warrior Conserves Power

The personal power that is reclaimed from the parasite can easily be lost again, if the warrior forgets his mission, and gets lost in the old dream.

If he takes something personally, or argues about who is right and wrong, or worries about what his mate or boss thinks about his performance, the parasite has taken the power back. The warrior must be constantly vigilant to keep his attention and energy out of the mitote, and focused on his love and acceptance.

ACTION!

If you want to increase your personal power, take action. Take good care of your physical energy, conserve your emotional energy by not taking things personally, and remind yourself often that you are perfect the way you are. Your personal power comes from your authority to be yourself without doubt.

Anytime you are lost in an emotional reaction, you will know that the parasite has taken back the attention and power. Emotional reactions are good opportunities for the new warrior to wake up and remember the truth of who he is. With awareness, he can conserve his emotional energy, and apply it to his continued awakening.

The warrior also conserves the energy of his body, by respecting and caring for it. He stays rested, eats good food, enjoys walking in nature, avoids alcohol, drugs, and medications, and celebrates his gratitude for his physical vehicle daily.

The Warrior Increases Power

You have already read about many of the ways the new warrior reclaims and accumulates personal power. The tools of recapitulation and others are specific to this purpose. Another important method is spiritual journeys to places of power, sometimes called "power journeys"! There are places all over the world that have been used throughout time for ceremonies and celebrations related to spirit and personal transformation.

The ancient cultures of Mexico, such as the Toltecs, Aztecs, and Mayans, built beautiful cities, including Teotihuacán, which are accessible today (see Chapter 20). In Peru, the lost Incan city of Machu Picchu is one of many magnificent spots for the warrior to absorb the energy of the past, as well as the spirit of the gods in the mountains there today. Spiritual journeys to places of power are an important aspect of a warrior's training. He knows he will return home with a radically new assemblage point, and a powerful new dream.

Chapter 17

Mastering Love and Acceptance

When the Toltec warrior has redeemed her parasite, and changed her knowledge into a strong ally, her entire victim dream changes. She becomes empowered in her freedom, and flies like an eagle in the dream of the third attention and the mastery of intent. In this chapter you will learn that the ultimate power of the warrior is true love. You also will learn how to use this state of being to create a happiness in your life that no one can take away from you.

The Mastery of Intent

There are many theories about humans' place in creation, and their ability to influence the unfolding of the health, wealth, and destiny of nations, wars, crops, romance, and individuals' lives. It is not surprising that humans have investigated these theories and possibilities throughout history—they have often felt powerless compared to the unknowable vastness of the universe.

Humans have created mythologies about the power and relative benefits of planetary influences, past lives, karma, animal spirits, punishing gods, benevolent gods, heaven and hell, mind control, tea leaves, the afterlife, human sacrifices, black cats, astral travel, card reading, prayer, séances, akashic records, willpower, affirmations, the law of attraction, love potions, amulets, voodoo, luck, rain dances, spilled salt, positive thinking, miracles, and lucky socks.

Every system of beliefs has its structure and form, and people who are attached to any one will be able to gather valid evidence that their system gives them power to understand and/or control the universe around them. Every mythology and belief listed here, and each of the many more like them, is valid and real—or not, depending on how you dream them.

The Quest for Power

Earlier in this book, the mastery of intent was compared to a firefighter who has a firm grasp on the nozzle of the fire hose, and is able to direct the stream of water exactly where she wants it to go. Although this analogy serves on one level, it misses an important aspect of intent on another. Intent is the same as the force that animates creation. To be able to harness and direct that force is the dream of most humans who seek empowerment from various sources and practices.

Teachers of the Toltec tradition share diverse explanations of the source and power of the warrior's intent. A common thread in these teachings is the relationship between intent and the force that creates and animates the universe. The Toltec student often wants to know how she can become a master of intent and use her power to control her world. It is a difficult question for the teacher to answer, because if the student were ready to hear the answer, she would not be asking the question.

Mastering the Power of Love

In the previous chapter you learned about the relationship among love, acceptance, personal power, and the life force that animates creation. Some Toltec teachers are now using "intent" and "love" to describe the same force. To master the power of love is to know yourself as love, as life, and as intent. The Toltec master is the nagual, manifesting the tonal. To live in this understanding is the essence of living a spiritual life—knowing you are the force of life that animates creation, enjoying being your creation.

In some of the older writings about the Toltec tradition, a great emphasis was placed on accumulating power—because crows were really witches, and unseen forces could attack at any time. Modern teachers tend to focus more on self-acceptance and love as a source of personal power, no matter what the danger.

To become a master of love (intent) you only need to accept the perfection of all of creation, including, always, yourself. Since creation is here, and has been here for billions of years, if not forever, and it is here doing what it does in perfect harmonious oneness with itself, it should not be hard to recognize its perfection. As you have learned through reading this book, the only thing that might be keeping you from knowing the perfection around you is your human mind, trained to take the universe apart and categorize the infinite pieces.

The master of love stops her mind's habit and puts the universe back together again in one whole being. Living in that wholeness she is life, and she has total control over her creation. Living in that wholeness, she has acceptance, and no need to control creation for her benefit. Thus, the student finds the answer to her question, and the question disappears.

The Dream of the Third Attention

The Toltec path has a beginning, a central point, and an end—more or less. It begins in the waking sleep of the dream of the first attention, symbolized by the serpent focused on its immediate needs, and not seeing beyond its limited environment. The serpent person follows the dream programmed into his mind; his parasite is in control of his emotions, so he does not question the nature of reality or his actions. He is very often outwardly content with his life, but does not want to be challenged about his masks or convictions.

ACTION!

Try using one or more of the wake-up tools described in Chapter 11. How often can you wake yourself up into the warrior's dream, and how long does it take to go back to sleep? Remember, do not judge yourself if you have not mastered these skills; it takes time and practice to become a master.

There is no way to understand why some people in the serpent life stir into awakeness and begin to ask questions, and others don't. Some are put back to sleep by the power of their domestication and the potions they are given, while others continue to awaken. If the process continues, the jaguar emerges and begins to ask questions. He learns to stalk his mind's mitote, and transform his beliefs and agreements in the dream of the second attention. This is the work of the mastery of transformation, when the seeker becomes the warrior, and uses the tools of the Toltecs to explore and heal his wounded mind.

Flying Like an Eagle

Many seekers of spiritual understanding and a better life are content to rest in the second attention, and live their human lives with increased awareness, acceptance, and satisfaction. The eagle invites those warriors who are beckoned by the prospect of absolute freedom to fly into the dream of the third attention.

There are many obstacles to the warrior's journey. By now he has triumphed over his personal importance. He has released his attachments to people, places, and things in his life, as well as attachment to his own suffering. He has faced and conquered the fear of letting go of his identity, and surrendered to the angel of death. Now, the flight of the eagle requires that the warrior release even his new loving, open, compassionate, and spiritually comfortable beliefs, and fly beyond them.

It is time to soar above all separation, all categories, and all beliefs. The eagle warrior leaps into the flow of life itself, into intent, and surrenders completely to love.

The Dream of Heaven on Earth

The eagle warrior uses his attention for the third time, to unhook himself from the illusion that he is separate from life. This is a major shift of the assemblage point. The warrior is no longer the jaguar, asking questions about the nature of reality, how to be impeccable with his word, or why he failed or is afraid. In fact, he has no more questions, since the answer is always "Because it is as it is."

FACT

The goal of the Toltec warrior is complete freedom from believing his own personal dream, as well as from the dream of the planet. The eagle warrior faces his fear of the death of his parasite, and ultimately, the death of his ally. When there is nothing left, the warrior becomes everything.

In the love that is life, in the flow that is intent, in the acceptance of the perfection of all that is, the warrior enters the dream of heaven on Earth. He dreams only peace. He does not need death to enter the kingdom of heaven; he is dreaming heaven on Earth every moment. Remember that the Toltecs call the force of life "the light." Now the eagle warrior lives in the light; he is one with the creative force of the universe. It is not surprising that he does not have to ask "why" anymore.

Acceptance Is the Highest Form of Love

Have you ever been fully and totally accepted by another person just as you are? If so, you probably felt loved in a way you were not used to from most people. To accept a person exactly the way she is, without judgment or resistance, is to love in a very different way from the bargaining in the dream of the planet. Love as acceptance says, "I see you, and I see the perfection that you are as a creation of the divine life. I am ready to receive you as you are."

To love in this way is a gift to yourself. Other people will like it and be attracted to it; however, if you do it for them you are not doing it. If you love as a strategy to gain approval, no matter how grand your love seems, it will not be true love. The eagle warrior loves because it is her nature. She has no attachment to how her love will be received, or returned. She loves because it makes her happy to love. The eagle warrior is so selfish that she loves all the time, so she is happy, all the time!

Getting Used to True Love

An apprentice was surprised the first time she went to hear the Toltec master teach: "It was strange! Everyone told me how loving he was, and I thought he was not paying any attention to me at all. He would look at me, but when I smiled, he just kept looking at me. He didn't smile back . . . well, he was smiling, but not really at me. He seemed happy, but he didn't respond to me the way I was used to.

Not very many people have actually experienced pure unconditional love, because very few humans are capable of offering it. People often reach out to religious deities or gods for love, but discover that the gods have been created by humans and require the same conditions, bargains, and punishments that humans dream for themselves.

"After meeting with him many times, I realized that he was loving me in a way I had never experienced. He was seeing my strategies and the masks I used to hook his attention and approval, I guess, but he was looking past them into the universal perfection that he knew I was. I couldn't understand what he was seeing (he made me a little uncomfortable, actually) because I had never seen it in myself. It was like looking into a mirror and not recognizing my reflection."

True Love Is Ruthless

In her story, the apprentice is describing an interesting quality of the Toltec master's love: It is ruthless. The master's love makes no bargains, takes no prisoners, and shows no pity. It does not accept the story of the apprentice's parasite that she must perform to be worthy of his love. The master gives his love freely, as absolute acceptance of each person exactly as he or she is.

Pity and feeling sad or sorry for someone's suffering are not love. These feelings are based on the belief that someone cannot take care of himself, and needs your help. The dream of the planet says you should be compassionate or sad about other people's pain, and if you are not, you are not a good person. Your inner judge will enforce the rules, and punish you if you do not show you are "caring" by having sympathy, pity, or sorrow for someone's suffering, and wanting to help him. Such helping is done from personal importance.

You will help by keeping your own judge from condemning and punishing you for not being a good friend, or a compassionate stranger. Real love is ruthless. Real love expresses its nature; it does not "help." Real love can be very helpful.

Practice Makes the Master

If you are like most people, you have practiced being a parasite your entire life. You have mastered being a victim, feeling powerless, and suffering because "it's not fair." You have mastered taking things personally, assuming you know what other people are thinking and feeling, and accepting responsibility for creating other people's emotions.

With dedicated practice, you have become a master at keeping your attention in the past and future, and avoiding your feelings in the present. You have practiced being a puppet and having your strings pulled by other people and events. Perhaps you have repeated their "you are not enough" mantra until you believed it with all your (broken) heart.

Beware of becoming discouraged when you read a book like this about how simple it is to transform your suffering into love and freedom. The transformation from fear to love is simple, but it is not usually easy. If you have mastered the lies, however, you can master the truth. The eagle warrior is a master, and knows the truth about love.

ACTION!

Become a student of love. Learn everything you can about true love. Research "unconditional love." Forget about the notions of romantic love in your culture, and go beyond them. Read Rumi and Hafitz, and feel the emotional, swirling, joyful love they celebrate for their divine beloved. Join them in the poetic dance with life.

The Truth about Love

The warrior knows that to make a new habit, he needs to change the behavior of his old habit. If he mastered self-rejection by practicing diligently, now he can change his behavior and thoughts to self-acceptance, and create a new habit. He knows he will only remember his new habit when he is awake in the dream, so he is also diligent about keeping himself awake. By the time he is an eagle warrior, he is a master at being awake and remembering the truth of who he is.

Some of the truths the warrior remembers about himself and true love are:

- Love is acceptance. It recognizes the perfection in everything.
- Love is life, the light, the one force animating the entire universe.
- The warrior loves because it is his nature—not to create reactions, obligations, or outcomes.
- Because it is his nature, he loves to love.
- The warrior's love is not personal; it radiates equally to all of creation.
- Love is ruthless; it does not pity self or others.

- Love is the open flow of the abundance through all of life.
- Love is the one antidote for the fear in the human mitote.
- The warrior's personal power comes from his authority to love all creation without conditions.

The eagle warrior continues to practice his new art, the art of love, until the habit is so powerful he becomes a master of love.

A Beautiful Romance with Yourself

Seekers on a path of love are often perplexed by the concept of loving themselves. They report that they take a bath with candles every few months as their time of self-love, or break the rules and eat an entire quart of their favorite ice cream. Or both at the same time! Although these may be pleasurable activities, the need and practice of self-love must be deeper and more consistent than these examples.

FACT

Romantic love is actually a fairly recent phenomenon; some authorities say it began around 800 years ago. Some of the characteristics of romantic love include that it lasts for a relatively short time, it is often a one-sided fantasy, it involves being in love with the love rather than a person, and it follows cultural models.

Love and acceptance have been used in this chapter and others as interchangeable concepts. Self-love and self-acceptance also are interchangeable terms. The eagle warrior becomes a master of self-love as self-acceptance. The master of self-love is the true king from the story in Chapter 10, who takes over the inner world from the false king and rules with love and acceptance.

When you accept yourself just as you are, in every moment, with every desire, fear, lust, love, excitement, doubt, thought, action, "mistake," wrinkle, and pound, you will be in a mad, beautiful romance with yourself. You will be accepted with no conditions, reservations, bargains, obligations, or standards you must meet for love. You will be your own best lover, and when you are loving yourself in that way, you will settle for nothing less from the world. You and all of creation will have a beautiful romance together.

Real Happiness Is Love Coming Out of You

Much of the energy of the parasite is used chasing the tail of the elusive "happiness" in life. The parasite believes it will come from the right friends, enough money, the perfect cosmetic surgery, the love of a perfect mate, the right position, a bigger home, well-behaved children, an early retirement, winning a lottery, or all of the above.

One of the difficulties of this pursuit of happiness is the inner judge and the outer judge, who keep raising the bar no matter how high you jump. Have you noticed yet that the judge never says, "Job well done. I won't bug you anymore." To have enough money and well-enough-behaved children is impossible for the parasite, because the judge is reading the "not good enough" rules from his book of lies.

An Apprentice and Her Moment of Happiness

"I was in the pyramids at Teotihuacán, in Mexico, on a power journey with my Toltec teacher, when I discovered happiness. I had my eyes closed as the group stood together holding each other at the end of a beautiful ceremony in front of the Pyramid of the Moon. The teacher had taken us into an amazing experience to recognize that we and creation are the same life energy.

QUESTION?

If I am happy from the inside, does that mean I won't care about being in love?
When you discover the happiness that comes from inside, you will not need to be in love with someone to be happy; however, you might choose to share your love with someone you are compatible with.

"I opened my eyes, and I saw life everywhere. I saw it in the pyramids, the vendors, my body, the clouds, my thirst, and in the eyes of my companions. I was looking at them and seeing myself, like looking in a mirror, and seeing the essence of life reflected back to me. In that moment, there was nothing but life and love pouring out of me into creation, and love pouring out of creation into me. I knew real happiness in that moment, and I brought it home with me. I will never be the same."

A Happiness No One Can Take Away

The happiness that comes from being in a heart communion with life in all of its forms cannot be earned, cannot be bargained for, and cannot be taken away from you. If your happiness comes from a perfect mate or automobile, it can be taken away—and will be, by the angel of death, sooner or later. Always in the back of your mind will be the fear of losing the person or object that makes you happy. Wherever there is fear, there cannot be true love or real happiness.

The eagle warrior practices loving all of creation without any expectations. She loves because she loves to love, and opens her heart to receive love from all of creation. She knows the stars are loving her, the trees and traffic are loving her, and every person is loving her—whether they know it or not. She sees her reflection as the divine perfection of life everywhere she looks. Her practice fills her with joy, and she dances with the sparkles of life all around her. This is the life of the Toltec eagle warrior.

Following the Path with Heart

These are times in the evolution of the human dream when many old mystery schools are opening their wisdom to the general population. Modern psychology is also developing more practical supports for emotional healing, and spiritual paths are accessible to more people. Books, magazines, television, and the Internet are bringing many alternatives into the awareness of a new audience.

The increased awareness of the emotional suffering of humans, and the possibilities for healing, are both exciting and intimidating. With so many choices in so many fields, many people are left wondering which services, teacher, or path to use. Every path has its benefits; however, it is important not to choose based on the logic of your mind.

Let your heart speak to you. What path draws you toward it, and which are neutral or uncomfortable? There is no psychological or spiritual perfection you must achieve in order to be a good person or worthy of love, so listen to your heart if someone tells you he or she can fix your defects. You already are love, remember? As love, as life, you are here to create, love, and play. You get to choose how you want to play, and what you want to create. Let your heart lead you to a healing or spiritual path where you can play, not create more suffering.

ACTION!

Practice being in the state of love and acceptance. Say "I love you" silently to everyone you see, every event that occurs, the news, every politician from every country, every star and tree, all wars, stray dogs, immigrants, your friends, and your enemies. Let love pour out of your heart like a beam lighting up your world.

For the Toltec warrior, there is no greater creativity and play than to explore his mind's mitote, and transform old fear into new love. He wonders to himself, "How happy can I be?" He knows that the more personal power he can reclaim from his parasite, the more he will love, and the more he loves, the happier he will be.

Chapter 18

Writing the Book of Truth

In this chapter you will explore many different concepts about the truth, and what it means to lie. The "truth" is your deepest feelings. It is a source of personal power, it comes from self-love and self-acceptance, and it is totally personal to you. The warrior knows he is lying when he describes his personal dream, but he is totally passionate about living it. He also knows how to control the crazy follies of his parasite, and dream into other people's dreams in order to share his love.

Honoring the Deepest Truth of You

In Chapter 11 of this book, you learned about the possibility of creating a new relationship with your feelings. In the old dream, feelings and emotions are problems to be solved, or embarrassing intrusions into daily life. In children, feelings are repressed, punished, or shamed, and in adults the habit of denial continues. How many men have experienced emotions in a movie theater, and when questioned by a surprised or pleased woman, blamed their tears on the bad air or their (occasional) allergy to popcorn?

The eagle warrior, alive in the new dream, recognizes and honors feelings as the truth of the moment. The warrior is no longer ashamed of what he feels. He honors his feelings the same way he loves a small child who comes running to him hurt, angry, afraid, or overflowing with joy. He honors and respects the feelings of everyone he relates to, whether a child, a mate, a friend, or a stranger.

Balancing on the Edge

The words *love*, *acceptance*, *honor*, and *respect* have been used throughout this book as important qualities of the warrior's life. It is important to remember that to accept a person as a perfect expression of the divine universe does not mean you have to like that person. Equally, to accept the perfection of the unfolding of an event, such as a dent in your car, a war, or the loss of a loved one, does not imply that you must like what happened.

The eagle warrior balances on the cosmic knife-edge between recognizing his human character and celebrating his divine oneness. When he is experiencing the human pain of an assault or loss, he also acknowledges the ongoing perfection of the universe of which he is a part. When he is experiencing the expanded awareness of his spiritual nature, he continues to stay connected to his human feelings and truth.

The warrior knows it does not serve him to use either his divinity or his humanness to deny or diminish the other. His wholeness includes the mystery of everything he is.

Using Feelings as a Guide to Life

The warrior who has released the old dream of his domestication—along with the rules and behaviors dictated by that programming—learns to listen to the instructions of his feelings. He is no longer a puppet of his emotional reactions. His recapitulation has revealed and rejected the lies from the past, and replaced them with the truth of self-acceptance and universal perfection. Without his emotional baggage, he is able to listen to the quieter truth that arises in him in every moment.

The warrior who surrenders to the truth of his nature as it arises in him in every moment has most of his personal power available to him at all times. Ending resistance to the truth of life as it is also ends the parasite's draining away of the precious daily allotment of personal power.

Like a child who goes to sleep when he is tired, or a dog that moves out of the sun when he is hot, the warrior listens to the simple truth of his feelings and his body, and responds to them appropriately. He does not reject his feelings, nor does he try to override the needs of his body. The warrior does not squander his personal power fighting the truth that arises in him; rather, he uses the power available to him to stay present and aware in each moment.

Using the Power of Truth

Truth becomes the warrior's ally. It is the angel of life, always present, always willing and able to know the deepest truth of what is present in each moment, within and without. Once the warrior lets go of the fear of other people's judgments about what she thinks, feels, and does, she is free to listen to her own truth. At every crossroads on life's journey, she looks within for the subtle nudgings that direct her choices.

The warrior must be resolute in her freedom. She knows that the dream of the planet will continue its attempts to make her afraid of being rejected and cast out alone in the wilderness of life. She knows she must keep her assemblage point open to her oneness with life, rather than her separateness from the rest of creation. She seeks out other eagle warriors to support her and accompany her on her personal journey.

Having Faith in the Power of Truth

It is a great challenge for the eagle warrior to maintain her faith in the power of her truth. She must learn from trial and error which feelings arising in her are the most important to listen to, and how to reconcile conflicts between them. She knows she is always doing her best, and does not judge herself for her choices. The warrior is absolutely clear that she does not, and cannot, make mistakes—they are a lie from the old dream, and she has left the lie behind.

FACT

When the warrior breaks her belief in the existence of "mistakes," she frees herself to be herself. The inner and outer judges are the only ones that label any action a mistake. When the warrior trusts that she is doing her best in every moment, and has no other expectation of herself, she is free.

The eagle warrior has faith that life expressing itself through her is the source of her subtle feelings and inclinations, and that if she follows their guidance, she is guided by the truth of life. She has faith that when the life in her expresses itself freely, and resonates with the life animating the universe, she will be in a perfect relationship with the universe—life resonating with life, creation embracing creation. This is the warrior's goal, and her joy.

An Apprentice Tests Her Truth

When the apprentice realized during a conversation with her teacher that she was not sure she really loved her fiancé, she decided it was time to trust telling her truth. She knew that if she waited until the "right time" to talk with him about it, she would put it off forever. She went directly home and told her fiancé she needed to talk. She asked him to just listen, and not try to fix anything or change her mind. The apprentice knew her feelings were not his responsibility, and doubting her relationship with him was not a judgment of him.

"This was the biggest test of faith in my truth I could have possibly imagined. I had let the persistence of my fiancé convince me to say 'yes' to his proposal, and I had never been comfortable with our engagement. When I started to talk to him, I could see the tears and hurt welling up in him. It felt good to be able to tell him without making him wrong, but I could see he was taking it very personally. He had so many great plans for our life together, and the truth of my doubt was shattering them.

"I thought maybe we could back away from the engagement and continue to date, but the more I talked the more I realized I was breaking his heart. There was a moment when I wanted to take it all back, and say I was sorry for doubting his dream, but I couldn't. I knew this was a time to trust my truth, and have faith that the outcome would be the best for everyone.

"We broke up, and two short months later, he met the perfect woman. They are married, have a new child, and are very compatible and happy together. Me? I continued to test my truth, and discovered that it serves me well. I am in a good partnership now, and know that I will never sacrifice what is true and right for me to try to control the outcome. I am trusting my truth to guide me, instead of my 'shoulds,' and I feel empowered to be me!"

The Book of Truth

It is very important for the new warrior to explore the judge's book of lies thoroughly. (You learned about the book of lies in Chapter 12.) Under the guidance of her teacher, she will transcribe the book, and become intimately familiar with the tricks and traps of the parasite. Revealing the lies is a vital part of the mastery of awareness. It strengthens the warrior, and prepares her to use the tools of the mastery of transformation.

When the warrior has transformed the mitote in her mind, and quieted her inner dialogue, it is time to write her book of truth—an important tool in the mastery of intent. It is impossible to write the book of truth until the judge is quiet, because he is afraid of truth and will sabotage her experience. The judge and parasite believe that the full expression of feelings, truth, and love causes trouble, pain, hurt, and rejection. The eagle warrior no longer believes those lies, and is ready to leap into life with love and an open heart.

ACTION!

You may need to continue writing down what you find in the judge's book of lies; however, for right now, bless and begin a new journal, your "book of truth." Use the suggestions in this section to guide you about writing down your new dream. If the judge gets in the way, go back to journaling his book of lies, and put him in there.

The Warrior's New Dream of Life

The book of truth is the warrior's description of the new dream of her life. It is where she writes the feeling truth of life that rises in her, without the interference of the judge and parasite. In the past, she might have been attracted to becoming a poet, firefighter, or computer programmer. The parasite would tell her she was ridiculous: She could not make a living as a poet, nobody hires female firefighters, or she could never learn something as complex as computer programming.

Every human develops a unique way of expressing life. It is a combination of DNA, domestication, new learning, chance meetings, and other factors. However it comes about, each human is the only one like him or her in the universe. The personal power of the eagle warrior comes through an expression of that uniqueness, without resistance or reservations. The eagle warrior embarks on a new journey of discovery, to recover the lost truth of who she came here to be.

Wants, Don't Wants, Desires, and Intent

With the voices of lies and fear silenced, the warrior is ready to listen to the deeper truth of who she is and what she feels and wants. She listens quietly, and writes whatever comes to her in her book of truth, without editing or censoring herself. She imagines all the humans going about their lives and jobs, and watches for what attracts her and what does not. She listens to her forgotten dreams, sidetracked ambitions, and unexpressed talents.

It is impossible to dream a new dream of life if the inner judge is making you wrong. Trying to create a successful book of truth before you have done the work to silence the judge might make you frustrated. Be gentle with yourself. Eagles have baby wings before they can fly.

The warrior uses her book of truth to write out everything she does not want (serious disease, loss of a loved one, and so on) and everything she does want (to study poetry, learn about computers, marry a rock star, live without fear). Although the warrior may never study firefighting or computer science, or marry a rock star, it is important that she allow her dreams to manifest themselves, at least in her book of truth. This is a time to let her repressed dreams come alive. Later, she can organize and prioritize her lists.

The Feelings Hidden in the Desires

As she adds ideas, wants, desires, and intentions to her lists, the warrior also looks for the feeling content beneath the things she wants. Perhaps she has dreamed of being a firefighter since she was little because she felt safe and loved when a fireman rescued her cat from a tree. Maybe as a teen she wished she could marry a rock star because she wanted to be envied and feel important (not feel hurt and alone).

When the warrior finds the emotional content behind what she wants and desires, she explores it to see if there is some way of meeting her emotional need within—perhaps without rescuing cats or enduring the complexities of being a rock star's wife. As she refines her discoveries, the warrior is clarifying and refining the meaning and direction of her new life. She is putting her faith in her truth, and trusting that it will direct her into the perfect relationship with life itself.

The power of the eagle warrior's intent is focused on accepting who and what she is, and riding the wild waves of life as herself.

Truth and Lies in the Dreaming Mind

The Toltecs teach that all humans are dreaming (Chapter 2). This means they are distorting reality according to their own individual filters and programming. What humans perceive as the world around them is not what is really there—it only exists in the little virtual reality ("dream") in their individual minds. No two people perceive the universe in the same way, which means that everyone lives in a different universe.

This piece of the Toltec wisdom is very profound. Everyone lives in a different universe. When any human describes the universe, that person is talking about the unique world he or she lives in, not anyone else's. This is why the Toltecs invite you to not take anything personally. If someone talks about you, he or she is actually describing the "you" that lives in that person's dreaming mind, not you. He or she cannot see you. What the person describes has nothing to do with you, so it is not personal.

The Truth of the Mind's Dream

When people describe their universe—how they feel about an event, a strong political opinion, the story of their difficult childhood, why the world is against them, what you did to hurt their feelings, or their new soul mate—they are telling the absolute truth. They are looking at the virtual reality of the world inside their mind, and describing it with precise accuracy, complete with all the visuals, dramas, and emotional content.

The eagle warrior knows that other peoples' descriptions have nothing to do with what is "out there" in the world, including the warrior. He is dreaming a different reality, and he is absolutely aware that his dream is the truth for himself, and no one else. The eagle warrior does not engage in conflict about whose dream is right, and he does not defend his version of reality. He knows that every person's dream is the truth for that individual, and for no one else. The Toltec warrior is free to live in the world, following his path with heart, seeing the truth in every dream.

The Lies in the Dreaming Mind

If everyone is dreaming and describing their dream, then nothing they say about the outside world will be the truth. No one can see the truth of the universe as it actually is, because everyone is distorting it. The human mind is an organ of self-deception: What it tells itself about what it sees is always a lie. The eagle warrior understands that he always tells the truth (describing his personal dream) and he is always lying (because he cannot see what is actually true).

QUESTION?

If everything I think I see is a lie, and not really out there, what *is* out there?

You can touch what is out there, but the minute you think about it, name it, ask about it, or describe it, you are dreaming something else. The warrior accepts that he can never really know what is out there.

The warrior gracefully holds the apparent contradiction between truths and lies. He absolutely believes everything he says, everything he stands for, and the perfection of his dreamed universe, knowing it is his truth and his alone. The warrior also knows that everything he believes and says is a lie, because he is describing a dream. The warrior knows he is a master dreamer, and lives passionately in the truth and lies of his dream.

Dreaming and Controlled Folly

The eagle warrior is a master dreamer, and purposefully cultivates her ability to dream. She opens new channels of perception, free from old distorting light, and hooks her attention in dreaming the oneness and perfection of every person and event she sees. Whether she goes into the wilds of nature or the wilds of the shopping mall, she sees with an assemblage point in her heart, rather than her mind.

The eagle warrior knows she will always be dreaming, and her goal is to dream a perfect replica of the divine truth she cannot perceive directly.

She keeps her attention on the wholeness of life, and does not let her mitote mind take apart, judge, and categorize creation. She loves and appreciates the multitude of ways life manifests and expresses itself, and is delighted to be part of life herself. She looks into creation as a mirror, and sees her own divinity reflected there. In the silence of her mind, she smiles and thinks, "No wonder the gurus are always laughing."

The Power and Love in Controlled Folly

The eagle warrior knows she is dreaming, and she knows everyone else is dreaming. This awareness gives her power in the world because most humans do not realize they are dreaming, and believe they are perceiving reality as it is. The warrior sees the parasites controlling all the humans, and understands that the humans have no choice about their fear and strategies. Her heart stays open to them, not in pity or judgment, but simply in acceptance of the perfection of what is.

Most of what the parasites make their humans do is folly. Their behavior is thoughtless, reckless, foolish, or worse. When the warrior is stronger than the parasite and has enough personal power to see and control its folly, she is able to choose her words and actions to promote the highest good for herself and others.

With her heart open in acceptance, the eagle warrior goes into the world to play, create, and love. Seeing deep into the dream around her, no matter where she is or who she is with, allows her to offer the humans whatever they need in order to dream her in a way beneficial to all. The Toltecs call this ability to dream into the dreams of others "controlled folly." The warrior's intent is to never go against herself, so she only uses her "seeing" with love and respect.

An Apprentice Changes the Dream

"About once a month, I drive to visit my mother in a nearby state. The drive usually takes about eight hours, and isn't very entertaining—so I drive as fast as I can. I used to brag to my mother about how fast I drove, and would always try to beat my record for how long it took. She would worry, and tell me to drive slower, but I would scoff at the suggestion that I didn't know what I was doing.

"As I learned to see the dream better, I realized that I was causing my mother a lot of anxiety. By the time I arrived at her house, she would be so agitated from worrying about me, we could hardly greet each other. I decided to practice my controlled folly. The next time I went to visit her, I called and told her I realized she was right, it was dangerous to drive so fast. I told her I was bringing a lunch along and would stop and picnic along the way. She was very pleased that had I listened to her, and relieved that I would be safe. I drove my usual crazy fast speeds. When I arrived at her house, she was relaxed and much easier to be with. It was an act of love for both of us.

"The funny thing about this story is that after telling Mom I was driving slow and picnicking a couple of times, it sounded like a pretty good idea, so I tried it. I discovered it was a more enjoyable way to drive for me, too. Now I always take my time, and it doesn't seem any longer. And I am relaxed when I arrive, too!"

A Final Word about the Truth

Sometimes it is difficult for the new warrior to fully accept that there is no absolute truth in the universe. All societies and civilizations are founded and held together by their common beliefs about what is true and right. Each human's identity is held together by what the individual believes is true. It is a major act of power on the path to personal freedom for the warrior to release his identity based on what he believes and his sense of belonging with others who believe the same things.

The entire concept of morals and morality is based on the assumption that there is an absolute truth in the universe, and someone or some group knows what that absolute truth is. It is easy, then, for that person or group to know that anyone who does not follow their rules is wrong and not part of "them." If the morality has been handed down from a powerful deity, then the authority of the rules is much stronger, and the fear of breaking them is greater.

FACT

Releasing attachments to all concepts about anything and everything in creation is one of the biggest challenges of the Toltec warrior. It does not mean that the warrior has no preferences or desires, only that he has no attachments to the outcomes. He knows that everything he believes is the truth and a lie.

If every religion, philosophy, and society believed in the same moral truths and social rules, it might be possible to agree that there is an absolute truth in the universe. Since that is far from the case, and there are different rules and expectations of behavior in every corner of the world (and wars everywhere, about who is right), the only conclusion seems to be that there is no universal truth. There is only the dreaming mind of every human, and the perfectly true lie they are dreaming in each and every mind.

The great truth that exists outside of the human dreaming minds can only be inferred. It is the Truth that cannot be spoken of, because speaking of it is dreaming, which is not the truth. The minute it is labeled "the divine" or any other term, it is being dreamed, not perceived.

Chapter 19

Living the Toltec Wisdom

To live the life of the Toltec warrior requires sacrifice, diligence, intent, and practice. The rewards are great, but not everyone chooses to follow the Toltec path. In this chapter you will learn some of the dangers and sacrifices the warrior faces, as well as the wonderful life of the artist of the spirit. The possibilities are appealing: Always being happy, feeling connected to spirit, and enjoying the abundance of the universe. As you read about these opportunities, dream that you are an eagle warrior, in love with life.

The Sacrifice of the Warrior

The Toltec path winds from its beginning, where the parasite (future warrior) is asleep in the dream of the planet, to its realization, when the eagle warrior launches her glorious flight into freedom. You have read about the challenges along the way, and the powerful tools of personal transformation offered in the Toltec tradition.

For any human considering walking this path, there are some cautions that should be addressed. There is a place on the journey, different for each person, that marks the point of no return—she can no longer turn back, go to sleep again, and resume her old life. The awakening that has been put in motion, aided and abetted by spirit, will stay in motion.

The Parasite Still Has Tricks

The parasite is happy to let the new warrior enjoy the imagined journey, and the fantasy life of freedom. As indicated in earlier chapters, the parasite has also dedicated all of its resources and power to prevent the imagined freedom from actually occurring. The warrior who battles the parasite for control of the human mind will often think she is winning, when she is actually still on the parasite's short leash. Vigorous vigilance is required by the warrior to keep from going in circles at the end of the leash.

It is also valuable, of course, to have the support and mirror of a teacher or Master who has walked the path and achieved personal freedom. The external warrior is an important resource, especially in the early stages of the journey. The parasites, both inner and outer, are formidable obstacles to personal freedom for the beginner.

The Warrior Becomes a Ghost

There is a pausing point on this journey when the new warrior realizes she is passing through a portal that leads her beyond the dream of the planet. She knows she is sacrificing her connection to everything that she knows and brings her comfort. By the time she reaches this point on her journey, the warrior is well aware of what she is about to do when she passes through the portal.

There is no way the warrior can know the full extent of her sacrifice until she makes it. She steps through the portal, leaves the dream of the planet . . . and becomes a ghost. She walks in the same physical world, but now separate from it. It is a moment she has been working toward, looking forward to, and fearing. She is free to live her life to the fullest degree possible, but the warrior also knows she now lives in a different world from almost every other human. She dreams differently, and her life will never be the same. This is the sacrifice the eagle warrior makes, in order to receive her gift: the dream of heaven on earth.

Each step on the Toltec path prepares the student for the next step. There are few surprises and no mistakes. There are, however, moments when the parasite is agitated about dangers ahead, and resists progress. The warrior recognizes these feelings, and accepts them as part of her journey.

Living Life as an Artist of the Spirit

Even though the eagle warrior knows he has left behind the old dream and everyone who dreamed it with him, he also knows he is free to love more and better than ever before. He may be a ghost to other people—they will not be able to see who he really is—but he is one very happy ghost. He is the master of his intent, a lover of life, and a Toltec artist of the spirit. The dream of heaven on earth is the dream of unconditional love and acceptance for every part of creation, and a way of life for the eagle warrior.

The eagle warrior remembers that he came into this world to play, create, and love, and his work on the Toltec path has restored him to his original nature. For many warriors at this stage on their journey, the best play they can imagine is to continue to clean leftover mitote madness from their minds. Some are drawn to help others do the same, through writing, teaching classes, or personal apprenticeships. Other warriors are content to play at personal forms of creativity, such as their art, inspired relationships, music, environmental protection, political participation, or learning new skills.

Living in Unlimited Happiness

There is a myth in the dream of the planet that says you cannot be happy all the time. Humans have been taught they need to suffer and feel pain so that they will recognize and appreciate their moments of happiness. The Toltec artist of the spirit has broken that old agreement. He knows he actually can be happy all the time, and he is. He keeps his attention focused on his emotional body, and if he experiences feelings that make him unhappy, he knows he has been hooked one more time by his parasite.

In those parasite moments the warrior goes quickly within, to play and love in his inner world. He becomes the jaguar, stalks his prey (a lie from the parasite), devours it, and replaces it with the truth of love and acceptance. When his feeling body has returned to its happy state, the warrior moves on. He will not tolerate anything but the joy and freedom that is his nature. The artist of the spirit is making beautiful art with his life. His love is his brush, and his paints are the many wonderful and unique qualities life has given him to share in the world.

Living a Spiritual Life

The beautiful life lived by the Toltec warrior is always connected to the life force of spirit that is in and through all of creation. The love and happiness that he experiences radiates out from him, and resonates with the love animating the universe. He sees the beauty of spirit in every person, in nature and cities, in all creatures, and in the events of his life and the world. He knows what he wants and what he doesn't want. He uses the movement of spirit as feelings and truth in his body to inform and direct his life.

The artist of the spirit absolutely knows that he is a unique manifestation of the Divine. He expresses his uniqueness as his gift of gratitude for every moment of his life. By staying present in each moment, the warrior embraces his life fully, giving and accepting the gifts of abundance that are the nature of spirit.

Living in the Abundance of the Universe

The Toltecs know there is but one universal presence here, and they call it the light (Chapter 2). It is one spirit, one life, one animating consciousness manifesting in limitless forms. They know there is nowhere the light stops and something else begins. All forms—the humans, clouds, rabbits, liver cells, galaxies, and the Earth—are animated by the same presence. The space in between the forms of atoms, planets, and humans is also filled with the same animating presence of life.

If forms and the space between the forms are all created by and animated by the light, the eagle warrior understands that he cannot be separate from the universal presence of life, no matter how it appears to his mind or his senses. He is made of and by the only thing here in the universe.

Living with a Wide-Open Heart

There are many theories and practices that have been proposed to increase abundance, especially financial abundance for humans. Most of these ideas have been dreamed by the parasites, who see themselves as separate from the rest of creation, and in a state of lack because of it. The parasites believe that they can have abundance if they use good sales tricks, clever prayer, or their mind power to attract what is "over there" into their realm, for their use.

ACTION!

Stop and reflect on your perception of abundance. Do you "wish" for abundance because you believe you live in lack? Remember that your word is everything you believe, as well as say. Believing in lack cannot bring abundance. What could you change about your thinking, to align your word with the truth of the universe's abundance?

The eagle warrior understands that the angel of death and life owns everything, and she lends it to humans according to her desires. She also takes back what she has lent when she is ready. The warrior has surrendered everything to the Angel, and his heart is wide open to the universe.

He knows that his oneness with creation means that everything is already his, because everything is him. He has no fear about having or losing anything. This is the life of the artist of the spirit.

Living in Gratitude for the Gifts

The gifts of the angel of death and life are limitless, and she gives them freely to all of life—insects, animals, plants, humans, and the galaxies. Her greatest gift is life itself, which she gives generously to every aspect of creation. The warrior lives in unceasing gratitude for the life that animates him and his playground, the Earth.

The artist of the spirit knows that his heart is a two-way door for all the gifts from the angel of death and life. He strives to keep it as open as possible, to receive the gifts that come, and to share the gifts she sends through him into the world. He knows that fear narrows the doorway, and love and gratitude open it. The warrior's gratitude for the gifts received, and for his opportunities to give, is his assurance that the door to his heart will always be opened wide.

Living in Healthy Relationships

One of the most beautiful arts of the artist of the spirit is her relationships of all kinds—romantic partnerships, child and parent relationships, and those with friends and strangers. All relationships are based on agreements, and in the old dream those agreements are mostly unspoken and unconscious. Living in the dream of heaven on Earth gives the eagle warrior entirely new agreements for her relationships.

FACT

Agreements are defined as a contract or arrangement between two or more people, wherein everyone involved agrees to the same terms and conditions. They can be verbal or written. The agreements between humans in the dream of the planet about relationships, child rearing, religion, and life are usually hidden and often silent disagreements.

Her new agreements are based on a love that expects no rewards, makes no bargains, holds no expectations, demands no conditions, and takes no hostages. She is free to love the entire universe from her spirit, and individual humans according to her human preferences. Parasites living in the old dream can never see who she is and how she dreams, so whenever possible she soars with fellow eagles, on the exhilarating updrafts of openhearted love and respect.

Living in Love in the New Dream

Because she is able to see how other people are dreaming, the eagle warrior does not take their perceptions of her personally, nor does she believe her opinions about them. She knows that everyone creates their own emotional reactions based on how they dream, so she respects the emotions of others, without feeling responsible for them or needing to fix them. If in doubt, she asks questions instead of assuming what her partner and others are thinking and feeling.

The warrior knows she is the source of love in her life, and she gives her love freely, without concern for whether it is appreciated or returned. She does not depend on the love or approval of others for her self-worth, nor does she expect them to make her happy. She is happy because she loves. She loves because it makes her happy.

The eagle warrior experiences the same love, as acceptance, in all of her relationships. She accepts her romantic partner exactly as he is, and chooses each day to be in the relationship. The warrior is never a victim of her partner, her relationship, or her commitment. She is always in choice, because she loves and honors herself first, and will not go against herself or use anyone else to go against her.

Living in Truth in Relationships

One of the most powerful agreements in the dream of the planet says, "You should consider other people's feelings before your own, and not do or say things that will hurt or upset them." The eagle warrior has broken that agreement as part of her journey on the Toltec path. Her new agreement affirms that her loyalty is to her own feelings and needs, and she is dedicated to living and acting on that truth in her life.

This new agreement is one of the most difficult to make and keep in the mastery of transformation. The parasite within is frightened by what will happen if the warrior is loyal to her own truth. It is afraid that if she gets too big, she will become a target of rejection or abuse again. Her parasite wants to keep her small to protect her. If her personal parasite fails, the parasites in the dream of the planet will do everything they can to domesticate her back into the old ways. The eagle warrior simply continues to love and comfort those frightened parts, and takes over the role of protector from them.

Living in the present moment is a gift the warrior gives herself. When she surrenders her attachments to the outcomes of her relationship, she can be present in them, in love, and without fear. She listens to her own inner truth, and relates to whomever she chooses, without having to take care of their feelings.

The eagle warrior uses her truth in all her relationships to guide herself and her relationships in harmony with life. She shares her feelings with her romantic partner; she tells him what she needs and wants, what she is afraid of, and what she loves. Her book of truth is open to him and she has chosen a partner who respects her feelings along with his own. Together they share their truth, and release their attachments to controlling the outcome. The warrior and her partner share and celebrate each moment in true love, free from the fear they knew in their old dreams. They dance in joy with the angel of life.

Living with Children in the New Dream

The eagle warrior's transformation has completely changed her relationship with children. She sees the perfection of all children and accepts them without reservation. She knows that everything kids say and do is the perfect expression of how they are dreaming. The warrior honors their dreams, and negotiates with them respectfully when necessary. Even when she must use her adult authority to enforce schedules and rules, she does it without judgment of their desires or behavior.

The warrior knows that children are never wrong or bad, but simply lack the experience and skills to perform at adult levels. She helps them develop the skills they need—pouring milk, wiping up spills, trusting their feelings, and discharging their emotions—without judgment or frustration. She has no expectations for them to be any different than they are, so they are free to be themselves, and evolve naturally. The eagle warrior's children are present, alert, responsive, cooperative, and express themselves freely.

Living with the Child Within

A large portion of this book has been dedicated to an understanding of the domestication and healing of the victim child in the inner world. The most important relationship in the eagle warrior's life is with the victim child. The warrior has worked hard, fought with the judge and parasite to win the child's attention, and revealed and healed the strategies the child developed to be safe and get his needs met.

The warrior has shown the child the judge's lies, and told him the truth about life. He has brought love and acceptance into a hidden world formerly filled with fear and self-rejection. The Toltec tools of transformation and the warrior's love have healed the wounds of the victim child, and integrated the split-off parts of his human mind.

Living with the Ally Child

Like children in the outer world, the warrior has learned that the child parts of his inner world are all dreaming perfect expressions of who they are, and what they know. They are never wrong or bad; they simply speak their truth as they understand it. The warrior has learned to hold a safe container for the feelings of all the parts of his inner world, and listen to their fears and concerns with an open heart and mind.

Now, the child has become an ally to the warrior. He is the voice of the subtle feelings that move through him as the truth of life within. The "ally child" is the warrior's reminder and guide to playing, creating, and loving in his life. They go into life together, the ally child in his magical innocence, and the Toltec warrior, present and powerful in every moment. Together, they are artists of the spirit.

An Apprentice Tells His Story

"When I started my work on the Toltec path, I had no idea about any victim child or warrior in my inner world. I knew my relationships didn't work out too well, and I was always pretty anxious, but, hey, beer kept me chilled out. Doesn't everybody have those problems? I just thought it would be cool to be a 'Toltec,' and do stuff like eat peyote and have hallucinations in the desert. I read some books and stuff, and then accidentally found a teacher.

QUESTION?

Are there many Toltec teachers who take personal apprentices?
When you begin to look, you will be surprised how many Toltec teachers there are doing workshops, writing books, hosting informative Web sites, and working with apprentices personally. Check Appendix B of this book for some possibilities.

"I was pretty surprised and pretty disappointed when he told me that he didn't believe in messing up my mind with plant medicine. He said the best thing for me to do was work at changing my mind a little at a time, to do it thoroughly, and be done with it. It didn't sound very exciting (like the desert thing) but something about him made me stick around. He was different—calm but energetic—hard to describe. I learned later he had a lot of personal power.

"So, anyway, the point of my story is, one day I went for a walk over at the town lake, because I knew I should be getting more exercise. My teacher had been talking about this idea of a child that was part of me, but I had pretty much blown off the idea. So, I'm walking fast, working out, getting my exercise, and totally in my head, thinking so fast I don't even know where I am.

"All of a sudden I hear this voice, like a kid, calling out my name, and saying 'Hey, wait for me, slow down!' I jerked around and, this is the truth, I wasn't hallucinating or anything, but sure enough, I saw this kid running up behind me, like in a dream. He reached out his hand for mine, and I couldn't help but do the same. The minute our hands touched, the whole world exploded into amazing colors and sounds. For the first time on the walk (or in my life?) I heard the creek gurgling, the birds chirping away, and I felt my body all alive and tingling.

"That is when I found out my teacher was telling the truth. That little kid was scared, because he was always getting left behind. But, man, he was also really alive! We got to be a team, and now we go everywhere together. We dig on the birds, sunsets, and little stuff like that. Wow, what a dream! Who needs peyote?"

The Living Dream of the Toltec Master

As you read about the life of an artist of the spirit in this chapter, know that this life is available to anyone who changes their dream. It is not a fantasy created by wishful thinking, nor is it reserved for some elite group with special connections to spirit. What you have been reading here is the direct result of using the Toltec tools of transformation and other teachings on this path to personal freedom. There is no magic or mystery—this is a path based on common sense, sound teachings, and good tools.

Even if no one knows for sure who the Toltecs were, and how they lived, you can be an artist of the spirit in your life right now. The dream is alive in many peoples' hearts, and getting stronger. The teachings are here, the tools are here, and your freedom can be here, now, in this modern world.

To live in the dream of heaven on Earth does require a focused intent. The traveler on this journey must be very vigilant about the short leash of the parasite. Just reading the many Toltec books available and discussing them with friends will probably not change your life. The Toltec path, above all else, is a path of action. It requires regular, deliberate, motivated action—to thoroughly master the lessons in the books or assignments from a personal teacher. (The value of personal apprenticeship with a living Toltec master can be very beneficial, of course.)

Imagine that you have followed this path, found a teacher, used the tools, created allies of your knowledge and child parts, and redeemed the parasite with your unwavering love. Imagine yourself as an artist of the spirit. See your life as a beautiful work of art. You have reclaimed your birthright to play, create, and love, and you are happy all the time. Imagine yourself enjoying the material and spiritual abundance of this beautiful world, and sharing it with everyone around you. Your relationships with your romantic partner, friends, children, and the strangers on the street are openhearted and overflowing with love and acceptance.

See yourself becoming the teachings. They are no longer concepts or stories to repeat to others, but have become the essence of who you are. Perhaps people are drawn to your light and you choose to teach them the tools and lessons you have learned. Or, you may simply be living your life quietly, sharing your love with all you meet. You know it does not matter—there is no authority watching or judging you about what you should do or how you should be.

Imagine yourself, the artist of your life, living the most beautiful life each and every day. You are the eagle warrior, the Toltec master, the perfect you. This is personal freedom, this is the goal of the Toltec path. This is the dream of heaven on Earth.

At the end of the film *The Matrix*, the hero Neo (the eagle warrior) says to the matrix (the parasite): "I didn't come here to tell you how this is going to end—I came here to tell you how it's going to begin. I'm going to show these people what you don't want them to see. I'm going to show them a world without you, a world without rules and controls, without borders or boundaries, a world where anything is possible."

This is the goal of "the one" in the film, and this is the goal of the Toltec path.

Chapter 20

A Spiritual Journey Through Teotihuacán

Teotihuacán is a living university of transformation, built for your use by an ancient culture of artists of the spirit. In this chapter, you are invited on a dream journey through the pyramid complex, to experience the healing and enrichment that this sacred site offers you. Each plaza and room of the site holds unexpected healing opportunities, and each ceremony along the way supports your journey to the dream of heaven on Earth. Perhaps you will be inspired to visit Teotihuacán and experience it in person.

20

Preparation for Your Journey

Teotihuacán is a place of great beauty, magic, and power. As you learned in Chapter 1, little is known about the people who gathered there and built the pyramids, temples, and other beautiful buildings that make up the core of the old city. Surely, they were artists of the spirit, great Toltec visionaries with knowledge of astronomy, art, agriculture, spirituality, and, of course, building. Their city reached populations of perhaps 200,000 people, with sophisticated systems for water, sanitation, and food distribution, with a government directed by their spiritual leaders.

In the centuries after Teotihuacán was abandoned, the ruined city was visited by the Aztecs and the builders of Tula, and honored in their mythology as the place where civilization began. The awe-inspiring pyramid complex, an hour northeast of Mexico City, is now a beloved national park and is visited by tourists, masses of Mexican schoolchildren, and spiritual groups throughout the year.

Teotihuacán is affectionately known as "Teo" to most who live, work, and visit there. The Aztecs called the city "the Place of the Gods" to honor their mythology about its origins. For the purposes of the following modern Toltec journey to Teo, the interpretation is revised to "the Place Where Humans Awaken and Remember their Divinity."

Visioning the Original Majesty of Teotihuacán

Archeologists have stabilized and rebuilt some of the edifices of Teo; however, they have not replaced the remaining plaster and murals that once graced all of the buildings there. The original builders covered the pyramids, temples, stairways, and priest houses with a thick layer of plaster, which was then painted white and decorated with murals and other brightly colored decorations.

The light of the sun is an important element of this ancient city, and to imagine it shimmering in the clear light of this high plateau is to dream unimaginable elegance. In addition, imagine rows of temple platforms on both sides of the mile-long Avenue of the Dead, with copal incense filling the air with its sweet smoke, and the magical music of flutes, drums, and voices singing spiritual praise. Thousands of people fill the avenue; priests, masters, apprentices, artists, and residents of the surrounding city, all here to share the glory and intent of their society.

The Home of the Sun

Most early cultures were very connected to the sun, and its seasons. In Teotihuacán, the light of the sun is unique and powerful, and the Pyramid of the Sun towers into the sky as though it were built as a ladder to the solar source. The sun represents spirit, the masculine element in creation, and the power of the sun and spirit are both very present in Teo. Of course, the feminine aspect is present here, also, in the earth, the Women's Quarters, and the Pyramid of the Moon.

▲ Murals adorned the cities built by the Toltecs.

This journey through Teotihuacán follows the three masteries of the Toltec path. It begins in "hell" (the dream of the planet) with its judgments, attachments, and suffering, and travels through the stages of transformation, through the feminine—until the final triumph of leaping free of the dream, into the "black sun" (the source of creation).

This journey offers you opportunities for deep surrender, letting go of beliefs and attachments that do not serve you, and opening yourself to your joyful connection with life. Teotihuacán is a place of spiritual pilgrimage for many individuals and groups, especially with teachers in the lineage of the nagual don Miguel Ruiz (including the author). Note that the journey described here takes place over several days.

Surrender and Surrender Again

Your spiritual journey in Teotihuacán begins in hell—in the Plaza of Quetzalcoatl at the south end of the Avenue of the Dead. This large plaza represents the dream of the planet, and the hell of judgment and fear that consumes most people's lives. In the center of the plaza is a small platform, which represents your "island of safety"—built from the beliefs and opinions that define your identity. Your island is surrounded by the vast "sea of the unknown," home of all the monsters that your mother warned were waiting for you if you broke the rules or went against your domestication.

Many people do not want to surrender anything, because they perceive it in the sense of "giving up." Although spiritual surrender does imply giving up something, it is not done as an admission of defeat, but done because you know that releasing will open space for something greater in your life.

This is your first surrender. In order to take this journey to the sun, you need to release your attachments to the ideas, concepts, and behaviors that you believe keep you safe. Take a moment here, and consider the dangers and rewards. Note that safety is an illusion you have learned to believe. Perhaps you can think of two or three major beliefs or agreements that keep you stuck here in your life. When you are ready, release them (with love) and prepare to face the sea of the unknown.

The Leap into Quetzalcoatl

The feathered serpent awaits your next surrender. The entire length of the Avenue of the Dead represents the body of your powerful guide Quetzalcoatl, the two-headed serpent, who is waiting to digest away everything you believe yourself to be. Find your way down the steps of your island, and into the sea of the unknown. Feel the monsters (parasites) trying to stop you from breaking away. The Pyramid of Quetzalcoatl is directly ahead. Climb the steps slowly, strengthening your resolve to give up the illusion of control, and open to the unknown.

As you climb, feel the power of this ancient pyramid under your feet. Feel the power of those who built it for you to use in this moment of your expansion, and express your gratitude. You are climbing to the head of the serpent. When you reach the top, you will find its mouth open, waiting for you. Without letting your mind interfere, without letting doubt trouble your resolve, step to the top and throw yourself into the waiting mouth of Quetzalcoatl. Your surrender deepens.

The Angel of Death and Sacred Ground

Feel yourself entering the body of the serpent. The digestion has begun. As you move through the serpent, you find yourself looking down the long Avenue of the Dead, with the Pyramid of the Moon beckoning from the far end. As you walk slowly down the broad avenue, perhaps your pulse quickens, because you know that the angel of death is waiting for you at the river, the crossing point into sacred Teo ground.

You walk slowly, preparing yourself for yet another surrender. You can feel the strong energy of the angel of death in the distance, and you know she is going to demand that you surrender everything you have to her, before you can go on. Are you willing? Are you willing to release the illusion that any of it is yours to own in the first place? Will you look into her eyes and acknowledge her and express your gratitude for what she lends you, including your life itself? Prepare yourself as you walk.

FACT

Death is an illusion to the life force that animates all of creation. The life that is the one thing, that is the wholeness of the universe itself, cannot die. It is everywhere and in all time. Death is an illusion created by the human mind identifying itself with the tonal of the material world.

As you approach the angel of death, know that you cannot fool her. Let her look you in the eye, and let go. If you are afraid, be afraid. Don't try to hide it. If you are truly ready to let go of your illusions of control and ownership, look the angel in the eye, and let her see your resolve. She is standing at the river crossing into the sacred parts of Teotihuacán. As she nods to acknowledge your intention, you cross the river and continue your journey through the body of the feathered serpent, Quetzalcoatl.

A Funeral, a Cleansing, and the Deep Feminine

As you climb the steps preparing to descend into the Plaza of the Earth, look back. You can see hell in the distance, and your island of safety. You can still turn back, but this may be your last chance. It is your choice, it is safe there, and you don't know what lies ahead. If you continue on this journey, the old you will die.

ACTION!

Close your eyes and dream Teotihuacán in all of its splendor 2,000 years ago. See, hear, and feel the energy of the place and the people here. Let the energy resonate with your energy, and imagine yourself an artist of the spirit—building, creating art, or participating in spiritual ceremony here.

If you choose to deepen your surrender to the serpent, turn and walk into the Plaza of the Earth. It is time to honor your commitment to your transformation. The person you were in the old dream has died, and this is a time of honoring, gratitude, and respect. Find a place in the plaza where you can hold a private burial ceremony. Perhaps you create a small cross or marker from twigs or stones to mark the spot, and sit quietly in mourning of the passing of the old you. There is no hurry; take your time.

Celebrating the New Warrior

As you finish your ceremony and prepare to continue your journey, you are suddenly transported 2,000 years back in time. You see the pyramids and temples shimmering white in the sun, decorated with brightly colored murals and motifs. You smell the incense, hear the music, and see the avenue lined with masters and students, welcoming and celebrating you. They offer you their love and wisdom, as they encourage you to continue. You realize that the Avenue of the Dead is truly the Avenue of New Life.

Quetzalcoatl leads you to the Plaza of Water, where he begins to digest away negative energies and unwanted emotional memories. As you pass through the water, feel the release and healing in your emotional body, and your rebirth into a new dream. Take time, surrender to this place of the heart, and let the digestion be complete.

Deep into the Feminine

Your journey now takes you out of the Plaza of Water, and into the sacred feminine. You descend the steps, and pass through the entrance into the dim light of the women's quarters. You open to access the deep feeling parts of you that have been denied and neglected for so many years. The energy from deep inside the earth mother enters you, and you merge with it, allowing it to awaken the profound truths of your feminine being. You are becoming more whole with each stage of your journey.

Filled with the energy of the Earth feminine, you bath in the healing energies pouring from the wall of this sacred temple. As they pass through your mind and body, your release transcends experience and expectations, and you are transported into total oneness with the earth mother. You rest there, in peace. In time, you return to present awareness, and as you walk silently out into the bright Teotihuacán sunlight, your heart opens in forgiveness of all mothers, including your own.

Redemption and Integration

As you return to the Avenue of the Dead, your journey through the serpent, Quetzalcoatl, takes you to the Plaza of Air. Breathe deeply, in gratitude for every breath of life-sustaining air you are offered in your new life. Breathe in the air with love, and breathe it out with love.

In this plaza you will use the rock of sexual healing and forgiveness to be born again into your new life. You approach the small pyramid, and stretch out your body in full contact with its stones. It has been prepared to receive you by your guides, and by thousands who have come before you.

> The burden of self-rejection and limitation carried by humans is based in lies. The life that animates creation is truth, love, and wholeness. Anything else cannot be the truth, and goes against your happiness. You have no need or obligation to continue to believe and repeat those lies. Leave them behind.

If you have used your sexuality to bargain for love, if you feel guilty about abortions, or if your sexuality has been abused by you or others, release the memories, guilt, and self-judgment here in this place. It is old, it is over, and you are new. Do not carry any of the guilt or self-rejection past this point. You are perfect, you have always done your best, none of it was your fault, and it is time to forgive yourself in this sacred place and time. Take all the time you need, and know that even as you leave this place, the forgiveness and healing continues until it is done.

The Underworld of Forgotten Feelings

There is a place deep in you that has long been blocked off and forgotten. It is the origin of all the subtle feelings and truth that have risen in your body since the beginning of your life. When you were small, those feelings were expressed in their full intensity and power, but you were taught to block and repress them. You built a wall at your throat, so they could not come up and out where they would be rejected or shamed. It is time to break open that wall, trust your feelings, and allow them to be expressed in your life.

Your guides take you to the underworld, where the Toltecs buried their early constructions, art, and beliefs, and built new forms on top of them. The wall has been broken open here, and you see the treasures revealed. You are inspired to reveal your hidden treasures. You sit in silent meditation, observing how the block at your throat stops the truth of your belly and heart from rising into your awareness and into the world.

Your intention to free the authentic expression of who you are and how you feel is strong. You see and hear the old agreements you made to deny your feelings, and perhaps even feel or see the wall at your throat. In the quiet of the moment, and with the power of Teotihuacán supporting you, the old agreements shatter and the juicy truth of you is liberated for all to honor and enjoy.

The Fire Burns Illusions of Separation

Your digestion by Quetzalcoatl continues as you enter the Plaza of Fire. Here you will face your beliefs and illusions of separation, and recognize your oneness with all of creation. What is your gender, and how do you identify with it? How does that identification separate you from others? How do you use your dream about "you" to deny your oneness with creation?

FACT

What has been done can be undone. Physical and emotional wounds heal. The free expression and discharge of trapped emotions is the healing they need. There is no danger in releasing the emotional shadows of the past. The danger is in holding on to them. The expression of deeper truth and honest feelings guides your life.

Throw yourself into the fire here. Let it burn away these illusions and lies that isolate you from life. You are life. You are the light. You are creation, and the force that animates creation. Any other belief is a lie. Burn yourself clear here. Use this place to return to wholeness, not only within yourself, but in the unity of the oneness that is the spiritual presence in all of creation. This is the fire of the sun of Teotihuacán; it is the fire of the ancients, and it is alive for you here in this place.

The Moon: Second Head of the Serpent

With the heat from the fire of integration still warming your heart, you prepare yourself for the long walk to the second head of Quetzalcoatl at the

▲ Stone carving of Quetzalcoatl.

Plaza of the Moon. There you will emerge into the light of your new world. To prepare yourself, you review everything you have done so far: You left your island of safety, and braved the sea of the unknown. You climbed to Quetzalcoatl and threw yourself into his mouth to begin your transformation. Surrender has followed surrender.

You faced the angel of death, and surrendered again. With every surrender, you have gained something precious: your life. You buried your old self in the Earth, in preparation for a new life, and were welcomed into Teo by the ancients. In each plaza, you healed, cleansed, changed agreements, opened to your depths, and liberated your truth. You are ready for the final release of the old you.

Your Walk with the Etheric Double

Ahead of you is the long, broad Avenue of the Dead. In the distance, the Pyramid of the Moon beckons you, and you are ready. You prepare by creating your "etheric double," a replica of your physical self that will accompany you on this journey. As you walk in meditation to the moon, you inventory and remove any final limiting beliefs, agreements, fears, sorrows, stories, denials, addictions, and other lies that do not serve you—and place them in the etheric double.

QUESTION?

Is it really possible to do all these things in the real Teotihuacán?
Yes, it is. In Mexico the rules are not as rigid as you are used to in other countries, such as the United States. Many Mexican people go to Teo to connect spiritually, also, and they respect your experiences there.

As you begin your measured walk, the Avenue of the Dead is alive with visitors and vendors, but they are not in your world. Once again, you are a ghost, and you move through them without their awareness. You hear your shoes crunching in the gravel, and the sounds of the clay flutes and children

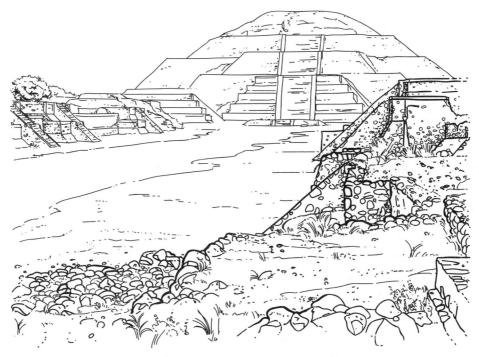

▲ Pyramid of the Moon, Teotihuacán.

around you, but your attention is focused only on your inventory. You scan your mind and emotional body, finding anything that does not serve you in your quest for absolute personal freedom.

The etheric double floats along beside you, receiving everything you are discarding. As you near the Plaza of the Moon, your pulse quickens, in anticipation of the powerful ceremony to come.

Emerging from the Serpent, the Double to the Sun

With deliberate steps, you climb the stairs to the Plaza of the Moon. You are emerging from the second head of Quetzalcoatl; your digestion is complete. Above you, the Pyramid of the Moon is alive in the strong Teo sun. As you approach an altar in the center of the plaza, you recognize your fellow travelers, gathering with you, for a special ceremony. It is time to send your etheric double, and everything it contains, to the sun.

You come close around the altar together, as a low hum begins to grow in the circle. The rose quartz crystal on the altar honors the feminine aspect of creation present here, and strengthens the vortex of energy opening in the center. The hum grows stronger, louder, and more powerful, until in one roar of power, each person in the circle throws his or her double into the vortex and up to the sun—to be burned in the fire of the sun's love.

Rituals and ceremonies are the most transformational when you are able to keep your logical mind outside of them. The mind always wants to know what is "real" and "not real." Tell the mind it is not real, and ask it to step aside so your can experience what you choose to be real.

You are restored to the pure and simple truth of your divine perfection. A gentle song begins, and the circle shares the love and power of their journey together. The song celebrates the love awakening in the heart of each individual, and recognizes that Teotihuacán is truly "the Place Where Humans Awaken and Remember their Divinity."

To celebrate the joy and liberation in your heart, you head for the Pyramid of the Moon, and climb its steep steps to the summit. The refreshing

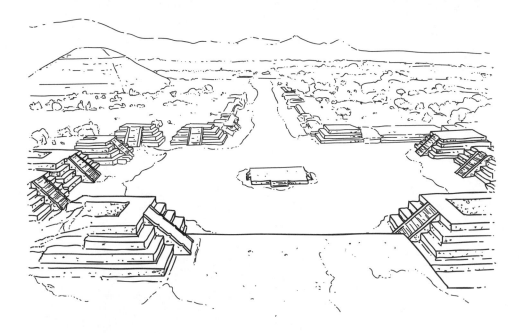

▲ View of the Avenue of the Dead from the top of the Pyramid of the Moon.

breeze is the perfect expression of what you have accomplished on your journey. You look out over the villages and the surrounding hills, and listen to the sounds of life drifting up from below. It is a very good day.

The Ultimate Surrender at the Pyramid of the Sun

A visit to "heaven" is the best way to follow your ceremony at the Pyramid of the Moon, and to prepare you for the Pyramid of the Sun! As you enter the Plaza of the Butterflies, you feel the soft presence of pure love. You are drawn to the center, and stand absorbing the sacred energy there. Your fellow travelers join you in a circle. There is nothing to say, and nothing to do—only to feel the presence of love in the place of heaven at Teo, and in your own heart.

As you continue in this special place, you are opening your heart and connecting with the sun. In the Toltec tradition, the sun is the source of all

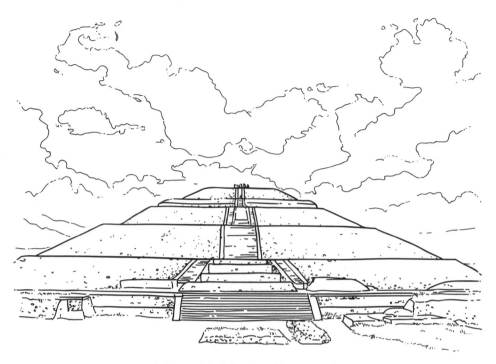

▲ Pyramid of the Sun, Teotihuacán.

life on Earth, and you are on your way to merge with it. When you know it is time, you walk back out onto the Avenue of the Dead, and toward the towering Pyramid of the Sun. You walk once again in meditation, opening and preparing yourself for the ultimate surrender: the leap to the black sun.

The Black Sun: The Hole in the Veil

A Toltec mythology describes the sun as the light messenger of creation. Every ray of the sun's light carries the message of a different form of life, which manifests itself as DNA. Every living being has its own unique ray of light from the sun, and its own unique DNA. The dream of the humans reflects back to the sun, and as the dream evolves, the sun changes its message. This is the time of the sixth sun, an important stage in the evolution of the human dream.

Manifested creation is the result of the sun dreaming. The unlimited potential for the dream is behind a veil, in the unmanifested side of the universe. There is a hole, through which the unmanifested becomes manifest—

this is the black sun. As you walk toward the pyramid, you set your intent to leap out of this dream into the black sun, where you will experience the ultimate expansion of pure potentiality.

Preparing Yourself, Preparing the Pyramid

You climb the many steps slowly, contemplating your intent. As you walk around each level of the stepped pyramid, you connect with the pyramid, the sun, and the black sun beyond. You climb higher and around, higher and around. You are awakening the pyramid, creating the spiral of the DNA, releasing any last attachments, and calling down your ray of the sun.

FACT

In order for there to be a manifestation, a real world, there needs to an unmanifested part also. The two are separated by the thinnest of veils, a mere idea, and yet so solid it is difficult for you to move from one to the other. It is good to get help from a pyramid and a guide.

As you climb the last steps and approach the center of the pyramid, you find once again that an altar has been prepared, and a powerful vortex is waiting for your energy. You sit down with your companions gathered there, and pour your personal intent into the vortex. You continue to release attachments that might hold you to the Earth, and your body begins to shake with the energy of the vortex. You are not sure what to expect, and that is good.

The Leap of Surrender into the Infinite

Suddenly, someone yells "now!" and you throw yourself into the vortex energy and leap to the sun. You do not know it yet, but there is no you. As you pass through the hole in the veil, you instantly expand into the totality of all that is, pure consciousness, absolute divine presence. The "lack of you" drifts there forever, until it is time to return to human form.

As your body stirs, you sit up and look around slowly. You have never seen this world before. It is brighter and more colorful than you remember.

Your DNA is tingling from the update into the sixth sun. Your mind is more peaceful than you ever imagined possible. You have nowhere to go, and nothing to do, but to be right where you are in this moment.

Your heart sings in gratitude for the ancient artists of the spirit who created this place for you to experience this moment. You feel their presence, and their gratitude that you are here, a human awakening, and remember your divinity. You are a Toltec artist of the spirit now, and Teotihuacán is part of you. A butterfly appears, and lands on your hand. It is the absolute perfect expression of what you are feeling.

In time, you notice that your human self is very hungry, and you remember that there are great enchiladas and tacos waiting for you back in another world. You gather up this new dream of heaven on Earth, and as you walk back down the pyramid, you carry the dream in your heart—where it stays for the rest of your life.

Glossary

action
The Toltec path is a path of action. To take action is to live life fully. The Toltec path has many tools that can change your life. To take action is to use the tools. Nothing changes without action.

agreement
A conscious or unconscious concept or opinion, especially one shared with another person. A goal of the Toltec path is to make all agreements conscious, and chosen with awareness. (See also *belief/belief system*.)

apprentice
A student of a master. (See also *Toltec master*.)

assemblage point
The point in the human from which perception occurs. May be fixed, as in the ordinary human, or flexible, in the warrior.

artist of the spirit
The name given to the early people of central Mexico, Toltecs and others, who built cities and pyramid complexes, created beautiful art, and demonstrated great spiritual wisdom.

attention
The ability humans have to discriminate and to focus only on that which they want to perceive. Attention can be focused on only one thing at any given moment. (See also *first attention*; *second attention*; *third attention*.)

awakening
First, you awaken into the awareness that you are dreaming a dream of hell, of the parasite, and the dream of the planet. Ultimately, you awaken into the awareness that you are the light and life; the divine itself.

belief/belief system
A conscious or unconscious acceptance of a fact or opinion that the mind believes is true. The program that results from all the agreements and beliefs programmed into the human mind by the outside dream. (See also *agreement*; *book of lies*.)

book of lies
All of the knowledge and beliefs about right and wrong, good and bad—and how you should be—that the inner judge uses to condemn and punish you.

channels of perception
The channels in the human mind that receive the light and process it into a virtual reality in the mind. Stored light (emotional memories, traumas, beliefs) in the channels distorts the incoming light and creates the personal dream. (See also *personal dream*; *dream*.)

divine/divinity
That power or intelligent life force that is in and through all of creation. To know your own Divinity is to know your oneness with all of life and all of creation (See also *awakening*; *nagual*.)

domestication
The process through which a child's caregivers download their beliefs and agreements (their dream) into his or her mind during childhood. (See also *dream*; *personal freedom*.)

dream
The virtual reality formed by light reflected from creation, distorted by stored light in the channels of perception, and projected into the human mind. (See also *channels of perception*; *light*.)

dream of the planet
The consensus dream of any society. It includes all the rules of society, its laws, its religions, its different cultural values; everything that is right and wrong, good and bad in any particular part of a society. (See also *personal dream*; *domestication*.)

dreaming
The controlled use of the attention to change the habits of perception, and thus change the dream. The ultimate tool of the warrior in the mastery of transformation.

faith
To have faith is to believe totally, without the need for proof. Toltec warriors have absolute faith in life to guide them.

first attention
The time in a child's domestication when her attention is hooked for the first time, and she is taught the beliefs of the dream around her: the dream of the first attention. (See also *attention*; *second attention*; *third attention*.)

happiness
The freedom from suffering. Your love in action produces happiness. Love coming out of you, as acceptance for yourself and all of creation, makes you happy.

heaven on Earth
For the Toltecs, heaven on Earth is the experience of love and acceptance for all of life in every moment. There is no suffering and no fear,

but rather, a keen awareness of one's own divinity and the oneness of all creation.

hell

The suffering that occurs when you feel victimized by judgment or rejection by an inner or outer judge. It is the realm of the parasite. It is normal life to most humans.

intent

Intent is life itself; it is unconditional love. Intent is the creative force that animates all of creation. The Toltec artist of the spirit directs that force to create her life as a masterpiece of art.

judge, inner

The inner judge enforces the rules in his book of lies. He makes accusations, passes judgment, makes condemnations, and punishes the victim child. He rules through fear and rejection, and is the guardian of the gates of hell. (See also *hell*; *warrior*; *book of lies*; *personal freedom*.)

light

The light is the messenger (the nagual) of creator, which manifests itself as the tonal, or creation. Light is the messenger that carries the image of creation from "out there" into your mind, where it is distorted into a dream. (See also *dream*; *personal dream*; *channels of perception*.)

love

The term used by the Toltecs to express the highest way of being. The animator of creation, truth, life itself; intent.

mastery of awareness

The first of the three Toltec masteries. To become aware that you are always dreaming, and everyone else is dreaming. To know that knowledge and fear have ruled your life, and to be prepared to use your awareness to change your beliefs. (See also *mastery of transformation*; *mastery of intent*.)

mastery of intent

The third of the three masteries of the Toltec path; also known as the mastery of love. When the transformation of the belief systems is complete, the warrior has the opportunity to release all beliefs, and live in the dream of heaven on Earth. (See also *heaven on Earth*; *mastery of transformation*.)

mastery of transformation

The second of the three Toltec masteries. After awareness of the dream has been achieved, the apprentice uses the tools of transformation to reveal and change his beliefs through his own choice. (See also *mastery of awareness*; *mastery of intent*; *book of lies*; *dreaming*; *second attention*.)

mitote

The ongoing chaos in the human mind, the result of domestication and self-rejection. The sound of the parasite arguing with itself, figuring out how to earn the love it knows it is not worthy of. (See also *dream of the planet*; *domestication*.)

nagual

The light, the messenger of creator, which manifests as the tonal (manifested creation). The nagual is everything that exists that you cannot perceive. It is the unknowable and the unknown. The title given to someone who identifies himself as the light. (See also *light*; *tonal*.)

parasite

A parasite is a living being that lives off of other beings, sucking their energy. In the human mind, the parasite is the dream of the judge, the victim, all the knowledge, the belief system. The parasite in the human mind feeds on the fear caused by self-rejection. (See also *self-rejection*; *judge*; *mitote*; *domestication*.)

perception

The recognition and interpretation of the light as it is received, distorted, and processed by the dreaming mind. Each human has a different perception of any given experience based on the stored light in his or her channels of perception. (See also *channels of perception*; *dream*; *assemblage point*.)

personal dream

Each human uses his organs of perception to receive the light reflected from creation. The light is distorted by light stored in his channels of perception, and a virtual reality is projected into the mind. The human looks at the virtual reality and mistakenly believes he is seeing what is "out there." (See also *channels of perception*; *dreaming*.)

personal freedom

The state of awareness achieved on the Toltec path, when the warrior has liberated himself from the limiting beliefs and agreements of his domestication and personal dream. (See also *domestication*; *personal dream*.)

personal importance

The illusion or dream that one is the center of the universe, and good and bad things happen because of what one does.

personal power

A state of clarity and effectiveness in the world achieved by the warrior when the distorted perceptions of the old dream are cleared. The love and intent available to the warrior in personal freedom. (See also *warrior*; *personal freedom*; *intent*.)

recapitulation

A central tool in the Toltec mastery of transformation. Examines all memories and beliefs in the mind, discovers the lies that create suffering, and changes them to the truth. (See also *mastery of transformation*.)

second attention

During the mastery of transformation, the Toltec warrior uses her attention for the second time to create a new personal dream of love and happiness. The dream of the second attention. (See also *attention*; *first attention*; *third attention*.)

self-acceptance

Coming to terms with the truth that you are perfect the way you are. Self-love. The opposite of self-rejection. The warrior is the master of acceptance; the judge is the master of rejection. (See also *self-rejection*.)

self-rejection

To deny the perfection of yourself as a part of creation. The result of domestication—the outer and inner judges make you wrong for who you are, and what you want. (See also *domestication*; *judge*.)

sixth sun
The recent change of the dream the sun is sending to humans, in response to the evolution of the human dream.

spirit/spiritual
The animating force throughout creation. An unseen force that is life, the divine, the nagual, the light. To live a spiritual life is to identify oneself as the animator of creation, rather than as creation. (See also *divine/divinity*; *nagual*; *tonal*.)

spiritual warrior
See *warrior*.

stalking
The warrior stalks the jungle of his mind like a jaguar. His prey is the parasite, and the fear created by the parasite. He stalks for places where he is leaking his energy because of his belief systems. Important skill in the mastery of awareness. (See also *parasite*; *belief/belief system*; *mastery of awareness*.)

stored light
Emotional memories, beliefs, opinions, agreements, and fears held in the channels of perception that distort the incoming light from creation into the personal dream. (See also *personal dream*; *dreaming*; *channels of perception*.)

suffering
The experience of the victim: "It's not fair. Why me?" The opposite of happiness. Suffering is the result of judging, resisting the perfection of cre-

ation, resisting the truth. (See also *surrender*; *happiness*.)

surrender
To surrender is to stop resisting life. In surrender there is no more struggle, no adversarial relationships with creation, and no suffering. You surrender to your true nature, and stop trying to please the judge. (See also *suffering*; *happiness*.)

Teotihuacán
A beautiful city and pyramid complex built by unknown ancients (Toltecs, artists of the spirit) in central Mexico. A national historical park, visited by many tourists, schoolchildren, and spiritual seekers. (See also *Toltec*; *artist of the spirit*.)

third attention
The ultimate goal of the Toltec path. All concepts and knowledge are released from the mind. The dream of the third attention is pure communion with the divine as and through creation.

Toltec
Toltec here means "artist of the spirit." To be a Toltec is a way of life, based on awareness and love. Ultimately, it is to become a master of intent, and create life as a masterpiece of art. A pre-Columbian culture that built cities and pyramids in central Mexico. (See also *Toltec path*; *Teotihuacán*; *artist of the spirit*.)

Toltec master
A warrior who has achieved personal freedom on the Toltec path. (See also *warrior*; *personal freedom*.)

Toltec path

A term used to describe the journey through the three masteries of the Toltec tradition, which leads from the hell of domestication and the dream of the planet to the dream of heaven on Earth.

Toltec wisdom

The great body of common sense and insight developed by the Toltec culture of pre-Columbian central Mexico. An ancient path of personal transformation and personal power that leads to liberation from the dream of the planet. Passed down through teachers and masters to apprentices for a millennium, before becoming available to the general public in the present time of the sixth sun. (See also *sixth sun*; *Toltec master*; *artist of the spirit*; *personal power*.)

tonal

All of manifest creation that humans perceive with their senses. The world of duality. The manifestation in physical form of the message of the divine, or nagual; the light. (See also *nagual*; *light*.)

warrior

A Toltec master. Also, the part of the mind that rebels against the abuse of the parasite. The spiritual warrior brings the expression of self-acceptance into the inner world, and changes the experience of the victim to one of empowerment and integrity. The warrior's dream is of pure love without conditions. (See also *Toltec master*; *nagual*; *parasite*.)

Resources

The following Toltec teachers, mentors, and authors offer valuable ways to begin a deeper exploration of Toltec wisdom. The list is by no means exhaustive, and the interested student is encouraged to also consult a local bookstore or library and the Internet.

Aaron Landman, Artist

Through his art, Aaron expresses the gift of the authentic life he received from Miguel Ruiz. He expresses his inner journey in many media, from paper to photography—and always with a great love for life. Aaron also leads journeys and supports personal apprentices.

✍ *www.AaronLandman.org*

Allan Hardman, Joydancer

Author of this book, numerous articles, and two anthology chapters, Allan is an expert in revealing and healing the hidden belief systems that limit and sabotage effective lives and relationships. He brings to his teaching an extensive background in emotional healing and spiritual counseling, along with his ten-year apprenticeship with Miguel Ruiz.

✍ *www.joydancer.com*
✍ *www.allanhardman.com*

Barbara Emrys and Gene Nathan, M.D., Sacred Legacies

Barbara Emrys has been designated by Miguel Ruiz to teach "Toltec dreaming" groups in his lineage. Her Web site shares her teaching through her writings, audio, and videos, along with schedules for the dreaming practice.

✍ *www.toltecsacredlegacies.com*
✍ *www.barbaraemrys.com*

Barbara Simon and Regina Cates, Romancing Your Soul

This dynamic teaching partnership guides you to romance your soul through body, mind, and spirit—power journeys, apprenticeships, yoga, and just the right clothing to make it all work.

✎ *www.romancingyoursoul.com*

Brandt Morgan, Thunderheart

A masterful teacher of the Toltec wisdom, Brandt Morgan is also deeply experienced in Native American traditions and wilderness skills. His new book is *Vision Walk*.

✎ *www.thunderheart.org*

Carlos Castaneda (Taisha Abelar and Florinda Donner-Grau)

When *The Teachings of Don Juan* was released in 1968, Carlos Castaneda became a favorite of the spiritual seekers of the time. His stories of meeting a Toltec nagual in the desert of northern Mexico, and his use of peyote and other mind-altering plants, inspired an entire subculture. There are nine books by Castaneda. His apprentices (names given in parentheses above) now use the Web site to share information about their teaching.

✎ *www.castaneda.com*

David and Linda Dibble, The New Agreements in Health Care

David Dibble combines a background in business consulting with his passion for healing individuals and society. He and his wife, Linda, have focused their intent on transforming the health-care system in the United States into a holistic wellness system, based on the Toltec wisdom.

✎ *www.thenewagreements.com*

Dr. Deborah Lord, Choosing Freedom

Along with her teaching of the Toltec wisdom, Deborah Lord is the creator and guardian of Eagles Landing Sanctuary, a retreat center on 200 acres in beautiful western Massachusetts. Her book *Choosing Freedom* and her CD sets offer additional ways to benefit from her love and experience.

✎ *www.dlordhealing.com*

Ed Fox, Intent Coaching

Ed Fox and Intent Coaching help empower students and clients by cleaning distorted perceptions to open and perceive truth. Ed teaches that understanding and embracing emotions is an integral part of living a dynamic and free life. Ed often teaches with his wife, Rita Rivera.

✎ *www.intentcoaching.com*

Gary van Warmerdam, Pathways to Happiness, Toltec Spirit

Gary is a longtime apprentice in the Toltec tradition who has created a simple and dynamic roadmap to a happy and fulfilling life. Changing old habits and agreements is not always easy, but good guidance makes it possible. Gary's site features many audio resources.

✎ *www.pathwaystohappiness.com*
✎ *www.toltecspirit.com*

La Doña Gini Gentry, Garden of the Goddess

La Doña is an insightful and powerful teacher, and a nagual woman in the lineage of Miguel Ruiz. She has created a beautiful retreat center, the Garden of the Goddess, near Santa Fe, New Mexico, for her workshops and residential empowerments.

✍ *www.nagualwoman.com*

Gloria Jean, Woman Reborn

Join Gloria Jean, along with Rita Rivera and a group of women seekers, for workshops or journeys to Teotihuacán and Iceland. Gloria also brings a fresh perspective to parenting through her work in the Toltec tradition.

✍ *www.womanreborn.com*

Heather Ash Amara and Raven Smith, Spirit Weavers

Heather Ash combines her rich experience in earth rituals, Wicca, and firewalks with her Toltec training to offer her students and apprentices a fresh and dynamic approach to personal growth. Her partner, Raven Smith, cofacilitates Spiritweavers Circles, journeys, and workshops.

✍ *www.spiritweavers.com*

Ken Eagle Feather

Ken Eagle Feather claims to have met don Juan Matus, the teacher of Carlos Castaneda, and has written several books about the Toltec path, including *The Toltec Path* and *Traveling with Power*.

Lee McCormick, Spirit Recovery

Lee McCormick enhances his Toltec teaching with his experience in guiding addictions recovery at his Ranch Recovery Center in Tennessee. Lee is the author of *The Spirit Recovery Meditation Journal.*

✍ *www.SpiritRecovery.com*

Lennie Tan, Transform Your Life

Lennie Tan began her own healing journey as a music therapist, and then discovered the Toltec wisdom through Miguel Ruiz. She shares her unconditional love on power journeys to sacred sites and through her mentoring in person, by phone, and through the Internet, from her home in Vancouver, Canada.

✍ *www.lennietan.com*

Leo van Warmerdam and Niki Orietas, The Dreaming Mind

A powerful teaching couple with insights into addictions recovery, Leo and Niki lead power journeys, guide individual apprentices, and present workshops in Southern California.

✍ *www.thedreamingmind.com*

Meghan and Jamie Gilroy, True Love Now

Meghan and Jamie Gilroy believe that it is absolutely possible to be living the life of your dreams. They are a loving and inspirational couple that teach from the heart of their own truth. Their full range of teaching offers support for many issues of modern relationships and daily living.

✍ *www.findyourtruelovenow.com*

Melissa Phillippe, Awakening Awareness

Melissa's love and wisdom gained on the Toltec path expresses itself through the power of her music with a message, and her messages with the power of music. Melissa combines her Toltec teaching with her experience as a science-of-mind practitioner to support individuals in their search for freedom.

✎ *www.melissaphillippe.com*

Miguel Ruiz and José Luis Ruiz

Miguel Ruiz is the author of *The Four Agreements*, *The Mastery of Love*, and other Toltec wisdom books. Don Miguel teaches and leads power journeys with his son, José Luis Ruiz, in the United States and Mexico, sharing ancient and modern Toltec wisdom. The teachers listed below have been trained by don Miguel. Most lead power journeys to Teotihuacán, Mexico, and other sacred sites in Latin America and beyond. Some are available for personal apprenticeships, some offer online courses and teleclasses, and many have written books about the Toltec path and related subjects. Check their Web sites for details.

✎ *www.miguelruiz.com*

Ray Dodd, The Power of Belief

Ray Dodd has combined his background in business and coaching with his apprenticeship in the Toltec tradition to create a teaching devoted to "real change, one belief at a time." His books include *The Power of Belief* and *Belief Works*.

✎ *www.everydaywisdom.us*

Rebecca Haywood, The Awakening Spirit

Rebecca Haywood was chosen by Mother Sarita (mother of Miguel Ruiz) to carry on Sarita's tradition as a *curandara*, or spiritual healer. Rebecca now offers traditional egg cleansings and healings along with her power journeys and private sessions.

✎ *www.TheAwakeningSpirit.com*

Rita Rivera, Toltec Mastery

Along with other master teachers, Rita Rivera offers teleclasses, power journeys, workshops, and private sessions to support the quest for personal freedom. The Toltec Mastery program offers support for every level of experience and interest.

✎ *www.toltecmastery.com*

Dr. Sheri Rosenthal, Journeys of the Spirit

Dr. Rosenthal leads spiritual journeys to sacred sites throughout the world. Her work with individuals and groups is dynamic, precise, and fun. She is the author of *The Complete Idiot's Guide to Toltec Wisdom*.

✎ *www.sherirosenthal.com*
✎ *www.journeysofthespirit.com*

Dr. Susan Gregg, The Dance of Power

From her home in Hawaii, Dr. Gregg offers her support to those with a desire to connect with their inner wisdom and divinity. Since her first book, *Dance of Power*, she has created several other books and audio resources for healing.

✎ *www.susangregg.com*

Théun Mares

In 1997 Théun Mares began to remember his training as a warrior in previous lifetimes, and has since dedicated his life to teaching the path to personal freedom through his many books and residential retreats.

✍ *www.warriorskeep.com*

Victor Sanchez

Victor Sanchez has written two books about the teachings of Carlos Castaneda and Toltec recapitulation. His books are a valuable contribution to understanding the sometimes complex writing and allegories of Castaneda, and offer practical applications of the teachings of ancient and modern Toltecs.

✍ *www.toltecas.com*

Victoria Allen, Dream Reflections

Victoria is skilled in helping her students understand both the dreaming mind described by the Toltecs, *and* the power and value of sleeping dreams. She offers her wisdom in a full range of personal and group teaching and journeys.

✍ *www.dreamreflections.com*

Index

THE EVERYTHING SERIES!

BUSINESS & PERSONAL FINANCE

Everything® Accounting Book
Everything® Budgeting Book
Everything® Business Planning Book
Everything® Coaching and Mentoring Book
Everything® Fundraising Book
Everything® Get Out of Debt Book
Everything® Grant Writing Book
Everything® Guide to Personal Finance for Single Mothers
Everything® Home-Based Business Book, 2nd Ed.
Everything® Homebuying Book, 2nd Ed.
Everything® Homeselling Book, 2nd Ed.
Everything® Improve Your Credit Book
Everything® Investing Book, 2nd Ed.
Everything® Landlording Book
Everything® Leadership Book
Everything® Managing People Book, 2nd Ed.
Everything® Negotiating Book
Everything® Online Auctions Book
Everything® Online Business Book
Everything® Personal Finance Book
Everything® Personal Finance in Your 20s and 30s Book
Everything® Project Management Book
Everything® Real Estate Investing Book
Everything® Retirement Planning Book
Everything® Robert's Rules Book, $7.95
Everything® Selling Book
Everything® Start Your Own Business Book, 2nd Ed.
Everything® Wills & Estate Planning Book

COOKING

Everything® Barbecue Cookbook
Everything® Bartender's Book, $9.95
Everything® Cheese Book
Everything® Chinese Cookbook
Everything® Classic Recipes Book
Everything® Cocktail Parties and Drinks Book
Everything® College Cookbook
Everything® Cooking for Baby and Toddler Book
Everything® Cooking for Two Cookbook
Everything® Diabetes Cookbook
Everything® Easy Gourmet Cookbook
Everything® Fondue Cookbook
Everything® Fondue Party Book
Everything® Gluten-Free Cookbook
Everything® Glycemic Index Cookbook
Everything® Grilling Cookbook

Everything® Healthy Meals in Minutes Cookbook
Everything® Holiday Cookbook
Everything® Indian Cookbook
Everything® Italian Cookbook
Everything® Low-Carb Cookbook
Everything® Low-Fat High-Flavor Cookbook
Everything® Low-Salt Cookbook
Everything® Meals for a Month Cookbook
Everything® Mediterranean Cookbook
Everything® Mexican Cookbook
Everything® No Trans Fat Cookbook
Everything® One-Pot Cookbook
Everything® Pizza Cookbook
Everything® Quick and Easy 30-Minute, 5-Ingredient Cookbook
Everything® Quick Meals Cookbook
Everything® Slow Cooker Cookbook
Everything® Slow Cooking for a Crowd Cookbook
Everything® Soup Cookbook
Everything® Stir-Fry Cookbook
Everything® Tex-Mex Cookbook
Everything® Thai Cookbook
Everything® Vegetarian Cookbook
Everything® Wild Game Cookbook
Everything® Wine Book, 2nd Ed.

GAMES

Everything® 15-Minute Sudoku Book, $9.95
Everything® 30-Minute Sudoku Book, $9.95
Everything® Blackjack Strategy Book
Everything® Brain Strain Book, $9.95
Everything® Bridge Book
Everything® Card Games Book
Everything® Card Tricks Book, $9.95
Everything® Casino Gambling Book, 2nd Ed.
Everything® Chess Basics Book
Everything® Craps Strategy Book
Everything® Crossword and Puzzle Book
Everything® Crossword Challenge Book
Everything® Crosswords for the Beach Book, $9.95
Everything® Cryptograms Book, $9.95
Everything® Easy Crosswords Book
Everything® Easy Kakuro Book, $9.95
Everything® Easy Large Print Crosswords Book
Everything® Games Book, 2nd Ed.
Everything® Giant Sudoku Book, $9.95
Everything® Kakuro Challenge Book, $9.95
Everything® Large-Print Crossword Challenge Book

Everything® Large-Print Crosswords Book
Everything® Lateral Thinking Puzzles Book, $9.95
Everything® Mazes Book
Everything® Movie Crosswords Book, $9.95
Everything® Online Poker Book, $12.95
Everything® Pencil Puzzles Book, $9.95
Everything® Poker Strategy Book
Everything® Pool & Billiards Book
Everything® Sports Crosswords Book, $9.95
Everything® Test Your IQ Book, $9.95
Everything® Texas Hold 'Em Book, $9.95
Everything® Travel Crosswords Book, $9.95
Everything® Word Games Challenge Book
Everything® Word Scramble Book
Everything® Word Search Book

HEALTH

Everything® Alzheimer's Book
Everything® Diabetes Book
Everything® Health Guide to Adult Bipolar Disorder
Everything® Health Guide to Controlling Anxiety
Everything® Health Guide to Fibromyalgia
Everything® Health Guide to Postpartum Care
Everything® Health Guide to Thyroid Disease
Everything® Hypnosis Book
Everything® Low Cholesterol Book
Everything® Massage Book
Everything® Menopause Book
Everything® Nutrition Book
Everything® Reflexology Book
Everything® Stress Management Book

HISTORY

Everything® American Government Book
Everything® American History Book, 2nd Ed.
Everything® Civil War Book
Everything® Freemasons Book
Everything® Irish History & Heritage Book
Everything® Middle East Book

HOBBIES

Everything® Candlemaking Book
Everything® Cartooning Book
Everything® Coin Collecting Book
Everything® Drawing Book
Everything® Family Tree Book, 2nd Ed.
Everything® Knitting Book
Everything® Knots Book
Everything® Photography Book

Everything® Quilting Book
Everything® Scrapbooking Book
Everything® Sewing Book
Everything® Soapmaking Book, 2nd Ed.
Everything® Woodworking Book

HOME IMPROVEMENT

Everything® Feng Shui Book
Everything® Feng Shui Decluttering Book, $9.95
Everything® Fix-It Book
Everything® Home Decorating Book
Everything® Home Storage Solutions Book
Everything® Homebuilding Book
Everything® Organize Your Home Book

KIDS' BOOKS

All titles are $7.95
Everything® Kids' Animal Puzzle & Activity Book
Everything® Kids' Baseball Book, 4th Ed.
Everything® Kids' Bible Trivia Book
Everything® Kids' Bugs Book
Everything® Kids' Cars and Trucks Puzzle
  & Activity Book
Everything® Kids' Christmas Puzzle
  & Activity Book
Everything® Kids' Cookbook
Everything® Kids' Crazy Puzzles Book
Everything® Kids' Dinosaurs Book
Everything® Kids' First Spanish Puzzle and
  Activity Book
Everything® Kids' Gross Cookbook
Everything® Kids' Gross Hidden Pictures Book
Everything® Kids' Gross Jokes Book
Everything® Kids' Gross Mazes Book
Everything® Kids' Gross Puzzle and
  Activity Book
Everything® Kids' Halloween Puzzle
  & Activity Book
Everything® Kids' Hidden Pictures Book
Everything® Kids' Horses Book
Everything® Kids' Joke Book
Everything® Kids' Knock Knock Book
Everything® Kids' Learning Spanish Book
Everything® Kids' Math Puzzles Book
Everything® Kids' Mazes Book
Everything® Kids' Money Book
Everything® Kids' Nature Book
Everything® Kids' Pirates Puzzle and Activity Book
Everything® Kids' Presidents Book
Everything® Kids' Princess Puzzle and Activity Book
Everything® Kids' Puzzle Book
Everything® Kids' Riddles & Brain Teasers Book
Everything® Kids' Science Experiments Book
Everything® Kids' Sharks Book
Everything® Kids' Soccer Book
Everything® Kids' States Book
Everything® Kids' Travel Activity Book

KIDS' STORY BOOKS

Everything® Fairy Tales Book

LANGUAGE

Everything® Conversational Japanese Book with
  CD, $19.95
Everything® French Grammar Book
Everything® French Phrase Book, $9.95
Everything® French Verb Book, $9.95
Everything® German Practice Book with CD,
  $19.95
Everything® Inglés Book
**Everything® Intermediate Spanish Book with
  CD, $19.95**
**Everything® Learning Brazilian Portuguese
  Book with CD, $19.95**
Everything® Learning French Book
Everything® Learning German Book
Everything® Learning Italian Book
Everything® Learning Latin Book
**Everything® Learning Spanish Book with
  CD, 2nd Edition, $19.95**
Everything® Russian Practice Book with CD, $19.95
Everything® Sign Language Book
Everything® Spanish Grammar Book
Everything® Spanish Phrase Book, $9.95
Everything® Spanish Practice Book
  with CD, $19.95
Everything® Spanish Verb Book, $9.95
Everything® Speaking Mandarin Chinese Book
  with CD, $19.95

MUSIC

Everything® Drums Book with CD, $19.95
**Everything® Guitar Book with CD, 2nd
  Edition, $19.95**
Everything® Guitar Chords Book with CD, $19.95
Everything® Home Recording Book
Everything® Music Theory Book with CD, $19.95
Everything® Reading Music Book with CD, $19.95
Everything® Rock & Blues Guitar Book
  with CD, $19.95
**Everything® Rock and Blues Piano Book
  with CD, $19.95**
Everything® Songwriting Book

NEW AGE

Everything® Astrology Book, 2nd Ed.
Everything® Birthday Personology Book
Everything® Dreams Book, 2nd Ed.
Everything® Love Signs Book, $9.95
Everything® Numerology Book
Everything® Paganism Book
Everything® Palmistry Book
Everything® Psychic Book
Everything® Reiki Book

Everything® Sex Signs Book, $9.95
Everything® Tarot Book, 2nd Ed.
Everything® Toltec Wisdom Book
Everything® Wicca and Witchcraft Book

PARENTING

Everything® Baby Names Book, 2nd Ed.
Everything® Baby Shower Book
Everything® Baby's First Year Book
Everything® Birthing Book
Everything® Breastfeeding Book
Everything® Father-to-Be Book
Everything® Father's First Year Book
Everything® Get Ready for Baby Book
Everything® Get Your Baby to Sleep Book, $9.95
Everything® Getting Pregnant Book
Everything® Guide to Raising a One-Year-Old
Everything® Guide to Raising a Two-Year-Old
Everything® Homeschooling Book
Everything® Mother's First Year Book
**Everything® Parent's Guide to Childhood
  Illnesses**
Everything® Parent's Guide to Children
  and Divorce
Everything® Parent's Guide to Children
  with ADD/ADHD
Everything® Parent's Guide to Children
  with Asperger's Syndrome
Everything® Parent's Guide to Children
  with Autism
Everything® Parent's Guide to Children with
  Bipolar Disorder
**Everything® Parent's Guide to Children with
  Depression**
Everything® Parent's Guide to Children
  with Dyslexia
**Everything® Parent's Guide to Children with
  Juvenile Diabetes**
Everything® Parent's Guide to Positive Discipline
Everything® Parent's Guide to Raising a
  Successful Child
Everything® Parent's Guide to Raising Boys
Everything® Parent's Guide to Raising Girls
Everything® Parent's Guide to Raising Siblings
Everything® Parent's Guide to Sensory
  Integration Disorder
Everything® Parent's Guide to Tantrums
Everything® Parent's Guide to the Strong-Willed
  Child
Everything® Parenting a Teenager Book
Everything® Potty Training Book, $9.95
Everything® Pregnancy Book, 3rd Ed.
Everything® Pregnancy Fitness Book
Everything® Pregnancy Nutrition Book
Everything® Pregnancy Organizer, 2nd Ed., $16.95
Everything® Toddler Activities Book
Everything® Toddler Book

Everything® Tween Book
Everything® Twins, Triplets, and More Book

PETS

Everything® Aquarium Book
Everything® Boxer Book
Everything® Cat Book, 2nd Ed.
Everything® Chihuahua Book
Everything® Dachshund Book
Everything® Dog Book
Everything® Dog Health Book
Everything® Dog Obedience Book
Everything® Dog Owner's Organizer, $16.95
Everything® Dog Training and Tricks Book
Everything® German Shepherd Book
Everything® Golden Retriever Book
Everything® Horse Book
Everything® Horse Care Book
Everything® Horseback Riding Book
Everything® Labrador Retriever Book
Everything® Poodle Book
Everything® Pug Book
Everything® Puppy Book
Everything® Rottweiler Book
Everything® Small Dogs Book
Everything® Tropical Fish Book
Everything® Yorkshire Terrier Book

REFERENCE

Everything® American Presidents Book
Everything® Blogging Book
Everything® Build Your Vocabulary Book
Everything® Car Care Book
Everything® Classical Mythology Book
Everything® Da Vinci Book
Everything® Divorce Book
Everything® Einstein Book
Everything® Enneagram Book
Everything® Etiquette Book, 2nd Ed.
Everything® Inventions and Patents Book
Everything® Mafia Book
Everything® Philosophy Book
Everything® Pirates Book
Everything® Psychology Book

RELIGION

Everything® Angels Book
Everything® Bible Book
Everything® Buddhism Book
Everything® Catholicism Book
Everything® Christianity Book
Everything® Gnostic Gospels Book
Everything® History of the Bible Book
Everything® Jesus Book

Everything® Jewish History & Heritage Book
Everything® Judaism Book
Everything® Kabbalah Book
Everything® Koran Book
Everything® Mary Book
Everything® Mary Magdalene Book
Everything® Prayer Book
Everything® Saints Book, 2nd Ed.
Everything® Torah Book
Everything® Understanding Islam Book
Everything® World's Religions Book
Everything® Zen Book

SCHOOL & CAREERS

Everything® Alternative Careers Book
Everything® Career Tests Book
Everything® College Major Test Book
Everything® College Survival Book, 2nd Ed.
Everything® Cover Letter Book, 2nd Ed.
Everything® Filmmaking Book
Everything® Get-a-Job Book, 2nd Ed.
Everything® Guide to Being a Paralegal
Everything® Guide to Being a Personal Trainer
Everything® Guide to Being a Real Estate Agent
Everything® Guide to Being a Sales Rep
Everything® Guide to Careers in Health Care
Everything® Guide to Careers in Law Enforcement
Everything® Guide to Government Jobs
Everything® Guide to Starting and Running a Restaurant
Everything® Job Interview Book
Everything® New Nurse Book
Everything® New Teacher Book
Everything® Paying for College Book
Everything® Practice Interview Book
Everything® Resume Book, 2nd Ed.
Everything® Study Book

SELF-HELP

Everything® Dating Book, 2nd Ed.
Everything® Great Sex Book
Everything® Self-Esteem Book
Everything® Tantric Sex Book

SPORTS & FITNESS

Everything® Easy Fitness Book
Everything® Running Book
Everything® Weight Training Book

TRAVEL

Everything® Family Guide to Cruise Vacations
Everything® Family Guide to Hawaii
Everything® Family Guide to Las Vegas, 2nd Ed.
Everything® Family Guide to Mexico
Everything® Family Guide to New York City, 2nd Ed.
Everything® Family Guide to RV Travel & Campgrounds
Everything® Family Guide to the Caribbean
Everything® Family Guide to the Walt Disney World Resort®, Universal Studios®, and Greater Orlando, 4th Ed.
Everything® Family Guide to Timeshares
Everything® Family Guide to Washington D.C., 2nd Ed.

WEDDINGS

Everything® Bachelorette Party Book, $9.95
Everything® Bridesmaid Book, $9.95
Everything® Destination Wedding Book
Everything® Elopement Book, $9.95
Everything® Father of the Bride Book, $9.95
Everything® Groom Book, $9.95
Everything® Mother of the Bride Book, $9.95
Everything® Outdoor Wedding Book
Everything® Wedding Book, 3rd Ed.
Everything® Wedding Checklist, $9.95
Everything® Wedding Etiquette Book, $9.95
Everything® Wedding Organizer, 2nd Ed., $16.95
Everything® Wedding Shower Book, $9.95
Everything® Wedding Vows Book, $9.95
Everything® Wedding Workout Book
Everything® Weddings on a Budget Book, $9.95

WRITING

Everything® Creative Writing Book
Everything® Get Published Book, 2nd Ed.
Everything® Grammar and Style Book
Everything® Guide to Magazine Writing
Everything® Guide to Writing a Book Proposal
Everything® Guide to Writing a Novel
Everything® Guide to Writing Children's Books
Everything® Guide to Writing Copy
Everything® Guide to Writing Research Papers
Everything® Screenwriting Book
Everything® Writing Poetry Book
Everything® Writing Well Book

Available wherever books are sold! To order, call 800-258-0929, or visit us at *www.everything.com*.
Everything® and everything.com® are registered trademarks of F+W Publications, Inc.
Bolded titles are new additions to the series.
All Everything® books are priced at $12.95 or $14.95, unless otherwise stated. Prices subject to change without notice.